COMMUNITIES OF FAITH

New Directions in Anthropology
General Editor: Jacqueline Waldren

COMMUNITIES OF FAITH

*Sectarianism, Identity, and Social Change
on a Danish Island*

Andrew Buckser

Berghahn Books
Providence • Oxford

First published in 1996 by

Berghahn Books

Editorial offices:
165 Taber Avenue, Providence, RI 02906, USA
Bush House, Merewood Avenue, Oxford, OX3 8EF, UK

© Andrew Buckser 1996

Library of Congress Cataloging-in-Publication Data

```
Buckser, Andrew, 1964-
    Communities of faith : sectarianism, identity, and social change
on a Danish island / Andrew Buckser.
    p.   cm. -- (New directions in anthropology ; v. 5)
    Includes bibliographical references (p.   ) and index.
    ISBN 1-57181-042-0 (alk. paper)
    1. Mors (Denmark)--Church history.  2. Christian sects--Denmark-
-Mors.  3. Sociology, Christian--Denmark--Mors.  4. Mors (Denmark)
5. Secularism.   I. Title.  II. Series.
BR987.M67B83  1996
274.89'5--dc20                                              96-25652
                                                                 CIP
```

British Library Cataloguing in Publication Data

A catalogue record for this book is available from
the British Library.

Printed in the United States on acid-free paper.

CONTENTS

❧ ❧ ❧

LIST OF MAPS

❧ ❧ ❧

ACKNOWLEDGMENTS

॰ঙ৯ ॰ঙ৯ ॰ঙ৯

*F*unding for this study came from several sources. A National Science Foundation Graduate Fellowship provided the primary support for my field research in Denmark; additional support came from the American Scandinavian Foundation, the Robert H. Lowie Memorial Fund, and a Humanities Research Grant from the University of California. The Commission for Educational Exchange Between Denmark and the United States, while not providing funding, generously extended the use of their facilities to me during my stay. My writing time was supported by a Berkeley Fellowship at the University of California.

My greatest scholarly debt is owed to Professor William Simmons of the University of California at Berkeley. Professor Simmons has provided generous advice and invaluable criticism throughout the course of this study; he has also offered a voice of consistent sanity in the chaotic world of Berkeley. He has my deepest gratitude for his confidence, encouragement, and wisdom. I would also like to thank Professors Stanley Brandes, John Lindow, Anton Blok, and Charles Lindholm for their perceptive observations and criticism. In Denmark, the guidance and friendship of Professor Palle Ove Christiansen of the University of Copenhagen were keys to the success of this project.

My greatest debt of all, of course, is owed to the people of Mors, both for their help in my fieldwork and for their warm hospitality and friendship. Mors has a somewhat forbidding reputation in Denmark, owing largely to its association with the writings of Aksel Sandemose. When I first arrived in the country, friends in Copenhagen warned me gravely of the intolerance and xenophobia I should expect to meet on the island. I never met it; indeed, I found on Mors an honesty, warmth, and openness that I had never encountered before. I am deeply grateful for the welcome that the island extended to me and my family. I would particularly like to thank Holger Vester and Esther Bech, whose help was critical in the success of this project, and whose friendship I shall always treasure. Many others gave me enormous help in my work, often without knowing it; space forbids mentioning them all here, but I would especially like to thank Gudrun and Mejnar Nørregaard-Jensen, Ellen and Karl Georg Holch Andersen, Kirsten and Erik Overgaard, Else and Erik Lau Jørgensen, Suzanne Overgaard, Vita Nissum, and Gunnar Boll.

Many people from the regions of Fur, Salling, and Thy also helped me understand the culture of western Jutland. I would particularly like to thank Gerda Jeppesen, Elisabeth Christensen, Ellen and Ole Tarri, and Esben Jeppesen of Fur; Trine and Benny Nielsen of Skive; Elisabeth and Hans Ove Svalgaard and Ingeborg and Per Skallerup of Thisted.

A number of institutions and associations on Mors assisted me with my work. Each of the religious groups described in the text allowed me access to its archives and members. The Morsø Frimenighed was especially generous; I would like especially to thank Erik and Kirsten Overgaard, Else and Erik Lau Jørgensen, and Dagmar and Jens Borg. Many members of the island's Indre Mission chapters discussed their lives and experiences with me; my thanks go particularly to Ejgil Dissing, Bodil and Egon Nielsen, and Edith and Gunnar Worm and their delightful children. The members of the Apostolske Kirke gave me an energetic welcome from the first time I set foot in the church. Bodil and Søren Viftrup, Jens Kristian Kristiansen, and Jette Jensen were especially helpful to my work. I would also like to thank Preben Nielsen of the Morsø Pinsekirke and Kurt Pedersen of the Frelsens Hær. In addition to these independent groups, the priests and deacons of the Nykøbing Folkekirke, especially Karl Aage Madsen and Per Thomsen, gave me the benefit of their valuable expertise about religion on Mors and in Denmark as a whole.

Mors has a tradition of local historical research which I relied upon heavily in my research and writing. I would like to thank the helpful and professional staff of the Morsø Lokalhistoriske Arkiv and the Dueholm Kloster Museum for their assistance, particularly Suzanne Overgaard and Per Noe. The staff of the Nykøbing Bibliotek gave me free acess to their rich collections of local history and geneology. Above all I would like to thank the island's premier historian, Karl Georg Holch Andersen, for his guidance and hospitality.

Though they did not directly affect my work on religious movements, I would like to offer special thanks to the doctors and nurses who cared for my daughter during our time in Denmark. They treated her with a combination of competence and tenderness that I have seen nowhere else, and which saved her great suffering. Dr. Franz Teschl and his nursing staff, the staff of the Nykøbing Sygehus, and the staff of Afdeling P16 of Viborg Sygehus deserve our lasting gratitude, as does the kind and distinguished Dr. Jørgen Haahr.

Several institutions at Berkeley provided great help during the writing of this dissertation. The staff of the Quantitative Anthropology Laboratory provided computer facilities and expertise. The Berkeley Scandinavian Department provided office space and resources, after the untimely demolition of the graduate student offices in my own department. The staff of the Anthropology Department gave me valuable administrative assistance.

A number of friends and colleagues have offered comments and advice on the work presented here. I would particularly like to thank Peter Redfield, Richard Hitchcock, Elise Marks, Ulla Thomsen, Timothy Tangherlini, Roland Moore, Max Olmsted, Bethany Caird, and Robert Anderson for their comments.

The revision of this work took place at the Department of Sociology and Anthropology at Purdue University. I am grateful to the department for the supportive environment and collegial atmosphere it has provided during the process. My colleagues have been invaluable sources of advice, and the staff of the Social Research Institute has given me excellent technical support. I would also like to thank my editor at Berghahn Books, Jackie Waldren, for her insightful suggestions on the revision of the manuscript.

My family has given me consistent encouragement and support throughout the course of this project. I would especially like to thank my mother, Carol Dolan, for her unfailing confidence and support. Thanks also to Douglas Buckser, Jeffrey Buckser, Alison Buckser, Lillian Jepsen, Dorothy Jepsen, Jim Dolan, Phyllis and Art Melden, Helen and Marian Coggshill, Harriet and Irwin Rofman, and Elaine and Sam Rofman. The memories of Ernest Overgaard Jepsen and Helen Christenson have been an ongoing inspiration to my work.

Finally, I would like to offer my deepest thanks to my wife, Susan Ann Buckser, whose love and intelligence have supported every aspect of this project. Her perceptive criticism, her constant encouragement, and her boundless confidence have helped me at every stage of my work; words can express only a shadow of the debt I owe her.

These people deserve much of the credit for the work presented here. The errors, however, are mine alone.

for my beloved children
Rachel, William, and Sarah

PREFACE

What is the place of religion in modern society? Why do religious groups survive, and even prosper, in places where scientific doctrines have undermined the central tenets of their theologies? What gives them their appeal, when even their adherents no longer believe their explanations of the origins and character of the world around them? How does that appeal relate to religion's construction of the individual and the human community? In this study, I will examine the place of religion in the modern world, focusing on the interaction of community, identity, and religion in times of rapid and confusing social change. I will look for the answers on a little island in the northwest corner of Denmark, where a series of religious awakenings broke out a century ago, and where they continue to shape society today.

In many ways, Denmark seems an unlikely place to study these questions. After all, the country has developed a reputation around the world for its apparent lack of religion. Church attendance is low, science and self-conscious modernity dominate the culture, and the nation's social policy often ignores the moral injunctions of traditional Protestantism. Denmark's liberal laws regarding sexuality, for example, have aroused international interest. When the state instituted a form of quasi-marriage for homosexuals in the early 1980s, many American fundamentalists denounced Denmark as an enemy of Christian values, an example of the shocking depravities possible in a land that has forgotten the Bible. Denmark appears to many outsiders as a country without a God, hardly the place to learn about religion.

My first days in Denmark seemed to confirm this impression. I settled on Mors, a small interior island in the rural hinterland of western Jutland. Mors lay far from the cosmopolitan culture of Copenhagen, in what I had been told was the least modern and the most religious region of the country; yet at first I could see no evidence of religious activity. The majestic church in the center of the market town stood mostly empty, drawing perhaps a tenth of its capacity on any given Sunday. People never talked about God, faith, or prayer; they talked about work, about family, about vacations and possessions, all the standard interests of a secularized society, but almost never about religion. Even folk religion seemed absent. The colorful world of gnomes, trolls, and elves so celebrated by folklorists was dismissed as the archaic superstition of a bygone era. Science and the welfare state seemed to define the universe and the people in it. The world of my neighbors held no place for religion, at least none that I could see.

Over time, however, I began to appreciate the profound significance of religious systems for the people of Mors. Not as an explicit cosmological theory; though the islanders almost all belonged to the Lutheran Church, relatively few could confidently state a firm belief in a well-defined God. But the ways that they understood the world, the ways that they classified people and social life, derived from a distinct set of religious views. These views traced back to a series of religious movements that had swept Mors, along with the rest of Denmark, between the 1830s and the 1910s. To understand attitudes toward family, education, government, or work, one had first to understand the nature of these movements, and the way that their ideas of person and community had transformed the island. To do that, I began researching the history of these movements, as well as their place in the lives of their members today.

This book presents the results of that research. I trace the rise of the three primary religious groups on Mors between 1837 and 1990, placing them in the context of the island's social and cultural life. I focus especially on their ideas about the nature of human beings, the temporal world, and the earthly community. In doing so, I try to explain why these movements arose when and where they did, and why some succeeded and others declined after World War II. I also explore the significance of these movements for our understanding of Western religion generally. For the movements have not disappeared, despite the well-publicized invasion of science and modernity in Denmark. The largest remains vigorous and growing, while the weakest owes its decline more to organizational problems than to any clash with the modern world-view. Their specific ideas about cosmology have indeed lost much of their clarity. But the ways that these groups classify the person, the community, and the world retain a powerful appeal for the people of Mors. It is these constructions of identity and community, I will argue, that attracted flocks of adherents during the wrenching social changes of the mid-19th century; those same constructions make them vital elements of local culture today.

In the course of this study, I also hope to present an ethnographic picture of a lovely and fascinating society. The culture of Western Jutland remains something of a mystery even to residents of Copenhagen; to the world beyond, it is virtually unknown. Its religious movements have often been the subject of caricatures and stereotypes, but only rarely of serious scholarly study. This study will try to convey some of the complexity, subtlety, and beauty of this little-studied culture.

Organization

This study is divided into four parts. In Part I I present a brief discussion and critique of secularization theory, the paradigm that has long dominated the study of religion in Denmark and the Western world. In Part II I turn to the island of Mors, to examine the ethnographic background against which the religious movements developed, and within which they function today. I discuss the island's landscape and settlement patterns; its history; its social organization; its institutions of authority and education; its seasonal and life cycle rituals; and some cultural aspects that distinguish it from the rest of Denmark.

In Part II, I turn to movements themselves. After a brief discussion of Danish church history, I describe the history and social structure of the island's two main religious groups, the Free Congregation and the Inner Mission. I also discuss a small independent Pentecostal group called the Apostolic Church. For each group, I cover history, theology, demographic structure, authority structure, financial systems, major rituals, leadership, and the place of the group in the lives of its members. I place special emphasis on how each group classifies people and the temporal world.

In Part III, I consider the significance of these movements for social scientific theories about the secularization of modern society. I argue that the experience of the religious groups on Mors poses problems for standard theoretical models, which tend to assume a basic opposition between religious and scientific understandings of the world. Such models cannot adequately explain the course of religious development on the island. Instead, I propose an understanding of religion that focuses on religion's role in creating identity and community for its members. This approach resolves some of the theoretical weaknesses of secularization theory, while providing a more persuasive explanation of the interaction between social change and religious awakening on Mors.

Field Methods

This study draws on data from three fieldwork visits to Mors between 1989 and 1992, the longest lasting from September 1990 to July 1991. The fieldwork involved interviews, participant observation, and the study of local archival materials. A brief description of my field methods may help readers evaluate the data in the following chapters.

The social organization of Mors presents a number of problems for traditional anthropological fieldwork. The patterns of daily life offer few openings for curious strangers; social life does not gather around public wells or outdoor entertainments, but behind the stout brick walls of family homes and meeting halls. Even in public areas, such as markets and churches, residents interact within established circles of family and business connections. This social system offers few openings for someone unconnected to the island's kin groups or voluntary associations, particularly someone unschooled in the local dialect. Moreover, local residents tend to respect the privacy of visitors; they eschew the nosy questions and curious visits that often give ethnographers their first social contacts. A large part of fieldwork on Mors, therefore, consists of solving the problem of how to enter into the relatively closed networks of local society.

I used three basic approaches to make an initial entry into these networks. The first was to make the most of the neighborhood, the only social group that one belongs to in Denmark simply by virtue of living there. With my wife and our infant daughter, I lived in a small two-family house near the center of Nykøbing. Next door to us lived a retired roofer and his wife, both of whom became good friends and valuable informants; not only did they help us with any questions we had about the island, they also introduced us to their own kin and social networks. Our landlady, likewise, introduced us to her own extended family. A second strategy was to approach the leaders of the island's organizations. Priests, association foremen, school principals, museum officers, factory owners, and other leading citizens were often happy to discuss their groups with an American scholar, and they provided introductions to other members of their organizations. The third avenue drew on my own family connections on the island, from which my great-grandparents emigrated around the turn of the century. I knew of only a few relations on Mors when I arrived, but a number of the people whom I met in other ways turned out to be cousins of some sort. Though the kin relationships were rather distant, such familial connections allowed me into the heart of the Morsingbo world.

Even with these connections, entering the networks of island society took considerable time and effort. Once inside, however, the connections multiplied very quickly. After learning about my purpose on the island, most informants were delighted to help, and they constantly referred me to others who knew more than they did about specific issues. Indeed, after an article about us eventually appeared in the local newspaper, we began receiving unsolicited journal articles and offers of help through the mail. Though Mors was a difficult society to enter, it was an inexhaustible source of information once people understood and took an interest in my work.

My daughter, Rachel, provided a fourth and rather unexpected means of getting to know people. Morsingboer respect adult privacy, and an odd-looking foreigner could wander the market street forever without being approached; babies, however, belong to everyone, and Rachel invariably drew attention when we walked through Nykøbing. Strangers came up to look at her, coo at her, pat her hand if she was happy, and offer advice if she was crying. From elderly grandmothers to burly factory laborers, everyone had a smile and a word for her. Indeed, discussions about Rachel's upbringing constituted most of our contact with Morsingboer during our first month on the island. These discussions introduced us to some of the core ideas that Morsingboer hold about people and the world. They also, I should note, provided real help; I learned to be a parent in Denmark, and I shall always be grateful to the people of Mors for the perspective on children which they taught me.

Most of my active data-gathering took the form of interviews, generally conducted at the homes of informants. After a few initial disasters with questionnaires, I kept the interviews as informal as possible; lists of questions tended to impose a stifling division into the conversation, reinforcing the outsider status that I had worked hard to overcome.

Most interviews took place over coffee, and covered a range of subjects about the informants' personal history and religious views. My hosts and I would sit in a kitchen or living room, drinking pot after pot of coffee and sampling a seemingly endless procession of pastries as we talked. Most informants were glad to help, and all were extremely hospitable, even when they found my questions rather bizarre. They talked most freely about their families, particularly their children. Farmers also took pride in showing me their farms, and I came to learn much more about agriculture than I had expected. Discussions of religion came with more difficulty; while informants could express themselves clearly about their views, they usually seemed anxious to avoid any appearance of preaching at me. Even priests took pains to acknowledge my freedom to disagree with them. I made most of my notes on the interviews immediately after I returned to our house. I took notes during the conversation only of important names and dates.

Participant observation provided another rich source of data. My family and I learned much simply by living the daily round in Nykøbing. Out of necessity, we learned to eat, dress, entertain guests, shop, and talk like Morsingboer. Neighbors taught us how to decorate our home, maintain our garden, and deal with the crises of everyday life. Visa restrictions barred us from having jobs, but I did visit most of the island's major worksites. Our success in these matters was naturally incomplete; a Morsingbo would never have mistaken us for natives. On our trips to Copenhagen, however, we passed easily as Jutlanders. In addition to everyday activities, I participated as much as possible in the island's religious rituals. I attended church services, revival meetings, parish meetings, weddings, baptisms, confirmations, funerals, and holiday services. I also attended such events as birthday parties, parades, dances, musical concerts, and the circus.

My archival work focused mainly on reconstructing the memberships of the different religious movements. The movements varied in the quality of their archives, from the voluminous membership lists and protocols of the Free Congregation to the nearly total absence of written records for the Apostolic Church. Even where records were available, they required considerable interpretation. Determining an Inner Mission chapter's membership from a list of contributors to the mission house, for example, requires a knowledge of the village social system as well as of the relationship between contribution and membership. Fortunately, Mors abounds with amateur historians, and I was able with their help to develop a fairly clear picture of the development of the movements described here. Members of the different groups were especially helpful in explaining their histories and archival systems. In addition, the professional staff of the Mors Island Local Historical Archive gave me unstinting and invaluable guidance.

A critical element in all of this fieldwork was the help of my wife, Susan Ann Buckser, who accompanied me on all three field visits. An anthropologist specializing in studies of early childhood, Susan conducted her own field research among the mothers and children of Nykøbing while I was working on religion. Her observations and opinions provided a constant supplement and contrast to my own, particularly since the feminine sphere in which she worked was less accessible to me. The data presented here owe a great deal to her ethnographic work.

Writing Style

Translating the lived experience of human beings on Mors into written English involves a host of stylistic decisions, all partially arbitrary and none entirely satisfactory. Writing about people inevitably distorts their world, not only because of difficulties of translation, but also because it places their free-flowing, occasionally disconnected, and ongoing experience into a focused and organized narrative. That narrative, moreover, generally reflects the conventions and biases of the writer's culture. The requirements of scholarly writing leave us with little choice; it may help, however, to make explicit some of the stylistic decisions made in writing this study.

Throughout the work, I have tried to make the writing as accessible as possible to nonanthropologists; I have avoided jargon specific to the social sciences, and tried to explain the technical terms that do come in. Unless specifically noted, therefore, all terms should be understood in their conventional usage. In addition, I have translated all Danish terms, and used the English versions wherever possible. For terms that posed particular difficulties in translation, I have discussed alternative translations in the notes.

In general, I have avoided fictionalizing events in the text. Mors is a real island, Nykøbing is a real town, and such figures as Rasmus Lund and Bette Wolle really existed. All stories are real as well, including the vignettes that open the chapters on the religious movements. Any departures from this rule are noted in footnotes. I have followed this policy partly out of necessity; Mors is a unique geographical feature in Denmark, and its religious life has often been the topic of nationwide discussion. No minor changes to its name and topography could disguise its identity from Danes. Using real names also makes this text easier for other scholars to use and criticize. Most importantly, though, I have simply followed the custom of the island's inhabitants. Morsingboer are proud of their strengths and honest about their weaknesses, and they would not appreciate my hiding their culture behind veiled descriptions.

The names of private individuals are a different matter; I assured most of my informants that our conversations would be confidential, and giving their names would violate that agreement. I have therefore used fictional names for all individuals who do not hold positions of public leadership. When describing individual life histories, as in Part II, I have also altered occupations and place names. For descriptions of prominent individuals, such as priests and civic leaders, I have used only published or generally available information. I have quoted such people only on issues relating to general features of the island's culture; I have treated their discussions of other individuals as confidential.

Another stylistic issue involves the use of pronouns. The common English practice of using the masculine pronoun to refer to sexually indeterminate individuals presents well-known problems of gender bias. In general, I have used constructions like "he or she" to minimize this bias. In some passages, however, particularly in Part III, such constructions would tend to confuse sentences that are already complex; I have reverted to the masculine pronoun for these occasions. In addition, I have routinely used the masculine pronoun to refer to the Christian deities God, Jesus, and Satan. This usage does not reflect my own theological views, but rather those of Morsingboer, who invariably describe their deities as male.

A final point regards my own biases. Recent studies of ethnographic writing have shown that anthropologists' backgrounds and beliefs exert a profound influence on their ethnographies. Awareness of this influence cannot wholly negate its extremely subtle effects. A brief statement of my own views on the subjects of this study may help others to evaluate the validity of my observations. I have tried to the best of my ability to keep these feelings from affecting the objectivity of the writing here; I know better, though, than to think that I have fully succeeded.

I have a strong personal connection to the people of Mors; my maternal grandfather's parents emigrated from the island around the turn of the century, and their children maintained strong ties with relatives there. I encountered many relatives while I was on Mors, some of whom became important informants. Such contacts provided a valuable entree to island society. My great-great-grandmother's affiliation with the early Grundtvigian movement gave me a particular affinity to the Free Congregation; she named my great-grandfather after one of the founders of the movement, and the mention of his name never failed to arouse interest when I talked to a Grundtvigian. Such connections, as well as the deep affection I developed for the island's people, may well influence the picture of the island presented here. Readers may want to compare my description with that of an avowedly hostile son of the island, Aksel Sandemose (1936), who wrote a brilliant and vicious description of Nykøbing that is available in English translation.[1]

Finally, in any discussion of religious movements, the author should say something about his or her own religious background. I was raised as a Unitarian in Memphis, Tennessee, a compromise between my father's Jewish upbringing and my mother's Lutheran and Congregationalist background. The teachings of that church have continued to influence my own belief; like most of its members, I believe in the existence of a divine will, but I have only a vague idea of what that will is or how it relates to human affairs. I regard all religious ideas as human constructions, structured not by divine revelation but by the requirements of human psychology and culture. Such ideas include the origin myths and heroic figures of the Jewish and Christian traditions. This view does not imply any disdain for these traditions. To the contrary, while I see reli-

---

1. On the subject of the Jantelov, for example, which I regard as a pervasive but fairly mild injunction against vanity (see p. 75), Sandemose is emphatic:

   ... he who has lived under the Law of Jante during the fifteen years it took him to develop, who has come to realize its bloody emphasis and its hysterical thirst for power, regards [it] very differently. By the means of the Law of Jante people stamp out each other's chances in life. All struggle against it and writhe beneath it, but all heartlessly exercise it against all others. Because of it the people of Jante are godless, without having first become human. Each is nailed to a cross of his own and requires no Christian symbolism. There they all hang, screaming, their brows wet with bloody sweat, turning and twisting in pain, and hissing to their brothers in crucifixion: "Do you think for a moment that anyone bothers his head about you?" (1936: 78)

   Clearly, Sandemose sees nothing mild about the Jantelov. Sixty years separate his description and mine, and I believe that the Law of Jante has moderated itself in that time. To some extent, though, the divergence in our descriptions simply reflects the divergence in our feelings toward the place. I, a newcomer and a visitor, loved the island; Sandemose, a native who fled to Norway, hated it. The truth may lie somewhere in the middle.

gion as a completely human invention, it is to me the most beautiful of such inventions. The assertion that the universe has a divine nature, and that human beings have a special place in it, strikes me as the most ambitious, optimistic, and potentially tragic statement that a human being could make; I have the greatest respect for those with the courage to make it. The psychological and cultural analyses used in this study are in no way intended to detract from the dignity of the religions and believers of Mors.

Literature

Like most of contemporary Scandinavia, 20th-century Denmark has drawn relatively little attention from ethnographers. A number of anthropologists have studied various aspects of the welfare state and the counterculture; Fuchs (1971), for example, discusses the dynamics of the Danish school system, while Lemberg (1980) examines alternative community housing projects. Community-based ethnographies, however, remain quite rare. Palle Christiansen (1980, 1978) provides some of the most comprehensive material in his studies of villages and manors in southeastern Sjælland. Christiansen focuses particularly on the influence of centuries-old power relationships on contemporary social organization. Robert Anderson also uses historical approaches in his ethnographies of a Sjælland maritime community (1964, 1975); Barbara Gallatin Anderson (1990) gives a more impressionistic account of the present-day community. Judith Hansen's (1970) study has less of a geographical focus, but her descriptions of core concepts of Danish culture could apply virtually anywhere in the country. The most recent ethnography, by Steven Borish (1991), examines the social and cultural organization of a Grundtvigian folk high school. Other ethnographic studies include Hendin (1964) and the articles published annually in *Ethnologia Scandinavica*.

Most of these works deal with eastern Denmark, near the powerful metropolis of Copenhagen. Jutland has attracted much less scholarly attention, and Mors hardly any. Yet the island boasts a surprisingly rich documentary record, with published works on many aspects of its history and social system. Local historians, led by archivist K.G. Holch Andersen (1990, 1989, 1983, 1975, etc.), have produced a wealth of meticulous studies. Such authors as F. Elle Jensen (1944, 1946), Erik Lau Jørgensen (1975, 1989), Sven Aage Brusgaard (1977), Suzanne

Overgaard (1988) and Christian Villads Christensen (1902) have written detailed and well-documented histories. The memoirs of Danish statesman Frode Jakobsen (1976, 1977) give a colorful portrait of island life in the early 20th century. The notes of folklorist Evald Tang Kristensen frequently deal with 19th-century Mors. For earlier periods, readers can consult Schade (1811), Pontoppidan (1769), and the various editions of Trap Danmark, as well as the historical journals *Jul paa Mors* and *Historisk Årbog for Mors*. All of these sources are directed toward local readers, and hence are written in Danish. The best source on the region for English speakers is Det Danske Selskab (1964).

An extensive literature exists on the religious movements we will examine, most of it written by Danish theologians. The classic study is by P.G. Lindhardt (1959), who discusses the connections between the different awakenings and corresponding social upheavals. Anders Pontoppidan-Thyssen has written and edited a huge range of material on the subject; his contributions include a study of the "new Grundtvigians" in the mid-1800's (1957) and a series of books on the history of the Danish awakenings. The cultural aspects of Grundtvigianism have attracted a great deal of interest, most prominently in the works of Margareta Balle-Petersen (1987, 1983). Other studies of Grundtvigian culture include Begtrup (1934), Nørgaard (1941), and Thodberg and Pontoppidan Thyssen (1983). Much less material exists on the pietistic movements, which have placed much less stress on history than the Grundtvigians. Anniversary studies such as Larsen (1986), Holt (1961), and Blauenfeldt (1912) provide the best information on the Inner Mission; for the Apostolic Church, Mortensen (1974) offers the only systematic history. Literary treatments like Kirk (1978) may be the best way to get an initial sense of these groups.

Readers may choose from a wide range of books about Danish religion in general. Lausten (1987) gives a concise and readable history of the Danish church. Iversen and Pontoppidan Thyssen (1986) cover the current state of religion in the nation, as does Salmonsen (1975). Rod (1961, 1972) discusses folk religion, and Piø (1977) analyzes aspects of ritual and folk belief. English speakers may best begin with Hartling's (1964) introduction to the Danish church.

For the broader issue of religious movements in modern Western society, readers can choose among a number of excellent studies. Some, such as Wilson (1970) and Stark and Bainbridge (1985), combine studies of a number of different religious sects. Others, such as Hunter (1983), Stromberg (1986), and Greenhouse (1986), focus on specific groups or movements. I will discuss theoretical studies in Part III; among the best of these are Berger (1967), Bellah (1970), Martin (1978), Stark and Bainbridge (1985), Finke and Stark (1992), and Weber (1976). Any study of religion in the modern West, however, must also consider the rich anthropological literature on non-Western religion and symbolic anthropology. Such authors as Mary Douglas, Victor Turner, Clifford Geertz, Melford Spiro, E.E. Evans-Pritchard, Emile Durkheim, Anthony Wallace, and Claude Levi-Strauss have profound relevance for the understanding of religion in the West today.

*   *   *

Note on Pronunciation

Most English speakers have difficulty pronouncing Danish words. Not only does Danish contain a number of characters not used in English, it also tends to vary the pronunciation of letters in different contexts. The frequent use of silent consonants, glottal stops, and dialectical variations adds to the confusion. I have therefore used English translations wherever possible in the text; the informal guide below should help readers with the few Danish words used repeatedly.

Danish Character	Pronunciation
Æ,æ	Halfway between a long *a* and long *e;* like the *ea* in *bear*
Å,å	Close to a long *o* in English
Aa, aa	Same as *å;* the letter *å* is a modern replacement for the traditional double *a.* Thus, *paa* is the same word as *på*, and both are pronounced much like *Poe*
Ø,ø	the *u* in *purr*
Y,y	Close to a long *u* in English. The Danish *y* is never used as a consonant
J,j	Like an English consonant *y*

xxiii

The following names and terms appear frequently in the text:

Mors *(morse)*
Nykøbing *(new'-curbing)*
Øster Jølby *(ur'-ster jurl'-by)*
Folkekirke *(folk'-uh-keer-kuh)*
Grundtvig *(grunt'-vee)*
Ansgarskirke *(ans-gars'-keer-kuh)*
Missionsfolk *(miss-yohns'-folk)*
Thy *(too)*
Viborg *(vee'-borg)*
Ålborg *(ohl'-borg)*
Århus *(oar'-hoos)*
Gågade *(go'-gaythe)*

It should also be noted that Danish makes many plurals by adding the suffix -er. Thus, *Morsingbo,* the term for a resident of Mors Island, becomes *Morsingboer* in the plural.

INTRODUCTION

⁊ ⁊ ⁊

*I*n the village of Galtrup in northern Denmark, a white stone church stands at the crossroads of the two main streets. It was raised around the year 1100, when the first Christian priests came to the region, and it has housed worship continuously since then. Through plagues and famines, through wars and invasions, through almost nine hundred cold Danish winters, the villagers of Galtrup have come to the church to receive the teachings and sacraments of the Christian faith. The massive stones in the walls are solid still, and the church may well stand another millennium. But over the past generation, the villagers have suddenly stopped coming. A typical Sunday service now draws a half-dozen parishioners, mostly elderly, who come more out of habit than out of interest. The church no longer has its own priest, but shares one with two neighboring parishes in a similar situation. This lack of interest has prompted the state church authorities to consider closing the Galtrup church and combining the three parishes in a single building. In a few years, the church that withstood the Black Death and the Reformation may collapse from simple lack of interest.

For the past fifty years, throughout the Western world, churches like the one in Galtrup have been closing their doors. Established religions have experienced a staggering loss of influence and credibility in Western Europe and North America; church attendance has fallen, levels of belief have declined, and the clergy have lost their influence in the larger society. The moral standards and unity once represented by the churches

1

seem to have evaporated. In their place has arisen a sort of moral anarchy, rooted in a scientific understanding of the universe, and lacking any theological basis. Areas of life once dominated by religion are now governed by market forces and government bureaucracies. Revivals and charismatic preachers may stem the tide here and there, but overall the trend seems unstoppable. The mighty foundation of Christian belief on which Western society was built seems to have crumbled almost overnight.

Social scientists call this process secularization, the decline of religious ideas and institutions in favor of worldly ones. For a long time, most social scientists have regarded secularization as an inevitable consequence of modernization. Since the West has led the world in modernization, it has experienced the greatest degree of secularization; over time, as science and technology spread, the rest of the world will become secularized as well. This paradigm has dominated the study of religion in the modern West, particularly for the ultra-modern nations of Scandinavia. It is a paradigm with serious shortcomings, however, which may distort the nature and development of modern religion. In this chapter, I will sketch the basic outlines of secularization theory, and consider its strengths and weaknesses for understanding religion in Northern Europe.

Secularization Theory

The basic idea of secularization is a simple one, and one that makes intuitive sense for many people in the Western world. Once upon a time, it says, religion permeated human life. The vast majority of people believed in some sort of god and attended some sort of church, while the churches they attended were powerful institutions in the larger world. Beginning with the Renaissance, however, and accelerating with the Reformation, the forces of modernization began to erode the power of religion. As science, rationality, individuality, and mass communication infiltrated Western consciousness, the influence of religion began to decline. People began first to doubt, then to dismiss the religious beliefs held by their ancestors. Church attendance fell, and the grip of the churches on human affairs weakened. As modernization progressed, religion gradually fell away, to be replaced by scientific thought and secular bureaucratic organization. As time goes by this process will continue, until religion is only a dim memory of an earlier and more credulous age. C. Wright Mills expressed it concisely in 1959:

Once the world was filled with the sacred – in thought, practice, and institutional form. After the Reformation and the Renaissance, the forces of modernization swept across the globe and secularization, a corollary historical process, loosened the dominance of the sacred. In due course, the sacred shall disappear altogether except, possibly, in the private realm. (1959: 32-33)

This notion is widespread in Western culture, and until recently, it was almost universally shared among sociologists and anthropologists. From the dawn of both disciplines, the assumption that religion is moribund was so widespread as to be seldom discussed, let alone questioned. The reasons for this assumption lay primarily in the circumstances under which these sciences developed (Hadden 1987). Both emerged out of Enlightenment philosophy, which tended to view Europe's established churches as archaic relics of the dark ages, soon to be eclipsed by the triumph of reason. Both also drew heavily on evolutionary models, by Darwin and others. These models posited a steady progress of both biology and culture, from primitive simplicity and ignorance to modern knowledge and sophistication. Religion, as the representative and guardian of ancient beliefs, became associated with a distant past that was by definition inferior. Marxist thought, another important influence, regarded religion as an adversary, a tool of the ruling classes that would disappear with the proletarian revolution. Even contemporary religious leaders lamented the decline of religious observance, and warned of catastrophic consequences if trends continued (Finke and Stark 1992). All of these views influenced early social science, which took it as a given that the age of religion was coming to an end. Many sociologists and anthropologists looked forward to the demise, which would pave the way for the ascendancy of their own viewpoints. Auguste Comte, arguably the founder of sociology, went so far as to devise a replacement.

With religion obviously dying, the question became one of explanation. Why had religion lost its appeal to modern humanity? What were its weaknesses, and how had the rise of the modern world exposed them? Was secularization something peculiar to the Western experience, or was it a general feature of social evolution? From the mid-19th century to the fourth quarter of the 20th, these questions dominated studies of modern religion within anthropology and sociology. The body of literature that addressed them came to be known as secularization theory. This theory was never a coordinated set of hypotheses; it embraced a variety of theoretical and methodological viewpoints, some in conflict with one another. Secularization theorists had differing conceptions of religion, of modernity, and of the nature of social change. What united them was not any particular facet of their argument, but the conclusion that all of them reached.

E.B. Tylor, for example, looked upon religion as an essentially intellectual system. In his work on primitive religions, published in 1871, Tylor depicted the history of religion as an evolutionary process, in which science and monotheism arose out of man's early attempts to explain the world. In the dawn of human consciousness, Tylor argued, men must have been puzzled by the figures they saw in dreams and hallucinations. To explain the mystery, they developed the notion of spiritual beings, insubstantial souls that animated the tangible world. These souls came to explain everything strange about the world, from the changing of the seasons to the mysteries of the human heart. Early on, people attributed souls to humans, animals, plants, and even inanimate objects. As time went by, however, humans learned more about their world; they came to understand the physical dynamics of nature, and it became less necessary to invoke supernatural beings to explain them. As a result, the range of beings to which souls were attributed gradually narrowed. First inanimate objects, then plants, then lower animals, and finally all animals lost their spiritual natures. As they did so, the number of deities in the cosmology shrank. The animistic world of the primitive, in which every forest and stream housed a god or spirit, evolved into polytheism and finally monotheism. The process reached its final stage with the rise of experimental science. Since science could explain the world, and even human beings, in rational physical terms, the supernatural lost the last of its practical value. Religion became a matter of ethics and morals, not explanation, and the stage was set for its decline to irrelevance.

Tylor's view of the evolution of religion was echoed, in varying forms, by James Frazer and other eminent anthropologists. Each proposed his own historical and functional model, but all shared a common view of religion as an explanatory mechanism, a naive attempt to explain the natural world using supernatural premises. The rise of science meant the end of primitive religion, and perhaps eventually of religion in general. This view sorted well with the prevailing evolutionary models of human history, and it certainly derived in large part from the 19th century's fascination with evolution. It survived, however, even after Franz Boas and his followers discredited cultural evolutionism in the early 20th century. The apparent collapse of religion in the Western world called for an explanation, and the Tylorian approach remained popular. As late as 1966, Anthony Wallace projected the future of religion in much the same terms:

> ...the evolutionary future of religion is extinction. Belief in supernatural beings and in supernatural forces that affect nature without obeying nature's laws will erode and become only an interesting historical memory. To be sure, this event is not likely to occur in the next generation; the process will very likely take several hundred years, and there will probably always remain individuals, or even occasional small cult groups, who respond to hallucination, trance, and obsession with a supernaturalist interpretation. But as a cultural trait, belief in supernatural powers is doomed to die out, all over the world, as a result of the increasing adequacy and diffusion of scientific knowledge and of the realization by secular faiths that supernatural belief is not necessary to the effective use of ritual. The question of whether such a denouement will be good or bad for humanity is irrelevant to the prediction; the process is inevitable. (1966: 265)

Max Weber proposed a very different approach to the decline of religion, based not on intellectual evolution but on social change. For it was not science alone, he said, that eclipsed religion in the modern world; rather, it was science as an element of modern capitalism. Capitalism for Weber had two features that distinguished it from other forms of economic organization. One was the endless pursuit of wealth for its own sake, rather than to fulfill some physical or psychological need. The other was the harnessing of science and rationality to produce this wealth. Together, these features made capitalism a virtually unstoppable engine, one designed in the long run to overrun and eclipse other economic structures. As it did so, it would impose a worldview that would have little or no place for religion. Capitalism would apply rational schemes to social organization, compartmentalizing its subjects into enormous bureaucratic structures. These structures would be motivated, like everything else, by a merciless and methodical quest to maximize profits; they would impose order and anonymity on the people who fit into them. Charisma, the basic force behind the religious experience, would have no place in such an order. Likewise, supernatural and transcendent experiences would cease to play any significant role in social life. As capitalism extended its irresistible grip, religion would be squeezed more and more out of the public world. While it might continue as a system of personal beliefs or otherworldly theories, it would lose any influence on the real world. Religion would die not because science proved it untrue, but because scientific capitalism would have no use for it (Weber 1976, Aron 1967, Lindholm 1990).

A third classic explanation of secularization comes from Peter Berger, who follows Weber in seeing social change behind the spread of the phenomenon. Whereas Weber finds its causes in the growing uniformity of the social world, however, Berger finds them in the world's growing disconnectedness. Modern society, he says, compartmentalizes and differentiates human life. In contrast to traditional societies, modern ones found separate institutions for their various activities; politics is enshrined in parliaments and Pentagons, economics in markets and stock exchanges, religion in churches and synagogues. Different spheres of life are cut off from one another, and the synthetic world of the primitive is replaced by a host of discontinuous institutions. Being separate, these institutions need not all operate by the same logic, and they may well compete with one another. The result is a loss of certainty, the loss of an overarching moral structure to which all activities are connected. In the primitive world, this structure constitutes a "sacred canopy," a web of meaning that relates all levels of life to one another. Modernization on the Western model destroys this canopy. It compartmentalizes religion into a single set of institutions, the churches; thus compartmentalized, these institutions can be ignored. Moreover, as economic, political, family, and other structures appear as competitors to the churches, religion loses its monopoly as a system for interpreting the world. Insofar as it faces competition from non-religious spheres, religion loses its plausibility for its adherents. As it does so, it begins a slide into secularization and irrelevance (Berger 1967; see also Wallis and Bruce 1992, Wilson 1985).

Other authors have presented other models of the secularization process, notably Bryan Wilson (1970, 1985) and David Martin (1978). Each of these models focuses on a different aspect of the tremendously complex phenomenon of modernization. Most of them, however, locate the key forces behind secularization in one of three aspects of the modern world. One is *rationalization,* the tendency of rational scientific thinking to replace mysticism and supernaturalism. Another is *social differentiation,* the increasing fragmentation of society into separate institutions and social units. The third is *societalization,* the erosion of local social networks in favor of large-scale, society-wide organizations. According to secularization theorists, each of these militates in some way against religion. As modernization irresistibly spreads across the globe, these forces undermine the irrational, synthetic, local bases of religion, and usher in a new age of scientific secularism. Religion may survive as a set of personal beliefs or as a philosophical system, but as a social and cultural force it is doomed to extinction.

This vision of religion's future has an intuitive appeal, one that has given it force well beyond the narrow confines of academic sociology. It answers in many ways to the everyday experience of Western laymen. For the sacred seems to have receded from the Western world. Ghosts, goblins, and the spirits of ancestors have lost their reality for us; they have been relegated to children's stories, to be believed by the young and then to be outgrown. Likewise, the charms and spells that our ancestors once used to heal and to harm have lost their power to us. When we are sick, we turn to medicine; when we are sad, we turn to psychology; when we are confused about the nature of our universe, we turn to science. As Weber said, our world has been disenchanted, and it is through technology, not the sacred, that we expect to solve our problems. This was particularly true after World War II, as breathtaking advances in medicine, astronomy, and other sciences swept away centuries of folk customs and beliefs almost overnight. Through the 1950s, 1960s, and into the 1970s, therefore, secularization theory remained virtually unquestioned both in and out of sociology. The discussion that took place concerned not whether religion was bound to die, but how long it would take to expire.

Critiques of Secularization Theory

A few objections to the secularization thesis did arise in the late 1960s; in 1969, for example, David Martin published a forceful attack on the theoretical validity of the term "secularization." Such criticisms were sporadic, however, and prompted no large-scale reconsideration of the theory. Social scientists did not begin to question secularization seriously until a series of political and cultural events starting in the late 1970s forced them to do so. In 1979, Islamic fundamentalists overthrew the Shah of Iran, one of the leaders in the Middle East most committed to modernization and secularization. During his reign, the Shah had forcibly imposed massive Western-style modernization on Iran. Such changes had aroused opposition in Iranian society, and the Shah had needed the help of a powerful military and a savage secret police to effect them. Even so, the success of his monarchy had seemed to confirm the inevitability of modernization and secularization in the non-Western world. The collapse of his regime, and its replacement by the Islamic authoritarianism of Ayatollah Ruhollah Khomeini, reversed the progression of religious decline long assumed by secularization theory. Over the next fifteen years, Islamic fundamentalism became a powerful political force throughout the Islamic world, challenging secular governments in Algeria, Morocco, and Egypt. Even Saddam Hussein, once an aggressive proponent of secular government, turned to Islam for support during the 1992 Gulf War. As religious fundamentalism came to dominate the politics of nation after nation, the notion that religion was becoming more and more ineffectual lost much of its credibility.

Across the Atlantic, the sudden visibility of Christian fundamentalism in America posed a similar problem. Jimmy Carter's election had brought fundamentalist Christianity into the national consciousness in 1976; in the 1980 election, the real power of the movement became apparent. Ministers like Jerry Falwell, Pat Robertson, and Oral Roberts linked fundamentalism to political conservatism, and they embraced Ronald Reagan as the savior of a nation headed for perdition. They made conservative Christianity a seemingly unified voting bloc, one of enormous importance for Republican party politics. Many observers credited Reagan's election to their influence, and for a time they appeared to dominate American politics. This appearance was deceptive; conservative Christianity never formed as large or as united a front as its leaders suggested, and its influence moderated in the ensuing years. Its seeming resurgence in 1980, however, dramatically exposed the weakness of secularization theory's predictions. Religion had not retreated from the public realm, it had not lost its power to affect political and social affairs. If anything, that power seemed to be growing.

The fall of Communism in Eastern Europe provided another potent example of the continuing power of religious groups. In Poland, the Catholic Church played a large part in the destruction of the Party; the Church was closely affiliated with the Solidarity movement, and it helped to organize and channel resistance to the state. To the east, the breakup of the Soviet Union in 1989 opened the way for a massive revival of the Orthodox Church. Long suppressed by the Communists, the Church became an emblem of the new era in the 1990s. Along with this resurgence came a revival of old religious antipathies. Scapegoating and persecution of Jews, for example, returned with a virulence not seen in decades. For better or worse, these developments gave strong evidence of religion's ability to endure. After the full resources of one of the world's most powerful modern states had worked for half a century to obliterate it, religion in Eastern Europe seemed stronger than ever.

These dramatic events forced a basic rethinking of secularization theory's premises and predictions. At the same time, improved research data collected by sociologists of religion cast doubt on its historical validity as well. Secularization theorists had posited a widespread historical decline in Western religiosity; they supported this view primarily with anecdotal accounts and reports from mainline religious groups. While this type of data lacked empirical rigor, no reliable source of historical religious statistics existed to challenge it. Beginning in the 1980s, however, sociologists began to develop such databases. When they did, they discovered a very different picture of Western religious history. In 1992, for example, Roger Finke and Rodney Stark published *The Churching of America*, the first rigorous and comprehensive study of religious affiliation in the United States. With a degree of detail unprecedented in studies of modern religion, Finke and Stark argued that, appearances to the contrary, religious participation in America had never declined in the way that secularization theory had supposed. Even at the widely accepted low water marks of religious participation – the early 19th century, for example, or the cultural upheavals of the 1960s – overall religious participation had remained largely stable. Individual denominations had often declined, and their supporters often described these events as general losses of faith; but new movements had always replaced them. In particular, fundamentalist and charismatic groups had steadily grown over the course of the nation's history. Overall, this and other studies have tended to undermine, not support, the general thesis of secularization (see also Stark and Iannaccone 1994, Stark and Bainbridge 1985).

These developments, in both the academic and the political worlds, have forced a widespread reexamination of secularization theory. Much of this work has focused on empirical questions – whether or not secularization is indeed occurring, and if so, whether the trend is irreversible. In one of the best-known works, Rodney Stark and William Bainbridge (1985) contend that secularization is one stage in a cycle of religious activity. Throughout history, periods of secularization have spawned religious revivals, which in turn have led to the formation of cults. These cults later become full-fledged churches, which eventually lose touch with their members' needs and become secularized. Stark and Bainbridge do not attack the notion of secularization; rather, they dispute the historical scheme that views secularization as the final death of religion. Similarly, most other critiques of secularization theory have focused on secularization's empirical foundation, rather than on the viability of the concept itself.

A few authors, however, have offered powerful critiques of the basis of the theory. Jeffrey Hadden, for example, has argued that secularization theory is not really a theory at all, but a group of loosely related ideas and arguments united by a vague orienting concept (Hadden 1987). Secularization theorists might all agree that religion is in decline, but they have widely differing ideas about what that decline consists of. Is it a loss of belief among the general population? Is it a loss of temporal authority by religious leaders? Is it a decline of participation in rituals? Is it a decreasing connection between private action and religious principles? These different meanings imply widely different causes and effects, and none of them presupposes the others (see also Martin 1969). Secularization theorists have generally assumed that they all go hand in hand, and have failed to produce a coherent theory that explains their interrelationships (for a notable exception, see Martin 1978). Karel Dobbelaere and others have recognized this weakness, and they have suggested breaking secularization into such levels as societal, organizational, and individual (Dobbelaere 1981). Such a solution, responds Hadden, only emphasizes the basic incoherence of the concept. If secularization's definition is so fragmented, and if its empirical basis is so weak, it might be better to dispense with it altogether than to try to salvage it.

These attacks have left secularization theory reeling, scrambling to rescue its basic premise while assimilating the wave of new data. Most sociologists have acknowledged the need to rethink many of the theory's most important predictions, and even its ardent defenders agree that the secularization thesis has been generally overstated. Yet the theory has by no means been discredited. Despite all the critiques, say its supporters, the evidence for secularization remains everywhere. Churches that drew large congregations a century ago stand empty today. Folk belief in the supernatural – in spirits, ghosts, goblins, and gnomes – has ebbed to near invisibility. In the most modern parts of the world, such as Scandinavia, religion has all but vanished as a regulator of everyday life. The religious standards that once governed sexuality, commerce, and public discourse have given way to private morality and market forces. And while one can argue that new religious movements may eventually replace the old mainline religions, they have not demonstrated the ability to do so. Movements like the New Age garner a lot of press coverage, but relatively few followers; most of those who have dropped out of the older religions have not joined the new ones (Wallis and Bruce 1992; see also Lechner 1991). While sociological critiques of secularization have shaken its foundations, the theory remains the dominant understanding of religion in the modern world.

Secularization Theory and the Meaning of Religion

The empirical and theoretical critiques of secularization theory have left a deeper question largely unexplored. Implicit in the notion of secularization is a distinction between the religious and the secular, between religious and nonreligious ways of understanding and organizing the world. Secularization is the process by which people and institutions move from one of these classifications to the other. A clear definition of these two categories is therefore essential to the theory – both because it establishes the baseline for measuring secularization, and because it establishes secularization as an intellectually viable concept. If no such nonreligious worldview exists, then the most interesting and ambitious claims of secularization theory evaporate. Secularization becomes, not a process of the worldwide decline of religion, but simply one religious change among others, a shift in religious consciousness occurring in a few industrialized nations. In order to claim cross-cultural and historical relevance, the theory must define the nature of both religion and nonreligion.

Most secularization theorists have solved this problem by turning to the supernatural. They define religion as a set of ideas or institutions predicated on the existence of supernatural agencies – what Wallace calls the "supernatural premise" (1966). Insofar as an institution bases its structure or authority on the supernatural, it is religious; to the extent that it rejects or ignores the supernatural premise, it is secular. This solution has a common sense appeal, and it allows a relatively clear division of the two categories. It also corresponds with a familiar division in our own experience, that between religion and science. It presents religion and science as competing explanatory systems, one based on ideas about an unseen world, the other based on observations of empirical experiments. The increasing effectiveness of science provides both a cause and a measure of secularization; secularization is, in large part, a movement of thought away from the supernatural to the real.

Despite its intuitive appeal, this approach to defining religion has a number of drawbacks. Some of them have to do with its theoretical consistency; the supernatural is a notoriously culture-bound concept, and it may well be impossible to define in a way that has cross-cultural validity. We will return to this problem in Part IV. Perhaps a more basic issue, however, is the narrow view of religion that this definition implies. By contrasting religion with science, secularization theory takes an essentially Tylorian approach to the subject. It casts religion as an explanatory system, a means of comprehending the mysteries of human experience and the natural world. It is the means by which religion does this – the invocation of the supernatural – that distinguishes it from scientific and secular thought. In their essential purposes, however, science and religion cover about the same ground. This characterization of religion has something to it. All religions provide some explanation of earthly existence, and most provide origin myths and explanations for the natural worlds in which they exist. Yet religion goes far beyond these activities. It has to do not only with explaining the natural world, but with constructing the human one. Religious systems define the nature of the person and the community; they structure the relationship of individuals to one another; they provide moral valuations of people and actions. They give a shape and a meaning to work, to child rearing, to gender, to family, to sexuality, to community, to all the identities and activities that make up human existence. It is these broader aspects of religion that make it so important to human life. To ignore them, to characterize religion as a system for explaining nature, is to ignore most of what religion is really about. In basing its understanding of religion on the supernatural, therefore, secularization theory takes a profoundly impoverished view of its subject.

This problem becomes particularly apparent when looking at religious systems in Northern Europe. Secularization is not a trend that has moved uniformly through the religious world of Scandinavia; it has affected some religious movements profoundly, and others only mildly. Pentecostal movements, for example, do not appear to have experienced the drastic fall-off of belief that has afflicted the state Evangelical Lutheran Churches. Within the state churches, some theological factions have lost far more participants than others. Yet the supernatural tenets of these various groups differ relatively little. A Pentecostalist is more likely to believe in gifts of the spirit than a Lutheran; the two will find broad agreement, however, on their ideas about the creation of the universe, the powers of God, the types of supernatural beings in existence, and the ability of modern science to explain the natural world. Within the Lutheran movements, the agreement on such issues will be almost complete. The differences between them revolve less around ideas about the supernatural than around ideas about the human world – how authority should be divided, how the morality of actions should be judged, how sexuality should be regulated, and so on. Their success or failure in the face of modernization must hinge in large part on these worldly dimensions. If we ignore these dimensions in our definition of religion, if we conceive religion essentially as a set of theories about another reality, we will find it difficult to explain adequately the differential success of these groups. To appreciate the complexity of the religious landscape, we need to see religion as something earthly as well as divine.

Such an approach has long characterized anthropological studies of "primitive" religion (e.g., Douglas 1966, 1970, Turner 1968, 1969, Leach 1954, Taussig 1983, Ortner 1989). When describing the beliefs of people in tribal societies, symbolic anthropologists link them with indigenous social and cultural categories. Beliefs about the spirit world both express and help constitute such categories as gender, rank, life-cycle status, wealth, and ethnicity. To describe them as abstract theologies, to remove them from the social context within which they are embedded, would be in a real sense to falsify them, to make an artificial intellectual construct out of a lived social reality. Anthropologists therefore seldom focus on the supernatural as a subject in itself, but look at it rather as one element of a cultural reality, as part of the process through which cultures create the worlds in which they live.[1] Most studies tend to follow Clifford Geertz's approach to defining religion; they see it not as a particular type of belief, but as a set of definitions that establish the basic nature of reality in any society (Geertz 1973: 87-125). Such an approach allows the integration of natural and supernatural in the definition of religion; both the nature of man and the nature of God are elements of cultural reality.

This book suggests that such an expansive understanding of religion is essential for understanding the development of religion in the modern West. Secularization theory's narrow conception of religion, it argues, produces a simplistic and distorted view of Western religious history. It reduces a rich and complex religious world to a few theories about other realities. In doing so, it makes it difficult to understand the differential development of specific religious groups. Only by moving beyond the notion of secularization, by taking an anthropological approach to understanding modern religion, can we understand why religion has changed so much over the past two centuries, and what it means in the contemporary world.

1. An exception to this general tendency has been the psychoanalytic literature, which has looked at the supernatural as expressive of psychological conflicts within a culture (cf. Spiro 1966). This literature, like the secularization literature, sees the supernatural as an objective category, which can be properly used to define religion cross-culturally. Unlike secularization theory, however, psychoanalytic anthropology does not cast religion and science as alternative explanatory paradigms. The value of the supernatural is primarily expressive, and is not particularly threatened by scientific explanations of the world.

I will begin with ethnography. Religion in the West, like religion anywhere, does not exist solely in churches and catechisms. It is intimately linked to the everyday experience of those who practice it. To get a sense of religion's meaning, and the way it has changed in the modern era, we must first get a sense of the lives and history of its practitioners. In the chapters that follow, therefore, I will undertake a close examination of a single community, the island of Mors in northwestern Denmark. This area presents an interesting test for secularization theory. The religious fundamentalism that has swept much of the Western world over the past twenty years has found few converts in the Nordic countries; there such measures of religious faith as attendance in church, belief in God, and respect for clergy have declined steadily for at least thirty years. Proponents of the secularization thesis cite Scandinavia as a type case, and even those who seek to reformulate the theory tend to regard Scandinavia as a secularized society (e.g., Martin 1978, Bainbridge and Stark 1987, Stark and Iannaccone1994, Hamberg 1994). If the secularization paradigm works anywhere, it ought to work here.

The next section presents an ethnographic sketch of Mors Island, covering such areas as geography, history, economy, family, and politics. After that, I will discuss in depth three of the island's most important religious groups, tracing both their histories and their current roles in the lives of their members. Finally, I will return to the question of theory, and of what this island can tell us about secularization and about the nature of religion in general.

Part I

THE SETTING

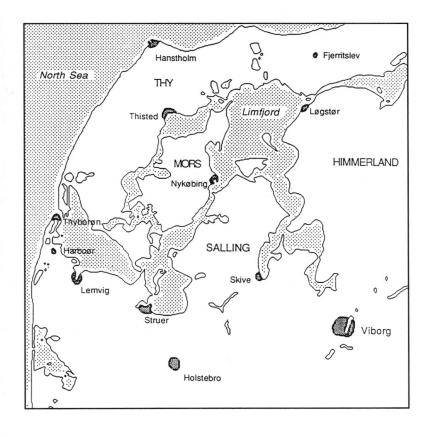

Map 1: Northwestern Jutland, Denmark *(showing major towns)*

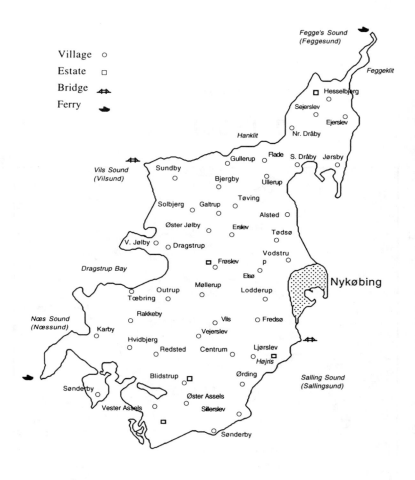

Map 2: Mors Island

1. MORS IN TIME AND SPACE

℞ ℞ ℞

The Island

*H*igh in the north of the Jutland peninsula, the gentle waters of the Limfjord cut a winding swath through the verdant countryside of western Denmark. They flow in from the Kattegat Sea, past the spires and factories of the city of Ålborg, through the narrow Aggersund channel at Nibe, and finally into the North Sea at the fishing harbor of Thyborøn. They reach their widest point as they pass the little town of Løgstør, with the provinces of Thy to the north and Salling to the south. In the middle lies the island of Mors, an irregular oblong wedged lengthwise into the channel. The people who live there call Mors the "Pearl of the Limfjord," after the rich oyster fishery that once flourished there. These people, and the faiths they follow, will be the focus of my study in the pages to come.

I will begin with the island itself. Until this century, Mors was divided into two regions, called *herreder*. The dividing line ran from Nykøbing to Dragstrup Bay, and marked both an administrative and a cultural boundary; each *herred* had its own royal administrator, and each tended to be endogamous. The division no longer exists officially, but it lingers on in popular vocabulary, particularly in descriptions of the landscape. Northern Mors is a land of rolling hills, dramatic cliffs, and Viking graves; Southern Mors is a place of rich fields, gentle countryside, and quiet har-

17

bors. The difference is noticeable almost as soon as one crosses the old boundary. In neither herred does the landscape reach such extremes as the rugged fjords of Norway or the broad plains of Sjælland, but the variety of landscapes in such a small area is remarkable. Morsingboer are very proud of this diversity, and they have a story to explain it. When God created the world, they say, He made Mors first, as a model; but in all the rest of His creation, He couldn't find room to reproduce all of its beauties.

The northern coast is indeed impressive. The northern tip of the island is Feggeklit, a massive clay peninsula whose cliffs rise 25 meters straight out of the fjord. Similar cliffs mark the whole northern coastline as it winds its way down to the Vilsund; the highest, Hanklit, reaches a height of 60 meters. Behind the cliffs, rows of steep hills parallel the coastline, gradually easing into the rolling hills and broad valleys that characterize most of North Mors. The land, as well as the coastline, becomes flatter as it moves south, sloping into marshes and sand flats around Dråby and Dragstrup Bays. All of it is intensively cultivated, even the top of Feggeklit; woods are almost absent.

Beneath much of this landscape lies Mors's only industrially significant natural resource. It is a special kind of clay, called *moler*, and the world's only known sources for it are here and on nearby Fur Island. It is not a particularly glamorous commodity, its main uses being for cat litter and certain kinds of heat-resistant brick. The deposits are quite valuable, however, and mining them is one of Mors's most important industries. Excavation pits pockmark the coastline around Ejerslev, Hesselbjerg, and Skærbæk, and a large processing plant sends a constant plume of smoke into the air near Skærbæk; political disagreements simmer constantly about the relative value of the industry and of the environment it is slowly eating away.

Southern Mors has no such excavations, nor many cliffs for them to devour. The coastline is low and in many places marshy, and the land is for the most part relatively flat. As in North Mors, the land is all intensively cultivated, and large areas of marsh have been drained to make fields. In several places, the cultivation includes small forests planted for wood production. In addition, much of the marshland on the small peninsula called Agerø has been set aside as a bird sanctuary.

Travelers to and from Mors have crossed for centuries using four ferries: the Feggesund ferry, from Feggeklit to Thy; the Vilsund ferry, to Thy near Sundby; the Neesund ferry in the southwest, from Nees to southern Thy; and the Sallingsund ferry, from just south of Nykøbing to Glyngøre in Salling.[1] Bridges have replaced the ferries at Vilsund (1939) and Sallingsund (1977), where most of the traffic comes across. A modern four-lane highway connects these two points; a smaller highway runs from Sallingsund up to Feggesund. Otherwise, traffic within the island moves on small paved or gravel roads, which are generally well maintained and nearly always passable.

Almost all the sea traffic comes into the harbor at Nykøbing, which lies by the sheltered waters of Kloster Bay. A few other harbors are scattered around the shores of the island, but none services more than a few boats; besides Nykøbing, only Sillerslev harbor on the southeast tip of Mors has facilities for large ships.

The weather on Mors, like the terrain, varies a great deal without going to extremes. The temperature ranges from an average of 0° C in January to 16° C in July, and seldom goes above 25° C or below – 5° C. Rainfall is high, an average of 65 cm per year; it rains during all seasons, but especially in the fall and spring. As in most of Denmark, winters are not very severe. While the frequent wind and hail storms do some damage, snowfall is relatively light, and in the two years prior to my arrival it was absent entirely. Summers are usually warm and pleasant – although intemperate weather can arise very quickly – and flocks of German and Swedish tourists fill the summer houses scattered all over the island during July and August.

The weather was not always this mild. Accounts from fifty years or more ago refer frequently to the bitter cold of the winters, and up through World War II it was not unusual to be able to cross the Limfjord to Glyngøre or Fur Island on foot. These days the harbor sometimes freezes, but shipping is seldom blocked for very long.

The one constant in Mors weather is the wind, which seems to blow all the time. It turns spring showers into driving torrents, and hailstorms into health threats. It also turns windmill blades, however, and furnishes Mors with a valuable power source; tall white metal windmills dot almost every hilltop on the island, contributing up to a tenth of the residents' electrical power.

Settlement

Settlements on Mors, as in all of Denmark, fall into two categories: town *(byen)* and countryside *(landet)*. Countryside includes the forty or so vil-

---

1. For a lively account of the history of ferry service in the area, see Holch Andersen (1974, 1989).

lages and hamlets scattered around the island, as well as the farm areas around them. Town refers only to Nykøbing, the market town on Kloster Bay on the eastern shore. Nykøbing has been the center of trade, government, and industry on the island for at least six centuries, and it has developed an infrastructure and social structure unique on Mors. Settlement patterns in the countryside, in contrast, are fairly standard across the island; a village in the northeast looks very much like one in the southwest, and both are subject to the same sorts of developmental pressures and problems. Some cultural differences do exist between villages, particularly between northern and southern ones, but these variations tend not to be reflected in village layout.

The countryside of Mors is divided into thirty-two parishes, or *sogne*, ranging in population from fifty to four hundred. In the heart of each of these parishes lies a village, usually consisting of a church, a few shops, and a number of houses; depending on the size of the town, there may also be a post office, a small bus station, a meeting house, a mission house, and perhaps a gas station. Most of these buildings usually stand fairly close together, often around the crossroads at the center of the village. The church, however, because of the space needed for the graveyard, usually lies a bit further away. For larger towns, several sidestreets with houses on them might cluster around this center. After these comes a ring of farms of various sizes; beyond these, farms are scattered across the landscape of the parish at odd intervals.

The buildings, like most of those in Denmark, are made mainly of brick. A determined searcher can find a few wooden buildings standing on the island, mostly abandoned fishing houses on the coast; the island's forests have been gone for centuries, however, and virtually all recent construction has consisted of masonry. The buildings are not, on the whole, particularly old, dating mostly to the 19th century. Roofs are steeply pitched, and are usually made of tile or tin; the beautiful thatched roofs so common in rural Fyn and Sjælland are quite rare in West Jutland. Houses tend to be boxy, plain, and very well maintained. They stand very close to the street, and usually have small gardens in the back. Shops look much like houses, although many have display windows and illuminated plastic signs. Villages have no monuments, courtyards, or parks marking their center, but the sudden cluster of buildings leaves no doubt that one has arrived.

Two kinds of building diverge from the general architectural uniformity. Government buildings, for one, tend to be large and sprawling, conforming to the latest architectural styles of the times they were built.

Most larger villages have a school, for example, and many have nursing homes; these usually lie a short way away from the center, and are landscaped in a way that is unobtrusive, but clearly different from the rest of the town. Most date to no earlier than 1950.

The other exception involves religious buildings. Nearly every village of any size on Mors has its own church, usually dating to the 12th century. Indeed, the concentration of churches on the island is one of the highest in Denmark, with a church every 11 square kilometers compared with a national average of one for every 22. The poet Jeppe Aakjær once remarked that the Morsingboer of old must have either loved church or hated walking. Most churches consist of a main hall, a chancel, and an entry hall; many also have a brick bell tower on one end, added centuries after the original building. The old churches are built out of large blocks of granite, with tile roofs. Most are painted white, and are surrounded by a small cemetery and an outer wall.[2]

Most of the shopkeepers, artisans, laborers, and professionals in a village live in this central area. The farmers, in contrast, live on their farms outside of the village. Morsingboer classify these farms in two broad categories, based on size. Homesteads *(husmandssteder)* are those with up to about 14 acres of land;[3] larger ones, ranging up to around 200 acres, count as true farms *(gårde)*. In the 19th century, 14 acres of land was around the minimum necessary for a farm to be self-sufficient. Those who owned less had to supplement the homestead's income with outside work, often on nearby farms during planting and harvesting. The low wages and unreliability of such work made homesteaders' subsistence meager and chancy, always vulnerable to disruption by illness or crop failure; such a disaster frequently led to beggary or the poor farm. Farm owners, in contrast, lived quite well, in spacious farmhouses with hands and servants. While that difference has changed radically in the past fifty years, the terms of reference remain.

The difference reveals itself in the architecture. A homestead generally consists of a small house and a simple barn, placed at right angles to one another on two sides of a small courtyard. A small vegetable garden might stand on the other side of the house, together with a chicken yard or pasture for a few cows. On a farm, in contrast, the house is usually

2. Borg et al. (1989) give a detailed description, complete with photographs, of every church on Mors. The introductory chapters on church architecture and maintenance are particularly helpful.
3. Some writers translate this term as "smallholding" (e.g., Det Danske Selskab 1964). *Husmand* means, literally, a "house man," and *husmandssted* a "house man's place."

fairly large, and the barn wraps in a U-shape around the other three sides of the courtyard. Additional outbuildings for farm equipment may stand nearby. A carefully tended lawn lies on the other side of the house, and a ring of trees or hedges surrounds the whole complex. Whereas a homestead is really just a house and barn, a farm is an enclosed little world.

Today, most of the homesteads have little or no land; as homesteading became increasingly untenable after World War II, most homesteaders sold their land to surrounding farms and became full-time wage workers. Many small farms have followed suit, and of the buildings one sees as one drives through the countryside, relatively few house working farmers. A typical farm today covers about 35 hectares, and is worked by the farm owner alone using modern farm machinery. Fields are often scattered over large areas, depending on where the farmer has been able to buy land. In general, each farmhouse holds one nuclear family; it is unusual for parents and adult children to live in the same house.

Another kind of farm used to exist on Mors: the estate, or *herregård*. These were huge farms, covering thousands of acres and employing dozens of servants and hands, which were established before the expansion of freeholding in the late 18th century. The owner was often a nobleman, and held legal authority over the people who lived on the estate's lands. These estates gradually sold off most of their lands during the 19th century, and today they have little effect on the life of the island. Some of the estate buildings remain, however, including magnificent moated manors with extensive lands at Højris and Ullerup. Others have been converted into schools and museums.

Crops on Mors include wheat, oats, barley, rape, mustard, and rye. Much of this production goes to support the island's most important agricultural product, pork. Mors has a large number of highly mechanized pig farms, which produce very high-quality pork. Pig farming, which yields a good profit using very little space and labor, works well in a land with relatively small, fertile farms and high labor costs.

The Market Town

The town of Nykøbing wraps around the quiet coastline of Kloster Bay, the largest and quietest harbor on the island. The name means "new market," and it must at some point have been just that. Now, however, it is at least seven centuries old, and it has served as the island's center of trade and administration for as long as the historical record can tell. In 1460, a royal decree restricted all trade on Mors to the confines of the town; though this decree lost its force in the 19th century, most of the significant commerce and industry still takes place there. Nykøbing also contains the island's governmental offices, hospital, gymnasium, trade school, museum, and 8,500 of its approximately 23,000 residents. The town has experienced several distinct waves of growth, and the current layout reflects these surges.

The oldest section of town stands on the north side of the harbor, between the shore and Østergade; called the "fishing town," it consists mainly of rows of low brick houses along narrow streets with narrow, deteriorating sidewalks. The houses are small and cramped, and until fairly recently most of the residents were poor fishermen and factory workers. Today the population is more mixed, although the section remains one of the town's poorest and worst maintained.

The areas to the west and south of the harbor bear the marks of the late 19th century, when the town's surging industry began to demand housing for factory workers. Rows of small brick houses with sharply pitched roofs line Nørregade, Nygade, Vestergade and the small streets around them. Before the 1950s, these cramped two-storey homes each housed two to four factory-worker families, in fairly squalid conditions; today most hold only one family, often elderly couples who have moved in from the countryside. In the middle of this section, between Nørregade and Nygade, lies the sprawling building complex of the Mors Island Ironworks *(Morsø Jernstøberi)*, the foundry that drew many of the workers here. The soot-stained brick buildings, up to five storeys tall and surrounded by a high brick wall with elaborate cast iron, tower over the heart of the town.

Another imposing edifice lies on the other side of town: Dueholm Kloster, once home to a monastery of the Knights of Malta. Built in the 14th century, Dueholm was converted to an estate after the Reformation, and it remained a manor until the beginning of the 20th century. It lost most of its buildings, including a sizable cathedral, during a series of fires that ravaged Nykøbing in the 16th and 17th centuries; it gradually sold off its lands during the 19th century, and in 1909 the remaining buildings were converted into the Mors Island Historical Museum. The museum includes the main building, an impressive white brick structure with arched windows and a high tiled roof, and two smaller buildings of the same style. Around it lies a grid of streets, laid in the early 20th century on land that had been the estate's gardens. The houses in this section of town, mostly built between 1900 and 1925, are larger and better furnished than those in the fishing and factory areas; they have more space and more land, and in some cases boast such architectural flourishes as false fronts and bay windows.

These areas of Nykøbing were almost entirely completed by 1940, and their appearance has changed little since then. The big postwar expansion in the town's area occurred to the north and south, where rising prosperity spurred a building boom that lasted until the late 1970s. To the north of town, along small paved and gravel roads that had previously led to summer houses, modern houses now stand on quarter-acre and larger lots. Unlike those in the center, these houses often stand back from the street, with well-kept lawns and gardens in front. The architecture is often very modern, with such touches as decks and sliding glass doors. Many have tall hedges surrounding the property; the resulting insularity of the home, sometimes nicknamed "hedge fascism" (*hækkefacism*), contrasts sharply with the close crowding of the town center. Such residences are expensive to build or buy, and the residents of the area include many professionals, artisans, and merchants.

A similar development took place on the south side of town, on the streets to either side of Fruevej and on the Refshammar peninsula. The areas closest to the center tend to have smaller houses and a greater mix of white and blue collar workers; Refshammar in particular has many small houses with young families. As one travels south along Fruevej, the houses become larger and the hedges somewhat higher. The road leads eventually to Fårup, a village that Nykøbing engulfed during the postwar expansion. Along this stretch of the road, no houses are visible at all from the main road; instead, tall plantings of brush line the road, with periodic breaks for small streets leading straight back. Each of these streets quickly ends at a perpendicular one, which in turn has dead ends at either end. The streets thus form a T-shape, along which stand large modern houses on immaculately tended lawns. People who live in the center of town jokingly refer to this area as the "oatmeal quarter," oatmeal being the food of poor people; some of the town's wealthiest inhabitants make their homes here.

Not all of the postwar construction was aimed at the upper class. Apartment buildings went up near the courthouse, next to the town hall, and just south of Dueholm Kloster. Their architecture varies from drab four-storey brick boxes to pleasant complexes with courtyards and balconies. Most of them are cooperatively owned by the tenants, and all are immaculately maintained; occupants range from young families to retirees.

The true center of town life lies just south of the ironworks, along the streets connecting Town Hall Square with Church Square, Little Square, and Kloster Square. For centuries these were the main streets in the town, and in the 19th century they were the site of the main shops and markets as well as several factories and hotels. In 1971, the town closed these streets to vehicle traffic and repaved them with flagstones; following a national trend in urban planning, it rechristened the streets as Gågaden, The Walking Street, a pedestrian center for town activity. Trees, planters, and picnic benches stand at intervals along the way, and cobbled plazas for meeting or picnicking cover the centers of the squares. The factories and hotels have all closed, leaving only shops and restaurants. The shops range in size from the Løvbjerg and Kvickly supermarkets, which lie at opposite ends of the Walking Street, to small clothing, furniture, radio, and housewares shops; the restaurants include three sizable sit-down establishments as well as several hot dog stands.

Nykøbing advertises its Walking Street as "Danmarks Utroligste Gågade" – "Denmark's Most Unbelievable Walking Street." No one seems quite sure who coined this slogan, or why; neither I nor anyone I asked could think of anything that made this Gågade very different from those that run through almost every market town in the country. In the local context, though, the Walking Street is rather unbelievable. On an island of small rural villages, in a town of factory houses and quiet streets, it bustles with the modern flair of a major city. Merchants display the latest wares and fashions behind smartly decorated plate-glass windows; shoppers pore over tables of merchandise set out in the streets; tourists sip coffee at tables with Carlsberg Beer umbrellas. Lighted signs and windows illuminate the street at night and on dark winter afternoons. While the rest of the island contents itself with pubs serving hot dogs, the Walking Street boasts Italian, Chinese, and nouvelle cuisine restaurants. To visit the Nykøbing Gågade is to taste a bit of the cosmopolitan world otherwise so removed from Mors. And it is a taste that Morsingboer enjoy; on Friday evenings, when the stores stay open until seven o'clock, people come from all corners of the island to shop, to socialize, and to stare.

Of course, there are other reasons to come to Nykøbing. The town contains most of the island's governmental buildings, for example; a large office building for the *kommune* stands on the shore next to the harbor, the island's police and court building *(tinghuset)* stands next to the cemetery, and a number of offices are located in the old town hall at Town Hall Square. The island's hospital is also here, overlooking the bluffs on the coast north of town. Two nursing homes, one psychiatric nursing home, and a number of complexes for housing the elderly are scattered through the town. In addition, just outside of town to the west lies the gymnasium and technical school complex, which draws students from the entire island.

Morsingboer also come to Nykøbing for work. Many of the island's industrial buildings lie along or near Limfjordsvej, which runs along the outer perimeter of the town. They include the finish-work plant for the ironworks, a plastics factory, a metal plating factory, a brick factory, a grain elevator, a small publishing shop, a stonecutting works, and several machine shops. Workers commute to these factories from all over eastern Mors. In addition, two large maritime enterprises sit on the Ørodde peninsula north of the harbor: the Mors Island Shipyard and the well-known (in Denmark) Glyngøre Limfjord Mussel Factory. Although some industries operate elsewhere on Mors, most of those not involved in excavation have their centers in Nykøbing.

As a full-size town, Nykøbing also has some facilities for recreation not found elsewhere on the island. It has two small sports arenas, for example, as well as a small soccer stadium. A movie theater showing first-run films lies just off the Walking Street, and the gymnasium and one of the schools each has stages for live theater. Two small parks, one north of the fishing village and one on Refshammar, offer pleasant walks and swans for children to feed during the spring and summer. And in a society where birthday and anniversary parties held outside the home are important social occasions, the concentration of restaurants in Nykøbing is a significant local resource.

Religious buildings in Nykøbing parallel those in the villages, although on a larger scale. The church, which stands together with the Church Center on Church Square, holds up to 850 people and is served by three priests. A splendid red brick building with a slate roof and a tall copper-clad tower, it was built in 1891 to replace an ancient but decaying church on the same site. The graveyard and a burial chapel lie near the courthouse on the north side of town. The mission house, one of the largest on Mors, stands next to the ironworks on Nygade. Several small free churches *(frikirker)* have their centers in the town; the Salvation Army, the Pentecostal Church, the Apostolic Church, and the Jehovah's Witnesses all have church buildings in Nykøbing.

Nykøbing, as we have just described it, sounds very different from the rest of Mors, and, indeed, it is. The trendy boutiques on the Walking Street, the computerized kommune offices on the waterfront, and the bustling factories on Limfjordsvej all seem a world away from the winding lanes, quiet farmhouses and manured fields of the countryside. This appearance, however, is deceptive. Nykøbing and Mors are part of the same world, and have been for a very long time; neither could exist the way it does without the other. Nykøbing draws from the countryside to provide workers for its factories, materials for its industries, consumers for its goods, clients for its services, citizens for its government, and worshipers for its churches. The villages look to Nykøbing for trade, for work, for medical care, for government services, and for a link to the world beyond. When looking at settlement patterns, or anything else for that matter, it is important to remember that the town and countryside on Mors work as a system. Morsingboer themselves see it that way. For all the differences between them, town and countryside work as, and are perceived as, elements in a single entity.

History

To understand Mors as it exists today, one must first know something about the island's long history. In any community, of course, the social groups and cultural symbols owe something to the events that have affected it in the past. Understanding history has a special importance when studying Mors, however, because history is so important to the inhabitants themselves. Morsingboer value history highly, and they put a remarkable amount of energy into reading, writing, and researching it. They place particular weight on local history, which most adults know in considerable detail. To be a Morsingbo is not only to live in a certain place on the earth, but also to live in a certain place in time, to be part of a stream of historical events that reaches back for centuries. The past is an almost tangible part of the community in which Morsingboer live, and any understanding of the community must begin there.[4]

4. Dates and names in the following discussion of Mors's history derive primarily from Pontoppidan (1769), Schade (1811), Christensen (1901), and Holch Andersen (1990). Much of the more general information comes from discussion with Morsingboer, particularly K.G. Holch Andersen, Erik Lau Jørgensen, Suzanne Overgaard, and Holger Vester, as well as conversations with Professors Palle Ove Christiansen and Margareta Balle-Petersen of the University of Copenhagen. As the discussion moves closer to the present, oral sources become progressively more important. Det Danske Selskab (1964) gives a wide-ranging English- language history of the Limfjord as a whole. For those interested in a more general history of Denmark, several good English-language histories exist. Lauring (1963) offers a conversational overview of Danish history, while Glyn-Jones (1986) provides a scholarly treatment. Oakley falls somewhere between them with his accessible but

Human history on Mors goes a long way back, for at least seven millennia. Archeologists have found settlements from 5000 BC elsewhere in the Limfjord, and similar settlements probably existed on Mors at the same time. The ancestors of the current inhabitants may have come to Denmark from Sweden in the 6th century AD, driving out the previous residents (Oakley 1972: 26). No one really knows, of course; details from this period derive mainly from the interpretation of archeological data, and even where some written sources exist, historical reconstructions are largely guesswork. It is fairly clear, however, that the economy involved both agriculture and fishing, and that the island was relatively densely settled by the end of the first millennium AD. The countryside was organized around estates, to which most peasants were bound by obligations of both work and military service. These estates were owned by a class of nobles, although in Jutland the social distance between nobles and peasants was relatively small, and there were many more freeholders than in eastern Denmark. The island lay under royal authority; a certain amount of local autonomy prevailed, however, including a limited democracy operating through village meetings *(tinger)*. Norse paganism dominated religion at least up to the 10th century. After that point Denmark became officially Christian, with bishops, priests, and monasteries, although pagan beliefs persisted up to the 19th century in some areas.

One of the island's earliest historical distinctions illustrates the difficulty of unraveling fact from folklore for this era. According to local legend, Mors was the birthplace of Christianity in Denmark. In 974, the story goes, Denmark went to war with the Christian Kaiser Otto of Germany. Led by King Harald Bluetooth, the Danes fared quite badly; Otto chased Harald's army up through Jutland, and finally cornered him on Mors. There, Harald agreed to undergo baptism, in return for which Otto withdrew from Denmark and allowed Harald to retain his throne. The baptism is supposed to have taken place in a holy spring near Dragstrup, which residents still proudly show off today. Since Harald ultimately imposed Christianity on the entire country, this spring can lay claim to being the baptismal font of the Danish people.

The basic elements of this story are quite sound, and indeed such historians as Erik Pontoppidan and Adam of Bremen report it as fact. The war did occur, Otto did run Harald to ground in western Jutland, and Harald did convert. Mors's role, however, is more dubious. According to folklorist Iørn Piø (1975), the precise location of the events was never recorded historically; the Icelandic and Norwegian historians who first wrote accounts of the war simply said it was probably an island in northwest Jutland. Adam of Bremen picked Mors as the island in his 11th-century account, and when Pontoppidan published his Danish Atlas in 1769, he relied on Bremen's judgment (1769: 530-31). The Atlas eventually found its way to Mors, where the residents assigned places for the events. By the 20th century, Mors's distinction as the birthplace of Danish Christianity was established both by historical sources and by a legend presumed to be ancient. Although Harald may never have set foot on Mors, his conversion there stands in the perception of many Morsingboer as an established part of their history.

The historical record becomes firmer by the 13th century, when Nykøbing appears to have been founded. The town was established as a market on the site of two earlier villages, Venner and Vettels, and served both as a market town and a fishing port. Soon afterward, around 1350, the Order of the Knights of Malta founded the Dueholm Monastery on the site of an estate on the town's southern border. Much of the town's area lay in royal hands; the largest landowners were the crown and the monastery, and most residents were bound either to the king or to the abbot. Relations between the town and the monastery were fairly friendly, although the town was clearly subservient to its powerful southern neighbor.

Conditions elsewhere on the island are harder to pin down, owing to the lack of documentary evidence. In the 15th century, however, Morsingboer appear to have shared in the general downturn of peasant living standards that characterized that century in Denmark. These involved both increased taxes to pay for royal military adventures and a tightening of the bonds that held peasants to their lands. A great deal of rural unrest resulted, and the farmers of Mors took part in a major peasant uprising in 1441. The uprising failed, though, and peasants remained under harsher conditions until the 18th century.

The town, in contrast, fared very well in the 15th century. It received official royal market status in 1460, meaning that no trade could take place anywhere on Mors but Nykøbing. In the same year, a royal decree forbade nonnative fishermen in the Limfjord to salt or sell their catch outside of a few sanctioned ports; as one of these ports, Nykøbing became an important fishing community. Moreover, still in the same year, the king retaliated against some of the nearby villages that had participated in the 1441 uprising by granting Nykøbing large portions of their lands. In the course of a few years, Nykøbing grew from a tiny market town feeding off the nearby monastery's business to a thriving center of trade and fishing. This new-found independence led to a good deal of friction between the town and the monastery, including a series of legal battles, which the monastery generally won.

The victories did not last long. In 1522, a civil war broke out in Denmark. The reigning king, Christian II, was challenged by a group of nobles led by the Protestant Duke Frederik of Holstein. Christian's relatively benign acricultural policies had made him popular throughout the Danish countryside, and many Morsingboer sided with him. Frederik ultimately won, however, and in 1536 he imposed a Protestant Reformation on the country. By the standards of other European countries, the Danish Reformation was quite mild; bishops were released and provided pensions after their forced conversions, and monks were allowed to remain on their monasteries for some time. Still, the monasteries eventually closed, and Dueholm was sold off by the crown as an estate. It remained a working farm until the end of the 19th century.

Although it now had independence from Dueholm, Nykøbing had little to celebrate over the next two centuries. Large fires ravaged the town in 1560, 1603, 1628, 1659, 1690, 1715, and 1748; their cumulative economic effect was catastrophic. Invading armies took an even greater toll. During a series of Danish wars with other northern European countries, Mors was occupied by Germans in 1627-29, Swedes in 1643-45, and a series of armies between 1657 and 1660. Each of the invaders extorted huge sums from the island's residents, in the process imposing crushing burdens on the peasants and stripping the possessions of the nobles and merchants. Not until the middle of the 18th century did Mors begin to regain the standard of prosperity it had enjoyed at the beginning of the 16th.

During all this time, the social structure out in the countryside had changed relatively little. Except for the freeholders, most peasants in the 18th century lived in the centers of the villages and worked the land of the estate to which they belonged. They used the same basic tools and methods that their great-grandfathers had used, with much the same results. Nykøbing had grown considerably, to 531 by 1787, but it was still not much larger than a large village. Taken as a whole, Mors in 1750 looked and worked very much like the Mors of 1550 – a quiet rural corner of Denmark's far western hinterland.

But not for long. In the next century, Mors entered a period of change more rapid and profound than any in its previous history. It began with a series of agricultural reforms enacted by the crown in the late 18th century. The reforms released the peasants from their obligation to live on their ancestral estates, and they made it much easier to sell estate lands for freehold farms. As a result, estate owners in need of money could sell off pieces of their holdings to the peasants who worked them. Over the next century, estates on Mors slowly began to shrink, and the ranks of the peasantry began to give way to an emerging class of independent farmers. At the same time, some of the peasants who could not afford to buy land began to make their way to Nykøbing; these peasants formed the basis for the labor force that Nykøbing would need to develop into an industrial town.

The expansion of freeholding meant major changes for the structure of the villages. For one thing, farmers no longer needed to live in the village center; they could build houses on their own land, and most of them did. The population thus spread out across the countryside, and the tightly clustered networks of the rural social system became somewhat looser. For another, classes of farmers based on size of holdings began to emerge. As mentioned earlier, the rural population divided itself into farm owners and smallholders, who often looked very differently at political and cultural issues. But perhaps most importantly, farmers who bought land suddenly found themselves with new political, economic, and cultural interests. Improved production methods could benefit them directly, as could better transportation systems, better slaughterhouses, better dairies, and better education. The new rural landowners, unlike their peasant predecessors, had strong incentives to change the shape of farming in Denmark.

In the first half of the 19th century, they gained the power to do so. This period was a hard one for the Danish crown, as a series of military and diplomatic disasters humiliated the nation and robbed it of most of its empire. Perhaps as a result of the crown's weakness, the lower classes saw their rights expand steadily. A school act of 1814 brought literacy to the entire nation; elected regional councils were established in 1837; elected county and parish councils followed in 1841. In 1849, Denmark adopted a new constitution, which effectively democratized the entire nation. It handed most of the royal power to a legislature elected by universal male suffrage, and it legalized alternatives to the national Lutheran Church. This constitution was quickly followed by acts that abolished service obligations for peasants, eliminated the distinction between the lands of nobles and commoners, and lifted the monopoly of the towns on trade and industry.

These changes brought a monumental increase in the freedom and political might of the rural population. Farmers acted on the opportunity in concert, forming cooperative associations to serve their needs and

31

promote their interests. They established populist political groups, which as the United Left Party gained control of the legislature in the 1870s. They built cooperative dairies and slaughterhouses, in order to benefit from economies of scale without surrendering control of production. They established cooperative stores and banks, to escape the power of merchants and financiers. And in some areas, they gathered around preachers of the folklife-affirming Grundtvigian religious movement (see pp. 106-151).

All of these developments affected life in the Mors countryside. A cooperative dairy was organized in 1877, and a cooperative slaughterhouse in 1903. Left Party chapters sprouted in villages all over the island, and politics became a matter of vigorous dispute. Farmers joined local and national associations to bring the latest agricultural methods to their fields; homesteaders formed an association to improve small farming. In general, the 19th century saw a florescence of self-help and education associations throughout rural Mors. These associations successfully raised both the living standards and the political influence of the farming population.

The movement reached its high point in the northwestern village of Øster Jølby. This village lay in the center of some of the most Grundtvigian-influenced regions of northern Mors; this romanticist religious movement, which I will discuss in the next chapter, celebrated rural folk culture and stressed the importance of free thought in education and worship. Such ideas accorded well with the new political and cultural mindset of the farmers. When the Gruntvigians built a church in Øster Jølby in 1870, therefore, the town became the center of a number of farmers' associations. Members of the new congregation established a "people's bank" *(Morslands Folkebank);* they formed a historical and cultural society; they organized gymnastics and shooting clubs; they held lectures and meetings to acquaint farmers with their historical and political situation. In 1876, they built a large eight-sided meeting house to hold both athletic and speaking events, and the building became a favorite stop on the nation's Grundtvigian and farm movement lecture circuit. Perhaps most importantly, followers of the movement built their own schools in the town. These "free schools" *(friskoler)* and "folk high schools" *(folkehøjskoler)* followed Grundtvigian educational principles, and they became a powerful force in the life of the island.

An equally powerful force was mounting at the same time in Nykøbing, which in the second half of the century emerged as an industrial town. Beginning with the iron foundry in 1853, a number of labor-intensive businesses arose in Nykøbing, drawing on the influx of unemployed former peasants from the countryside. They included several cigar factories, textile factories, a shipworks, and the island's cooperative slaughterhouse. The harbor became increasingly important both for fishing and for commerce. These factors made for major changes in the character of the town. The population exploded, rising from 1,168 in 1831 to 4,507 in 1901. The rising population necessitated paved and lighted streets, gas and electric works, water works, and a rudimentary railroad. The increased wealth of the town brought with it a new church, a new cemetery and chapel, the planting of parks and small woods, and the erection of new schools, statues, and institutions for the poor and old. The increased population brought pollution, disease, and rows of cramped factory housing.

The social effects of the changes in Nykøbing differed drastically from those in the country. Whereas the farmer's movement had unified the rural population through cultural and political action, the rise of industry in Nykøbing divided the town more sharply between the rich and the poor. Merchants, artisans, and factory owners saw their wealth increase as the town grew. The steadily swelling ranks of the factory workers, however, saw only more cramped working and living conditions, increased pollution and disease, and worsening poverty. In the course of half a century, Nykøbing developed a laboring underclass it had never had before. These workers generally supported the quasi-socialist Social Democratic Party after its establishment in 1876, and Nykøbing remains the party's stronghold on the island today.

Not all of those who left the countryside went to Nykøbing; many of them left Denmark altogether. While Danish emigration to America never reached the scale it did from Norway and Sweden, almost 10,000 Danes left every year during the last two decades of the 19th century. No precise figures are available for Mors, but the number was considerable, and today it is virtually impossible to find a Morsingbo who does not have family in America. Most of the emigrants were young, from the countryside, and male. Many of them were third or fourth sons in their families; since eldest sons usually inherited their fathers' farms, emigration represented one of the few chances for a younger son to get land of his own (see Hvidt 1971).

Mors endured occasional economic crises during the 19th and early 20th centuries, as well as several severe epidemics and an occupation by Germany in 1864.[5] On the whole, though, prosperity increased

5. Holch Andersen (1976) details the experience of Morsingboer during the war of 1864.

steadily. Productivity and living standards rose for the farmers, while industry and commerce expanded in Nykøbing. Denmark's neutrality made even World War I a boon for a while; export prices rose for grain and manufactured goods, with little regard to quality. But in the long run, the war marked the end of the island's growth period. The price fall afterward hurt farmers, and many merchants who had invested in war industries found their investments worthless. A rash of bankruptcies followed, which in turn brought the island's major bank to the brink of failure. The island's economy did slowly recover, but the depression that swept Europe after 1929 dragged Mors down with it. Grain and meat prices dropped, some factories in Nykøbing closed, and living standards took a sharp fall. And just as the island began to regain its footing in the late 1930s, World War II and the German invasion brought everything to a halt.

Denmark's experience of World War II was unique in Europe, and it had a strong influence on the nation's subsequent development. When the Germans invaded in 1940, the national government decided that resistance would be futile; instead, they opted to maintain a limited sovereignty by cooperating with the invaders. As a "model protectorate" of the German Reich, Denmark was to retain its own government and police force, and be spared the repressive policies applied to most nations conquered by the Nazis. This policy infuriated many Danes, who considered any cooperation with the Nazis immoral, but for a while it shielded the country from the worst of the Germans' tactics. In the long term, it proved unworkable. The Germans quickly abrogated the treaty, forcing the Danish government to sign treaties and pass laws against its will. They also required Danish industries to produce for the German war effort, paying for the goods with funds "borrowed" from the Danish treasury. The Danish population, angry to begin with, soon organized a startlingly effective underground to sabotage factories and railroads. This sabotage brought German reprisals, which increasingly strained the protectorate agreement. Finally, in August of 1943, following an impasse over the punishment of saboteurs, Germany dissolved the government and placed the nation under martial law. A month later, Gestapo troops moved to round up the Danish Jews for transport to concentration camps; in one of the few bright moments in the history of the Holocaust, outraged Danes from all social strata managed to rescue almost all the Jews and smuggle them to neutral Sweden. The Gestapo controlled the country for the rest of the war, exercising considerable brutality in the big cities before they withdrew in May 1944. Over its course, the war cost Denmark dearly in lives, capital, and national trauma. Compared with the rest of Europe, however, Denmark fared very well; the government's submission to the invasion prevented significant damage from the Germans, while the underground's effectiveness in sabotage meant that the British did relatively little bombing. Although its suffering and popular resistance gave it a war record to be proud of, Denmark emerged essentially intact from the conflict.

The same could be said of Mors. The German army occupied Mors from 1940 to 1944, with a headquarters in Nykøbing and a small number of troops in farmhouses around the island. They took over government, rationed and appropriated goods, and controlled all traffic going in and out; otherwise, they left the islanders mostly alone. Nearly all older Morsingboer, however, have vivid and angry memories of the occupation. Some were forced to work for the Germans, whose emplacement building offered the only employment during several harsh winters. Many men joined the resistance, which was primarily oriented toward aiding the English in the event of an Allied invasion. British planes dropped packages of guns and ammunition at night, and the farmers who formed the movement used them in secret night drills. Secret radios kept resistance leaders in close contact with the British; on the southern island of Agerø, the schoolteacher climbed the church tower nightly to guide British bombers with a hidden radio beacon. The Gruntvigian congregation in Øster Jølby played a particularly significant role. Not only did some of its members organize the local underground newspaper, but the son of the free school's teacher, Frode Jakobsen, became one of the nation's underground leaders.[6] The British invasion never came, as the Germans withdrew without a fight. As soon as they were gone, the resistance rounded up and shot male collaborators; girls who had dated German soldiers were paraded naked through the streets.[7] These were powerful events for a quiet rural island, with strong effects on Morsingboer's attitudes toward themselves and the outside world. As in most of Denmark, however, physical damage was very light, and at the war's end, Mors was intact and ready for prosperity.

6. Jakobsen has written a number of books about his personal and political life, some of which give fascinating details of his childhood on Mors. See especially Jakobsen (1976, 1977).
7. None of the underground members I met expressed any remorse for shooting collaborators. Many, however, regretted the treatment of the girls, and thought it a shameful event. As one older woman said, "How can you blame someone for falling in love?"

The prosperity came. The next thirty years saw an unprecedented rise in living standards throughout Denmark, as a hungry Europe devoured Danish agricultural and industrial exports. On Mors, the industries of Nykøbing blossomed, as new factories were built and old ones expanded. Incomes rose enormously, as did the availability of credit for building homes and shops. The changes altered life in Nykøbing drastically. Families who had previously lived in cramped apartments built houses to the north and west of town. Ordinary families gradually came to have electricity, indoor plumbing, clothes washers, kitchen appliances, telephones, and televisions. Cars became commonplace, making all of the island and the region accessible to townspeople. More distant travel became commonplace as well, and islanders whose parents had never left Mors began to travel as tourists around the world. As blue- and white-collar workers streamed in to fill the new factories and offices, the social network became larger and more anonymous. In addition, as people moved to separate houses farther away from one another, the old neighborhoods broke up. Like many Danish towns of the time, Nykøbing gained tremendous material benefits at the same time as it lost some of its social cohesion.

It was the countryside, however, that changed the most. Farm machinery revolutionized the old social system; as they gained access to tractors, harvesters, planters, hay balers, and stock feeders, farm owners found the farmhands they had formerly employed superfluous. Unable to find farm work, the hands went to Nykøbing, never to return to agriculture. As mechanization increased yield and lowered prices, smallholders found themselves unable to survive on their small plots, and most sold off their land to nearby farmers and took up wage work. Even many of the farm owners came into difficulties from falling prices. By the 1980s, only the larger farms could survive without either the farmer or his wife working outside the home. In a relatively short space of time, the old rural social system nearly dissolved. The lively society of farmhands and serving girls who flocked to village social events disappeared, as did the leisurely lifestyle of the prosperous farmers. With them went much of the impetus behind village activities; community houses that had once bustled with activity fell into disuse, and churches and mission houses stood nearly empty.

Families changed as well. The advent of widespread birth control and higher living standards in the 1960s led to shrinking families throughout Mors. Whereas her mother might have had seven children, a typical woman of the 1960s or 1970s would have two; she might even decide to have none at all. As a result, even though Nykøbing expanded its area and workforce tremendously, its total population remained largely stable from 1950 to 1990. The national turmoil of the 1960s affected sexual norms on Mors, making premarital sex and childbearing out of wedlock fairly common. The entry of women into the work force in the 1960s and 1970s affected families as well; as mothers left the home, childcare came increasingly into the hands of schools and paid caretakers.

Educational opportunities increased dramatically during this period, with mixed results for the island. The government built and staffed good primary schools all over Mors, as well as a large gymnasium and technical school in Nykøbing. Morsingboer welcomed the schools, which brought an excellent education within the reach of every child on the island. For the children, this meant enhanced employment prospects in Denmark's increasingly high-tech economy. For the island community, however, the effects were less favorable. Students who attended the gymnasium had to leave the island in order to continue on to a university; afterward, they could find no work on the island appropriate to a university education. The education system thus began to drain the brightest of the island's youth out of the area. The effect hit particularly hard in the countryside, where the farm economy offered little opportunity to use a gymnasium education. The young farmers who would once have become leaders in the rural churches and associations never came home from school.

Another critical development during these years was the introduction of the welfare state. Beginning in the 1950s, the Danish government began to provide a comprehensive welfare system, including national health insurance, unemployment insurance, pensions, vacation and leave policies, and adult education. To some extent, these developments replicated existing systems; in the countryside, for example, cooperative health insurance programs had existed for a century already. But the welfare state operated on a much larger scale than local organizations. The Nykøbing hospital was enlarged and modernized; elderly housing and nursing homes were built; pensions and unemployment insurance became universal. Poverty on Mors vanished, taxes rose drastically, and the national government assumed a direct and important role in the lives of individuals.

This striking increase in living standards, welfare benefits, educational opportunities, and work mechanization hinged on the steady expansion of the Danish economy. Inflation and climbing interest rates put a damper on this expansion in the 1970s, and by the late 1980s the economy began to show signs of serious trouble. High wages and taxes were encouraging manufacturers to move operations abroad, and the debt load acquired during the building boom began to strain financial markets. As national resources diminished, the government began to cut back on social services. Mors, like many rural areas, has felt the effects; schools, childcare institutions, and medical care have all been cut back. Industries on the island have cut back operations as well, and several factories have closed entirely. Unemployment has become a serious problem, and many islanders have had to leave in search of work. Mors remains an active place, and it has faced the recent problems more successfully than many areas in Jutland. The boisterous expansion of the postwar period, however, has moved into the realm of history, along with the German invasions, the herregårds, the Knights of Malta, and the dubious baptism of Harald Bluetooth.

2. THE SOCIAL WORLD

૨૧ ૨૧ ૨૧

Earning a Living

*E*arning a living, like everything else on Mors, takes different forms in town and countryside. Work in the villages revolves around agriculture and the trades that support it. In town, in contrast, work derives mainly from industry, commerce, and government administration. The two economies have strong links; Nykøbing's governmental sector, for example, could not exist without a countryside to administer. In terms of everyday experience, however, they are largely separate, and we can understand them most easily by taking them one at a time.

In both economies, work is more than just a way to earn money; it is also an important facet of individual identity. A person's occupation says something about who he or she is, what his or her education was, what his or her family is like. Telephone books and tombstones list occupations immediately after names. A job implies a social circle, both in and out of the workplace; it implies a political interest and affiliation; for some occupations, it may even imply a particular way of envisioning God. A person without a job, especially a man without a job, is in a sort of limbo, lacking a critical piece of his personal identity. The importance of occupation to the individual's sense of self accounts partially for the meticulousness and high standards of agricultural and industrial work on Mors. It also explains why, despite one of the world's most generous systems of unemployment insurance, unemployment is one of the most keenly felt social problems in Denmark today.

Whether this identification with occupation constitutes a class system depends on ones viewpoint. Occupations do tend to run in families, and they tend to shape a worker's social contacts and interests. And some do connote more status than others; being a business manager, or a successful merchant, or a doctor commands a respect that being a factory laborer does not. The gulf between these occupations seventy-five years ago was certainly a class difference. Today, however, the welfare state has significantly evened out differences in income, while the educational system has made social mobility possible for anyone. A factory worker's son may well become an educated professional, and a businessman's son may become a laborer. Honorific terms of address have largely disappeared. Thus the differences in wealth and status that do exist may or may not constitute a class system, depending on how one defines class.

Occupations in the Countryside

Work in the countryside falls into four general categories: farming *(landbrug)*, trades *(håndværk)*, shopkeeping *(købmænd)*, and the professions. Each area requires special training for its practitioners, and each carries social roles and requirements with it. None carries a special rank; while a few specific occupations bring with them a special visibility or authority, no type of work is considered inherently superior or inferior to others.

The largest area, both in terms of numbers of workers and cultural importance, is farming. Most farms average around 35 hectares of land, and are worked by a single nuclear family using motorized equipment. The husband ordinarily does most of the daily work himself, although he may require the assistance of a paid farmhand or grown son at planting and harvest times. On a larger farm, his wife may assist with feeding livestock and arranging business matters; usually, however, she supplements the family income with nonfarm work outside of the home. Most farms could not survive without this income, although both husbands and wives downplay its importance. School-age children also assist in agricultural tasks, and the one chosen to inherit the farm devotes himself increasingly to them as he grows older.

The titular owner *(gårdejer)* of the farm is generally the husband. His wife may also be referred to as a farm owner *(gårdejerinde)*, and she inherits the farm if he predeceases her. Few farmers own much mechanized field equipment themselves; while they usually have their own tractors, most either rent equipment for planting and harvesting or share ownership with a group of neighbors. Many farmers do invest heavily in mechanized barns and livestock feeders, which enable a single person to care for several hundred pigs. The debt load that such investments require is considerable, but seldom crippling. No strict rules govern inheritance of the farm by children. Since few farms are large enough to survive if divided, a single child usually takes it over; while this lot most often falls to the eldest son, it may go to any son or daughter whom the farmer considers especially suited to the task. The choice is made while the children are still young, so that the one who will inherit can direct his education toward agriculture. This transfer often takes place when the parents reach 65 years of age and become eligible for state pensions. The inheriting child moves into the farmhouse with his or her family, and either builds or buys a small house for the parents. While the new house may stand on a corner of the property, parents more often move into the village center or to Nykøbing, where shopping and medical services are closer.

Much of the education for farming comes from working with the father; the responsibilities of the inheriting child grow as the parents age, and by the time of actual inheritance, he or she has been effectively running the farm for several years. He or she has probably worked at a number of other farms as well. Before the last war, when most farms had several hired workers, farmhands changed locations twice a year.[1] This system not only protected hands from abusive employers, but it also exposed them to farming techniques from all over the island. While the advent of agricultural mechanization broke up this system, some exchange of farmhands still goes on. In addition to this practical education, moreover, most young people contemplating a future in farming spend a year or two at an agricultural school *(landbrugsskole)*. These boarding schools teach the latest techniques in livestock breeding, field management, crop fertilization, pest control, and the use and repair of farm machinery.

This combination of practical and theoretical education produces extremely capable farmers and immaculately tended farms. The thor-

---

1. This is something of an oversimplification; while changing twice a year was common practice, it was by no means required, and a farmhand in a particularly congenial situation could stay an extra half year or two. Notice of positions passed both by word of mouth and through newspaper advertisements. Religious affiliation sometimes played a role; families in the Inner Mission often preferred to have servants of the same persuasion, and would advertise for hands or servant girls from the YMCA/W (see Part II).

oughness of this education can take an outsider by surprise. On my first visit to a farm, I asked the owner why one set of fields seemed to be yielding better than another. From his rustic dialect, weather-beaten features, worn overalls and old wooden shoes, I had expected a quaint speech about the vagaries of Mother Nature or the spirits of the fields. Instead, I received a short lecture on soil chemistry, crop rotation and changes in fertilizer formulas. While tradition is extremely important to the way farmers view themselves and their land, it plays a secondary role in their techniques of land use. Farming is a modern enterprise, and those who practice it generally embrace the scientific methods it involves. [2]

A farmer cannot master all of the skills required for an agricultural community, however; hence the need for the second category of occupations, the skilled trades *(håndværker)*. This group includes such workers as mechanics, masons, roofers, carpenters, electricians, and plumbers. Most work in small companies, generally compring a single master artisan *(murermester, tømrermester, etc.)* and several assistants *(murersvend, tømrersvend, etc.)*. Most are male; although no government or union rules bar them from entering the trades, women on Mors do so only rarely. Sons of artisans often enter the same field as their fathers, and in such a case usually rise to partnership in the firm. Farmers' children who do not go into agriculture may also enter the trades, although they have more difficulty securing a position. Education for this work operates mainly through apprenticeships, which aspiring tradesmen generally find through personal contacts. In addition, the unions for each trade operate technical schools in various parts of Denmark; most tradesmen spend six months to a year there at some point in their careers. Most unions also have local buildings for seminars and social events for members of the trade. As with farming, standards of work are very high, and tradesmen set great store by their expertise.

Merchants constitute another important occupation in the countryside. They come in two general varieties: shopkeepers *(købmænd)*, who sell prepackaged goods, and merchants who process food in their shops. The latter group includes butchers and bakers, and operates very much like a skilled trade. The owner is a master of his trade, and may employ assistants to help with the work. Education operates through appren-

---

2. This attitude toward modernity stems partly from the farmer's movement of the 19th century. The propagation and development of new techniques were a primary focus of the movement, and they made possible the emergence of small farmers as a potent political force.

ticeships and technical schools, and strong unions organize the trades-men. Shops are often run as a family, with the father processing the food and the mother and older children handling sales and paperwork.

Shopkeepers operate somewhat differently. Most shops in the coun-tryside are small kiosks with one or two rooms, selling a large variety of prepackaged goods. These include frozen, boxed and canned foods, fresh vegetables, milk, cheese, eggs, a small assortment of housewares, and garden supplies. Shopkeepers often purchase these goods from a single source, a buying chain that sets standard prices for its distributors across the country. A few villages contain radio or furniture shops as well. Most shops are owned by a single person, often a woman; the owner's spouse usually holds a separate job in addition to helping with the store. Shops ordinarily have an apartment behind or above the sales floor, where the shopkeeper's family lives. Two or three clerks assist in running the store. Since a shopkeeper plays no part in producing the goods he or she sells, education for the trade focuses on the mechanics of commerce and finance; after two years or so in a business school *(handelsskole),* aspiring shopkeepers work as clerks in stores for their apprenticeship. After completing this work, they may either work per-manently as clerks, or attempt to buy shops of their own. Such a pur-chase necessitates a substantial bank loan, which makes shopkeeping a chancy affair at the beginning.

One notable exception exists to this kind of shop: the cooperative market, or *brugsforening.* These shops, found in most larger villages, are owned in shares by a number of residents of the parish. The sharehold-ers elect a board of directors to oversee the shop, which in turn hires a manager to run it. A national association of cooperative markets buys for and supplies the shops, which sell their goods at standardized prices. Profits range from small to nonexistent, and while they should theoret-ically be divided among the shareholders, in practice they usually remain in shop accounts. Cooperative markets originated in the farmers' move-ment of the 19th century, as a way of allowing farmers the advantages of large-scale purchasing enjoyed by merchants. Until the last few decades, they constituted the only markets easily accessible to the rural popula-tion, and they were often vital centers of town life.

Recently, however, like other rural shops, they have encountered severe difficulties. The decline in the rural population after World War II depleted the customer base in the countryside; more importantly, the increasing presence of automobiles has brought village merchants into a withering competition with the larger markets in Nykøbing.

Butchers and bakers have disappeared from most of the smaller villages, and from some of the larger ones. Several cooperative markets have closed, while some others remain open only because of contributions from local farmers. The days of merchants in the Mors countryside appear to be numbered.

The future appears brighter for the last major class of workers in the Mors countryside, the professionals. This category covers those whose work involves a seminary or university education: teachers, nurses, doctors, managers, and priests. Rural professionals usually work either for the government or for private nonprofit groups, and they enjoy better pay and security of employment than most people in the countryside. They often come from outside the area; while one seldom meets a farmer on Mors who was not born on the island, one seldom meets a doctor or priest who was. Both men and women work in all professions, although gender distribution within occupations varies. Most nurses are women, for example, while all but one doctor and all but one priest are men. Professional workers' numbers are relatively small, and depend on the particular social services available in a given parish. The larger parishes have schools, which typically employ ten to twenty seminary-trained teachers. Most have nursing homes as well, which employ a dozen or so nurses and nursing assistants, all educated through nursing seminaries. Doctors are rarer; only five of the largest villages have a local physician. Larger villages usually have a resident priest, but in less populated areas, one priest may serve two or three parishes. Both doctors and priests require extensive university education as well as ongoing professional education throughout their careers. All professionals belong to trade unions, which bargain collectively with the government over wages and working conditions.

Occupations in the Town

Some occupations in towns work very much like those in the countryside; a town tradesman or a doctor, for example, earns his living essentially the same way as his rural counterpart. The industrial and governmental sectors of Nykøbing, however, create several occupational groups not found in the countryside. Moreover, work in general occurs in a more institutional context. Most people do not work for themselves or a single master, but for a firm or agency over which they have little control.

No one experiences this difference more directly than the industrial laborer (*arbejder*), a class of worker seldom found outside of Nykøbing.

Unlike most workers in the countryside, laborers possess neither productive capital nor special education; they work in the factories of Nykøbing, and receive their training on the job. They receive the island's lowest wages, and most have little opportunity for professional advancement. They include both men and women, although women are most likely to work in food-processing plants like the mussel cannery. Recruitment goes along family lines in some factories; in several families, for example, the men have worked at the iron foundry for five generations. Other factories have no such traditions. Laborers in Nykøbing constitute about a quarter of the work force.

Another contrast with the countryside is the number of professionals in the town. In addition to its doctors, nurses, teachers, and priests, Nykøbing has the lawyers, accountants, architects, professional managers, journalists, and other specialists associated with a regional commercial center. The factories also employ managers, designers, chemists, and a number of other professionals. Like those in the countryside, these workers have university or seminary education, and receive relatively high wages. Altogether, professionals in Nykøbing make up about 7 percent of the work force.

Many of these professionals work for the government, whose presence in Nykøbing dwarfs that in the rest of the island. Government institutions in the town include the local government offices, a regional post office, a small hospital, the island's court and police station, the civil defense station, a wastewater treatment facility, three nursing homes, several elderly housing complexes, and the tourist bureau. These offices employ another category of worker virtually unknown elsewhere on the island: civil servants, the secretaries and office workers who administer the government's business on Mors. Civil servants typically have either a gymnasium or business school education, and receive somewhat higher wages than factory workers. They are equally likely to be men or women, and are most often natives to the island.

The situation for merchants in Nykøbing differs radically from that in the countryside. While operating a village store might afford a comfortable subsistence for a family, owning a store in town can bring real wealth. The stores on the Walking Street offer a large variety of goods to a market that includes the entire island. Even the smallest employ a few clerks, and the largest have staffs of a dozen or more. Store clerks thus form a substantial occupational group in the town that is nonexistent in the countryside. Store owners also occupy a different station; unlike the humble shopkeepers of the villages, Nykøbing's larger storeowners are wealthy and influential members of the community. Their status has declined from that of two hundred years ago, when the town's wealthy merchants effectively dominated the town government; even so, some of today's store owners are descendants of those merchants, and many live in the expensive districts to the north and south of town. Merchants take a direct hand in running their businesses, and generally own them alone.

Few Morsingboer work directly in the tourist trade; aside from the staff of the tourist bureau and those who own and operate campgrounds, very few people cater specifically to tourists. Nonetheless, tourism brings in a lot of customers, and most shops in Nykøbing depend on it to survive. Thousands of tourists come to Mors annually, mostly from Germany and Sweden. The Germans usually come in the summer and stay in camping trailers or in rented cottages *(sommerhuse)*, of which there are 513 on the island. Families from all backgrounds and all parts of the island own rental cottages, which augment income from work. Most of the tourist money, however, goes to the restaurants and shops in Nykøbing. In addition, the Jesperhus Flower Park just south of Nykøbing, owned by a private family and employing a large staff of gardeners, draws over 200,000 visitors every year.[3]

Nykøbing has one other occupational category that we should note: retirees. The Danish government pays a standard pension to retired workers of all kinds, and while retirees come from many different occupational groups, most enter a similar situation after they stop working. Retirees come into Nykøbing from all over the island; with its hospital, its nursing homes, its elderly housing, its bus system, and the nearness of its stores, Nykøbing appeals strongly to people with frequent medical needs and limited mobility. Most retirees live in their own houses or apartments, together with a spouse if living. They constitute 25 percent of the town's population, and together they represent a potent cultural and political force in the community.

Living Standards

In return for the work that they do, Morsingboer enjoy one of the highest standards of living in the world. Annual wages range from 200,000 kroner for a factory worker to 500,000 kroner for a doctor. Taxes take more than half of this, and prices are very high, but the remainder still allows a comfortable existence. A standard home on Mors has indoor

---

3. Many of these visitors are from the island or nearby areas. Jesperhus is, incidentally, the largest park of its kind in Scandinavia.

plumbing, electric heat and lighting, telephone service, kitchen appliances, a clothes washing machine, well-kept furniture and linens, a set of china, a television set, a videocassette recorder, a stereo set, many books, and assorted decorative art. Most families that want them have automobiles, although the high price of cars and gas limits the amount of driving. The state provides excellent medical care and education, as well as pensions for the old and disabled. Poverty is virtually nonexistent, as are violent crime and serious property crime. Morsingboer do not lead a lavish existence; material possessions of even the wealthiest seldom rival those of a middle-class family in the United States. But when the security provided by the welfare state is taken into consideration, their standard of living is one that most nations in the world would envy.

Most Morsingboer expect a decline in this living standard in years to come. Denmark's recent economic difficulties have placed a strain on the welfare system; some cutbacks in social services have resulted, and more are likely to come. Unemployment has become a serious problem, while bank foreclosures on property are rising. Anxiety over these problems has led to some resentment throughout Denmark against Turkish guest workers and refugees, who make a convenient scapegoat for the strains on the welfare system. Mors has only a handful of such workers, and they are generally well-liked. But the island shares in the general perception that the Denmark's era of prosperity is on the wane.

Government and State Services

Governmental Organization

The island of Mors constitutes a *kommune*, the smallest unit of government in Denmark; its official name is Mors Island Kommune *(Morsø Kommune)*. The kommune is part of Viborg Province *(Viborg Amt)*, a regional entity centered in the city of Viborg, about 45 kilometers southeast of Mors. This province is one of sixteen in the nation, which has its capital in Copenhagen on Sjælland's eastern coast. Mors is thus part of three levels of government – national, provincial, and "kommunal." Each level has a directly elected council to make and administer laws, according to procedures laid out in the Danish Constitution. The national parliament, called the Folketing, makes the most important policy decisions; the provincial council *(amtsråd)* and kommunal council *(kommuneråd)* work primarily on implementation of Folketing directives and on allocation and collection of revenues. Every Morsingbo over 18 years of age may vote in elections for all three councils. Most choose to do so; in the December 1990 elections, almost 90 percent of eligible voters went to the polls.

Political Parties

A system of political parties influences politics at every level in Denmark. All candidates for all offices declare affiliation to one or another party; on the ballot, a voter can either choose a specific candidate or vote for a party slate. Each party takes a stand on the issues before the council, and when votes take place in the councils, members usually follow their party's line. Most parties have local chapters in every kommune in the country. Local members run these chapters, which serve both to promote local party solidarity and to relay members' sentiments to the national party organization. Chapter organizers come from all walks of life, and are elected periodically by the local members. The system allows private individuals to participate in the political system, and most Morsingboer feel capable of having a voice in their own government.

Danish political parties fall into four main groups. The Conservative and the Left parties make up the liberal, or bourgeois *(borgerlig)* wing; generally conservative on social and international issues, these two parties usually act as a unit. The Conservative party draws much of its support from affluent urban areas, while the Left party is based among rural farmers. On the other side of the spectrum stand the leftist parties, the Social Democratic Party and the Socialist People's Party, committed to a program of state controls and welfare services. Rooted in the working class, the Social Democrats constructed the current Danish welfare state during their heyday in the 1950s. Between them the liberals and the leftists dominate Danish politics. Neither, however, constitutes a majority. The third group, swing parties, therefore determines which of the major blocs controls the government. These include such small parties as the Progress Party, the Center Democrats, the Radical Left, and the Christian People's Party. Swing parties tend to follow narrower agendas than the major parties; the Progress Party opposes taxes and the European Community, for example, while the Christian People's Party arose in opposition to the state's legalization of abortion in 1973. The final group, fringe parties, have little impact on Danish elections, although they occasionally achieve a brief celebrity. The Humanistic Party, for example, a thinly disguised front for an Eastern religious group appealing to university students, drew considerable media attention during the 1990 election.

In that election, the Social Democrats won more votes than any other party in Denmark. The liberal parties, however, entered a coalition with most of the swing parties, and together they formed a national government led by a Conservative. Mors followed a similar pattern; while the Social Democrats' 38 percent of the vote far exceeded the liberals' 27 percent, the liberal parties combined with the swing parties to dominate the kommune council. The results showed considerable differences between town and countryside. The Social Democrats captured 49 percent of the vote in Nykøbing, compared with 31 percent for the rest of the island. The Left party, in contrast, received only 11 percent in Nykøbing but 22 percent in the countryside. The Progress party also did very well in the countryside, with 25 percent as against 13 percent in town, while the Conservatives fared poorly with 7 percent in the country and 12 percent in town. No other party won more than 5 percent in either area.

The State in Everyday Life

The Danish national government occupies a powerful place in the everyday life of Mors. Not directly – most programs relevant to Morsingboer are administrated on the kommunal or provincial level, and contacts with Copenhagen are rare for most people. But the programs and policies of the national government provide structure for important areas of life on Mors. They do so partly through the legal system, which establishes the rules and boundaries for individual conduct, and over which local authorities have little discretion. In addition, they have created a number of institutions that deeply affect the way that people plan their lives. Three of these have particular importance: the welfare system, the educational system, and the church.

Welfare

Denmark's welfare system protects its citizens from the financial problems associated with illness, disability, unemployment, and old age. It does so with a thoroughness that has few parallels in the world. While Danes, Morsingboer included, frequently decry the shortcomings they find in the system, outsiders are invariably dazzled by the variety and quality of the benefits it offers.

Many of these benefits involve income replacement. If a Morsingbo cannot work, whether because of illness, disability, or simply loss of a job, the government gives him or her money to replace the lost wages as long as he or she needs it.[4] In most cases, the government payment is the same as or close to the worker's regular wage. At retirement, all Danes receive a government pension of a standard amount; in some well-paid occupations, employers may also provide a private pension. In addition, Danish law mandates certain amounts of paid leave for employees. Employers must give five weeks of paid vacation per year, for example, as well as paid maternity leave of up to three months before and six months after childbirth. These programs profoundly affect life for Morsingboer. The threat of poverty does not exist; regardless of the misfortunes a person may suffer, he can count on an adequate income for the whole of his life.

The welfare state also provides medical care. The national health insurance system pays for all medical treatment, whether by a local physician or by a regional hospital. It also subsidizes prescription drugs and dental work. The system relies heavily on nurses, many of whom make regular rounds of the countryside to care for patients in their homes; infants receive special priority, getting visits from nurses twice a month. Such a system imposes a number of restrictions on patients. Since the government allocates all health care resources, for example, patients may have to wait months for certain complicated procedures. The quality of care is superb, however, and ordinary illnesses are treated immediately.

Education

Morsingboer, like most Danes, value formal education highly. One reason, they say, is necessity. Denmark has a small population, few natural resources, and little military power; the chief strength of the nation is the minds of its people. Innovations in science and manufacturing have brought the nation unprecedented prosperity in recent decades, just as the agricultural education programs of the farmers' movement revolutionized rural life in the 19th century. Morsingboer therefore argue that unless they place a priority on education, they will not survive. In addition, though, education has a value in itself. People speak proudly of the schools they attended, whether they mean the university in Århus or the agricultural school in Kolding. They accord a special respect to those

4. This is something of an oversimplification. The money may come either from the government or from the trade union, depending on where the person works and why he or she had to stop. Nonetheless, the rules for payment are established by agreement with the government, and the outcome is essentially the same from the employee's perspective.

who have had higher education; the high status of doctors and priests stems largely from the extensive education that their jobs presuppose. Many attend seminars and adult education courses throughout their lives, and those who die possessing a university degree often have it inscribed on their tombstones. For all its utilitarian value, education on Mors is also a matter of prestige.

The core of the state educational system is the *folkeskole*, which all children must attend from ages 7 to 16. The folkeskole teaches the basics of a Danish education: reading and writing Danish, mathematics, Danish history, world history, basic physical and life sciences, and two foreign languages, of which English is primary. Teaching takes place in classrooms, in which around fifteen students are instructed by a single teacher. Each teacher instructs several subjects, so that a student taking six subjects rarely has more than three teachers. Moreover, teachers remain with their classes over the years; although the level of the material taught changes, a student usually has the same Danish teacher from the first year to the ninth. The relationship between them accordingly takes on a familial flavor. Teachers speaking of their students sound like Danish parents speaking of their children – sometimes stern, often annoyed, but always with a strong undertone of affection. Students become attached to their teachers as well, and regard a change in teachers due to illness or retirement as a real misfortune. Teachers and students use first names for address, and classroom interactions are fairly informal, although teachers are careful to maintain firm authority.

This system does not function without problems, of course, but on the whole it works very well. Schools on Mors tend to be orderly and clean, and both students and teachers speak about them positively. By the end of their time there, almost all students can read and write Danish well, and have a good grasp of math, science, history, and English. They also have decided, in consultation with their teachers and parents, what they want to do next.

Most choose to study further. While graduation from the folkeskole fulfills government requirements, it opens few doors; any skilled or white-collar trade requires additional education. This education takes three main tracks. Students who wish to enter trade or agricultural work enter technical schools for the specific work they would like to study. This training may last from six months to two years, and is ordinarily followed by an apprenticeship. Students interested in business-related work enter business schools, where they learn about economics, finance, and practical business skills. Finally, those wishing a theoretical education enter a gymnasium, where they continue their folkeskole studies at a higher level. Continued education often requires students to travel; students from around the island must travel to Nykøbing for the gymnasium and the business school, while those entering trades must travel to one of the technical schools scattered around Denmark.

The gymnasium education lasts three years, and takes place in a less personal environment than the folkeskole. Students have a different teacher for each class, and classes tend to be rather formal. Unlike folkeskole teachers, who attend a teacher's seminary after gymnasium, gymnasium teachers must have university education. In addition, the gymnasium involves more specialization than the folkeskole; students choose between a language-oriented curriculum and a science-oriented one, and within each curriculum they choose a specific focus. Business school involves similar choices. Both gymnasium and business school students finish their schooling with a rigorous examination called a *studentereksamen*. The various sections of this examination receive separate grades, and these scores determine admission to programs in the universities. The test therefore weighs heavily on a student's future plans, and it brings severe emotional strains on those taking it. Those who complete it, however, achieve the impressive title of graduate *(student)*, and are honored with a parade through Nykøbing and a series of parties lasting up to two weeks.

Afterward, most gymnasium graduates seek admission to one of the Danish universities. They apply to specific university departments, each of which has its own test-score requirements. Most graduates can find a place somewhere; a prospective doctor whose scores are too low for the medical school, for example, might be able to get into a dental school instead. The universities all lie far from Mors, in the cities of Copenhagen, Århus, Ålborg, and Odense. Graduates must therefore leave Mors for the vastly different world of an urban center, from which many never return.

All of these institutions – folkeskole, business school, gymnasium, technical school, and university – are operated by the state.[5] Students need not pay to attend, and those who must live away from home receive a stipend from the government. The national ministry of education sets curricula and teaching standards, as well as grading systems for major tests. It also organizes and underwrites the adult education center in

---

5. Technical schools are actually more complicated than that. Some are state-owned, others are run by trade unions, and a few are self-owned nonprofit institutions.

Nykøbing. The state thereby gains a strong influence on the way people on Mors think and learn about the world. Even those students who never leave the island get a powerful dose of the outside world.

One alternative exists to this system. Danish law permits private organizations to create "free schools" *(friskoler)* of their own, and it allows such schools to receive substantial public funding. This option has been exploited primarily by followers of the Grundtvigian religious movement. Grundtvig's romantic religious philosophy led him to advocate Kristen Kold's informal method of education, modeled on folk storytelling and stressing creativity among students. Kold actually developed this method while teaching on Mors in the 1830s, and the island's Grundtvigians have ardently supported free schools since the first one was established in 1864. Located in the villages of Galtrup and Bjergby, the schools today cover the same age range and curriculum as the folkeskole. They form an important center for the Grundtvigian community, and the members of the movement generally consider the schools' creativity and spiritual atmosphere ample repayment for the low tuitions they charge.

The Grundtvigian movement's most famous creation, the Danish folk high school *(folkehøjskole)*, is absent on Mors.[6] Study at one of the folk high schools elsewhere in Jutland used to be a standard event for Grundtvigian children after the folkeskole. Such travel has diminished in recent decades, however, perhaps because of the increase in other educational opportunities (see Borish 1991 for an account of the folk high school movement).

The Church

No discussion of the national government's presence on Mors can ignore that of the church. Denmark has a state church, funded from tax revenues, that operates in every town and village of the nation. Most Morsingboer are members of this church, whose theology and policies are largely determined by the Church Ministry in Copenhagen. The church's reach extends into a number of administrative areas; priests register births with the social services bureaus, for example, and confirmation classes are part of the folkeskole education. Membership in this church is not mandatory, and other faiths do thrive on the island. When Morsingboer take part in religious activities, however, most of them do so as part of a state institution.

6. A *højskole* established in 1864 foundered in 1883, when its leader refused to join the Free Congregation in leaving the Folkekirke. See Part II.

The state church, and the alternatives to it, will be the focus of Part III. I will now briefly discuss its structure and theology, as well as those of its main rivals.

Religious Groups

The State Church

In 1849, the Danish constitution established freedom of religion in Denmark. At the same time, however, it restated the preeminence of the Danish Evangelical Lutheran Church in the religious life of the nation. Founded under Martin Luther's supervision during the Reformation, the Church had served as an instrument of state policy for four centuries. Pietistic kings had made weekly attendance mandatory, and the crown circulated its civil edicts through the local priests. The constitution ended such coercive measures, but it retained the church as part of the state system. Rechristened as the *Folkekirke,* or Church of the People, the Church was to embody and enrich the spiritual nature of the Danish people (cf. Lausten 1987).

Today, nine Danes in ten belong to the Folkekirke. A church stands at the center of nearly every sizable village, and such rituals as baptism, confirmation, marriage, and burial bring virtually everyone into close contact with it. Members pay a church tax of about 1.5 percent on their income, and receive all church services free of charge. Others must pay for weddings and funerals themselves. While most Danes are members of the church, though, most seldom enter it; on a given Sunday, only three in a hundred members attend the weekly services. Participation in both weekly and other rituals varies widely by region. Whereas around 50 percent of Copenhagen children go through confirmation, for example, over 90 percent of those in Jutland do so. No precise pattern governs these variations, but in general, church participation rises with distance from Copenhagen. No place in the Danish mainland lies farther away than West Jutland, and the area around Mors is popularly regarded as one of the Folkekirke's strongest bastions.

The church bases its organization on geographical divisions. The smallest of these is the parish, or *sogne,* which ordinarily covers one or more villages, a town, or a region of a city. A parish usually has its own church. Ideally, at least one priest should serve each church, but because of the recent depopulation of rural areas, a single priest must often take care of two or three rural churches; in such a case, the areas involved are grouped into a single parish. Priests administer most of the church's business, and their positions carry lifelong tenure. In addition, an elected parish council *(sogneråd)* oversees church management and selects new priests when necessary.[7] Mors has thirty-two parishes, most of which cover several villages and employ a single priest; Nykøbing, because of its size, employs three. All of these parishes together form a *provsti,* the church's next level of geographical organization. A provsti's priests elect one of their number to serve as its administrator, or *provst.* The provst oversees church buildings, budgets, and parish boundaries, and negotiates with the regional authorities over church taxes and funds. Each provsti, meanwhile, belongs to a larger geographical area known as a *stift,* or diocese. A bishop heads each diocese; bishops are elected for life by a vote of the leaders of the parish councils. Unlike provsti boundaries, which usually correspond to kommunes, boundaries of dioceses do not follow any other civil divisions; while Mors belongs to Viborg Province, it belongs to the diocese centered in Ålborg. Over the bishop stands the Church Ministry in Copenhagen, headed by the Church Minister. This minister is a member of the Folketing and a cabinet officer, and runs the national church according to the government's policies. He or she need not have clerical credentials; indeed, some Church Ministers have been outspoken socialist atheists. Even the socialist parties, however, value the church as a cultural resource, and have endeavored to preserve it.

The Folkekirke's theological principles derive from the Protestant Reformation, and are based on the New Testament and Luther's Little Catechism. The church sees Jesus Christ as the son of God sent to redeem mankind. Those who accept this gift by believing in His divinity will be resurrected after death and given eternal life with Him in Paradise. Those who do not will be sent to Hell. Jesus's life and words also provide a moral code for this life, and although redemption or damnation hinges solely on belief, those who believe have an obligation to act morally. The Folkekirke lays great weight on infant baptism, a ritual that redeems the child by bringing him or her into the community of believers. The church also values communion very highly, as a symbol of the presence of Jesus among the faithful. It does not, however, accept the

7. Theological conflicts between priests and parish councils are fairly rare, since parish councils ordinarily select priests whose views suit them. Should such a conflict arise, the council has little direct authority over the priest, whose lifelong tenure effectively shields him from coercion. Hans Kirk paints a vivid picture of such a conflict in *Fiskerne* (1978), in which the council ultimately triumphs through social pressure.

idea of transubstantiation. The Danish language is used in all rituals and texts, including the highly valued Apostolic Creed.

Within this theological framework lie vast opportunities for disagreement. How literally, for example, should the Bible be interpreted? What are the details of the moral code endorsed by Jesus? What is the nature of Hell? Does baptism alone confer redemption, or are ongoing avowals of faith necessary? And perhaps most importantly, what is the nature of earthly life? Is it a gamut of temptations to be shunned by the faithful? Or is it a soil outside of which the soul cannot properly develop? Different Danes have different answers for such questions, and the Folkekirke therefore encompasses a range of theological positions. Individual priests have wide autonomy in this area, although they must stay within the church's overall framework.

On a local level, the Folkekirke performs a number of services. The most visible and important involve the conduct of rituals. Each priest holds at least one service (*gudstjeneste*) each Sunday at the church, in which the congregation prays together, sings hymns, recites prayers, listens to scriptural readings and a sermon, and takes communion. The service, like all those performed in church, follows a standard format laid out in detail in the hymnal. Sometimes the service includes a baptism, which takes place just before communion. Services may also include seasonal elements, such as special songs and decorations for Christmas and Easter. The priest also holds wedding ceremonies and funerals; both of these are modeled on Sunday services, though neither is normally held on a Sunday. An assistant (*kirkebetjent*) helps the priest with these services, and one or more deacons from the congregation may assist as well.

The church also performs some administrative services. Each local church keeps a record of all births, deaths, marriages, and confirmations among its parishioners; since these events all involve church rituals, the priest can keep notes on them very easily. These church records constitute the primary archival information for individual Danes prior to 1900. Today, the priest also transmits this information to the state, which keeps detailed electronic records on all citizens.

The church also extends certain services to members with physical or emotional problems. The priest, for example, regularly visits parishioners who are debilitated by illness or old age. By doing so, he ensures that community members who cannot participate in the life of the parish do not completely lose contact with it. He also visits parishioners after births, marriages, and deaths in the family, offering advice and counseling during periods of emotional strain. Members may themselves seek the priest's advice about emotional or financial problems. Since church rules require him to keep such problems confidential, these consultations provide a safe place to talk about sensitive or embarrassing subjects. In the tight social network of the village community, such places are few and valuable.

Almost all local churches own at least two properties: the church and churchyard themselves, and a house for the priest *(præstegård)*. Priests' houses usually contain facilities for parish meetings, confirmation instruction, and large dinners, as well as sleeping quarters for guests of the parish. Larger churches may own other buildings as well; the Nykøbing church, for example, owns a separate funeral chapel and a building for parish meetings. The church pays for maintenance of these buildings out of its own budget, usually employing a hired caretaker.

The Lutheran Movements

In the 19th century, two powerful theological movements arose within the Folkekirke: Grundtvigianism, led by the romantic theologian N.S.F. Grundtvig, and the Inner Mission, led by the pietistic priest Vilhelm Beck. These two movements proposed radically differing views of the Christian life, and their followers developed bitter and lasting antipathies to one another. While the broad framework of the Folkekirke's doctrine prevented an actual schism within the church, religious differences created deep divisions within many rural communities. Today the fervor felt by both sides has subsided greatly, and the personal animosities have mostly healed. But the movements still shape religious views throughout the Danish countryside, including the island of Mors.

I will discuss these movements in detail in Part II. Here, I will just briefly mention what they are, where they are located, and a something about what they do.

The Free Congregation

At the beginning of the 19th century, a Copenhagen priest named Nikolai Frederik Severin Grundtvig began a singlehanded rebellion against the Rationalist theology then reigning in the Folkekirke. Rationalism, he felt, had removed the soul from the Danish church; religion had become a moral system, a set of rules for the earthly life, without any real connection to the divine. He longed for the emotional connection to God that had electrified both the early Christian congregations and the first

Protestant reformers. The church, he argued, had to rekindle that connection in the hearts of its followers. His quest led him through a series of studies, travels, and occupations, during which he applied his considerable talents to theology, folklore, literature, politics, and poetry. His writings stressed the importance of the congregation to Christian worship. Each child, he said, enters the world as part of a community, and the traditions and beliefs of that community are essential to his or her development into a complete person. Only such a person can truly understand and appreciate Christ's love and sacrifice. Accordingly, the church should value the folk communities in which it operates, studying and celebrating their traditions, teaching them about their history, and cultivating their folklife. No brief summary can possibly convey the breadth and virtuosity of Grundtvig's scholarship, nor his dazzling gifts as a poet and speaker. Few figures in history have made more of an impact on the Danish mind, or achieved a greater following. All around the nation, especially in the countryside, people flocked to churches where his followers preached. They built Grundtvigian community centers, Grundtvigian schools, and Grundtvigian historical societies. And in some places, where local Folkekirke priests did not share Grundtvig's views, they built their own churches.

In 1871, the Grundtvigians on Mors built Ansgar's Church in the village of Øster Jølby, near the road from Nykøbing to the Vilsund. It quickly became the center for the Grundtvigian movement on the island, and the next few years saw the erection of a meeting house, a bank, and two schools in the immediate area. Originally, the church was to be part of the Folkekirke; as a voluntary congregation *(valgmenighed)*, its members could transfer their affiliation from their home parish to the new church. Conflicts with the Folkekirke's authorities, however, led the church to declare itself a free congregation *(frimenighed)* in 1883. As the Mors Island Free Congregation *(Morsø Frimenighed)*, it soon grew into the largest and one of the most influential Grundtvigian congregations in Denmark.

The Free Congregation today has about 1,500 members, and is one of the most active and well-attended churches in Western Jutland. A majority of the members live in northwestern Mors, although some drive to services from Nykøbing, southern Mors, and even Thy. A large proportion are farmers, and most support the Left party in politics. In its daily operation, the Free Congregation works like any Folkekirke church; the priest conducts services and sacraments, visits the sick and old, and holds meetings and confirmation classes. Its theology remains strongly

Grundtvigian. The church has altered some of the Folkekirke rituals, but its relations with the state church, once very poor, have become cordial.

In addition to the church itself, several local institutions have strong ties to the Free Congregation. The free schools in Galtrup and Bjergby were founded by members of the Congregation, and they work very closely with it today. Members of the Congregation also built the Eight-Sided Meeting House *(Den Ottekantede Forsamlingshus)* in Galtrup, which houses educational, religious, and athletic meetings; the People's Bank of Mors *(Morslands Folkebank)*, one of the island's largest; and the island's daily newspaper, the *Morsø Folkeblad.* The church itself owns a housing complex for the elderly in Øster Jølby.

The Inner Mission

While Grundtvig was formulating his ideas of worldly involvement and folk tradition during the early 19th century, a very different movement was taking shape in the fishing communities along Jutland's west coast. Like Grundtvig, its adherents disapproved of the abstract morality of Rationalism, and wanted to bring the emotional fire back into Christian worship. They did not seek it, however, in the worldly pursuits of folk culture. Such secular attachments, they argued, merely distracted people from the most important project of human life: the pursuit of salvation through belief in and obedience to the word of Jesus Christ. True Christians should rather reject earthly pleasures, and devote themselves to leading moral lives and celebrating Jesus's love. Members of the movement therefore shunned drink, dancing, card playing, fashion, and the theater, living in tightly knit groups often removed from the larger community. The movement spread during the 19th century, ultimately becoming organized in 1853 as the Church Association for the Inner Mission in Denmark *(Den Kirkelige Forening for Indre Mission i Danmark).* Led by the charismatic preacher Vilhelm Beck, the Inner Mission built mission houses (*missionshuse*) all over Denmark for its revival meetings and bible study groups. It also established a youth movement to guide children in the ways of proper morality. The Mission, which never broke from the Folkekirke, eventually came to include hundreds of thousands of Danes. It began to weaken after the World War II, and today has ebbed considerably from its high point in the 1920s; even so, it constitutes a powerful force in the nation's religious and political life.

The Mission came to Mors relatively late; the first mission house was built in 1896, the last in 1952. Chapters were formed all over the island, though the movement found its greatest strength in southern Mors and on the northeastern peninsula. A powerful force on the island before World War II, its membership has fallen sharply in recent years to about three hundred adults. Fourteen mission houses stand on the island, but only half still hold meetings. Meetings are held weekly; a revival meeting with a speaker usually alternates with a bible study group. In addition, most houses hold weekly Bible classes for children. A local chapter, headed by a lay member, runs each mission house. The chapters together form the Mors Island Circle of the Inner Mission, which is led by a priest and organizes several large meetings throughout the year. It also organizes an annual Christian summer camp for children, and it has strong ties to the local chapter of a mission-influenced trade union called the Christian Labor Movement *(Kristelig Fagbevægelse)*.

Many local members attribute the decline in membership to a break in the 1970s between the national Mission and the leaders of its youth program. The program had brought a constant stream of young people into the movement, and its loss was keenly felt all over the island. The Mission has recently begun a new program, which it hopes will turn the tide that seems to be slowly washing it away.

The Free Churches

The vast majority of Morsingboer belong to the Lutheran ministries of the Folkekirke and the Free Congregation. A few, however, about two to three percent, have cast their lot with one of the three independent churches operating on the island. Morsingboer refer to these institutions as free churches *(frikirker);* they include two Pentecostal churches and the Salvation Army *(Frelsens Hær)*. Free churches have no ties to or support from the state. Their operations are organized and financed by their members, who in turn do not pay taxes to support the Folkekirke. All the free churches on Mors draw on beliefs and theologies developed outside Denmark and brought into the country by missionaries.

The Pentecostal Churches

Two Pentecostal groups operate on Mors: the Pentecostal Church *(Pinsekirke)* and the Apostolic Church *(Apostolsk Kirke)*. Their beliefs differ in a few minor respects, but both derive from a movement begun in Wales in the early 20th century. Pentecostal theology agrees with Lutheranism about the redeeming role of Jesus Christ and the importance of belief to salvation. It differs, however, in its stress on the role of the Holy Spirit. In the Pentecostal view, the Holy Spirit is an agent of God that transmits His will directly to those who will accept it. It was the Holy Spirit that transfigured the apostles and their followers on the first Pentecost, causing them to speak in tongues and convert thousands of onlookers to their cause. Christians today can receive it as well, by opening their hearts to Jesus and asking him to enter them. The glosso- lalia that ensues may or may not be understandable to the speaker, but it will always provide spiritual enrichment and a cathartic feeling of con- tact with the divine. This direct interaction with God has tangible con- sequences for earthly life. The Holy Spirit may send instructions or enlightenment from God to help solve practical problems of living. It may carry believers' prayers for material and spiritual help up to God, who may choose to grant them. And at times, acting through the medium of a believer, the Holy Spirit may heal the sick. The only qual- ification for access to this enormous power is belief in Jesus. Priests may use their knowledge of the Bible to guide their followers, but they have no special access to the Holy Spirit. Believers become members of the church by choosing to undergo baptism. Pentecostalists take a literal approach to biblical injunctions; accordingly, only full immersion in water qualifies as a real baptism.

The Pentecostal and Apostolic Churches differ slightly in their organi- zation and format of worship. The Apostolic Church has a more struc- tured national organization than the Pentecostal, and it uses more structure in its ritual services. Otherwise, though, they follow the same theological principles, and members of the groups on Mors regard them as essentially interchangeable. Both have church buildings in Nykøbing, and both employ priests on a part-time basis. They cooperate in many activities, and members of each church regularly visit the services of the other. Their origins are similar as well, stemming from a Pentecostal awak- ening in southeastern Mors in the late 1920s. The Apostolic Church is the larger of the two; in addition to ritual services, it also operates a Christian bookstore and cafe in Nykøbing, a craft workshop in Karby, and a statu- ary garden depicting biblical scenes in Nykøbing. Its has a membership of about forty adults, about twice that of the Pentecostal Church.

The Salvation Army

The Salvation Army is a worldwide religious organization dedicated to converting people to Christianity and performing charitable works. It operates on a military model: a "general" heads international operations, "lieutenants" run local chapters, and "soldiers" make up the congregations. Lieutenants serve as local priests, and receive theological training from Salvation Army schools in England. The religion stresses faith in Christ as the key to salvation and eternal life. It regards sacraments as signs of faith without efficacy in themselves, and therefore does not sanction baptism. Local chapters hold weekly evangelical meetings to convert the unbelieving and to strengthen the faith of the converted. They also hold open-air meetings in public places, often supplementing their preaching by playing band music. Beyond faith in Jesus, the religion demands that its adherents lead a moral life; they may not drink liquor, dance, gamble, or attend theaters. They should also work to aid the less fortunate in society. Commitment to this task has made the Salvation Army a highly visible charitable organization in many countries, and has often obscured its religious aspect to outsiders.

The Salvation Army sent its first missionaries to Nykøbing in the 1890s. After a difficult start, the church built up a substantial and highly visible following among the town's workers, particularly at the iron foundry. The excitement of its band concerts and the self-sacrificing charitable work of its leaders made it a well-known and highly regarded organization by the 1930s. Membership began to fall drastically in the 1960s, however, and today only a handful of elderly soldiers make up its ranks. It operates from a sizable church building in Nykøbing, under the leadership of a married couple. Since the Danish welfare state has obliterated the poverty that the Salvation Army used to relieve, charitable work is limited; most of the proceeds from the church's used clothing store go to ensure that low-income families have enough supplies to celebrate Christmas properly. Weekly evangelical meetings are still held, and are regularly attended by about ten soldiers.

Other Religious Movements

Not all religious groups in Denmark are Protestant. A small Catholic population, for example, worships at a church in Copenhagen. Jews have lived in Copenhagen for centuries, and a synagogue there serves about 7,000 members today. The increasing numbers of Turkish immigrants in Copenhagen and other cities have brought Islam with them, and are currently planning the nation's first major mosque. In university cities, Eastern religions and their Western derivatives gain periodic popularity, as do such pseudo- religious movements as the New Age and natural medicine. None of these religions, however, has gained a sizable following on Mors. The largest non-Protestant sect is a small group of Jehovah's Witnesses that has built a Kingdom Hall on the outskirts of Nykøbing; in addition, the town's health food shop attracts a number of customers who ascribe magical powers to certain herbs and crystals. A Hare Krishna devotee and a pair of Dianetics proselytizers also pass through the island once in a while selling books. Generally, however, Morsingboer follow Protestantism, which has reigned here for four centuries, and respond to these newcomers with a smile and a shake of the head.

Voluntary Associations

On Mors, as in most of Scandinavia, voluntary associations *(foreninger)* play an important role in the organization of social activities (cf. Barnes 1954). These associations are made of private individuals interested in a specific activity; while some associations develop fairly broad concerns, most are devoted to a single recreational or political matter. Their organization is usually fluid, based on a constitution written and easily amended by the local members. While an elected chairman *(formand)* ordinarily heads an association, he or she seldom acts without the general support of the group. Decisions are made by discussion and consensus. Should serious divisions emerge within an association, fission into two new groups is more convenient and more likely than an ongoing conflict. Associations are financed entirely by their members, usually through a set system of dues. Membership is usually open to any interested person, although such groups as residents' associations and youth associations impose obvious requirements.

Associations fall into several categories. Political associations are generally local chapters of national political parties, organized locally but geared toward national concerns. Residents' associations promote the interests of a particular area; the little hamlet of Vodstrup just north of Nykøbing, for example, has formed the Vodstrup Property Owners' Association *(Vodstrup Grundejerforening)* to represent its concerns to the kommune. Business associations organize local shopkeepers to improve business conditions. The Walking Street Association *(Gågadeforening)* in Nykøbing does so by periodically redecorating the Walking Street and establishing uniform business hours. Trade associations are local chapters of national trade unions, like the Danish Kommune Employees Union and the Masons' Union. Religious associations, like the local chapter of the Inner Mission, promote belief among their adherents.

Many associations organize recreational and educational activities. Sports associations, for example, sponsor local leagues in soccer, gymnastics, cricket, badminton, handball, sailing, rowing, tennis, and shooting, among others. Several scouting organizations conduct activities for boys and girls. Cultural associations support historical lectures, the island museum, scientific education programs, folk music and dance groups, family history research classes, and many other activities. Some recreational associations have distinct ideological tilts; Danish gymnastics, for example, has a close association with Grundtvigianism, while each of the scouting associations is connected with a different political or religious ideology.

The variety of associations on the island can be bewildering. In addition to the categories just mentioned, Mors has such miscellaneous associations as the Housewives' Association, the Asthma and Allergy Association, the Police Dog Association, the Christmas Charity Committee, the Recreational Fishermen's Association, the Soldiers' Friends, and the Pensionists' Association. The island's address register lists 190 different associations on the island; an equal or greater number of unlisted ones surely exists. Many of these are local groups formed for playing cards or sewing. Together, these associations make up a tremendous source of social and intellectual activity on the island. Every Morsingbo belongs to at least two or three, and is an active member of at least one.

Association membership often runs along the same lines as that of social groups. This tendency was more marked before the advent of the welfare state, when class divisions were clearer. In most villages around 1900, for example, an citizens' association *(borgerforening)* would include the wealthiest and most influential of the area's residents; to be asked to join it was equivalent to being invited into polite society. The 17th of February Association in Nykøbing likewise gathered the town's upper crust for cultural and educational activities. Today, increased social mobility and education have eroded the social distinctions that underlay these groups. Still, a factory worker is unlikely to belong to the Citizens' Club in Nykøbing, and the manager of the ironworks would not join a card club formed by the workers.

3. Being a Morsingbo

In the last chapter, I outlined some of the social structures that frame the lives of people on Mors. Life is more than structures, though; it is also emotions and attitudes, the way that people experience and feel about the social world that surrounds them. Some of these attitudes are peculiarly Danish, and some are specific to Mors. In this chapter, I look briefly at three matters that shape the experience of being a Morsingbo with particular force: the construction of the family, the cycle of the seasons, and the identity of the island.

Family

The notions of inside and outside are important on Mors, as they are all over Denmark. Outside has connotations of coldness, strangeness, and danger, while inside implies warmth, familiarity, and security. This dichotomy applies to a whole range of cultural activity, from architecture to mythology. It also applies to social life, and no institution in Danish society embodies the idea of inside more than the family. The ideal family is a place of warmth and affection, where ties are based on a deep and unshakable foundation of love. No matter how heartless the world may be, no matter how difficult and disheartening the problems of everyday life, acceptance and security await in the bosom of the family, especially in the bond between mother and child. This ideal is, of course, illusory;

like all human families, those on Mors are prey to disagreement, rivalry, jealousy and dislike among their members. Yet the ideal provides a model for what family life should be, and people try remarkably hard to achieve it. For all its problems, the average family on Mors is indeed a place of warmth and refuge for its members, and one with which most people keep close contact throughout their lives. While Morsingboer frequently express irritation with family members, I never heard one express actual dislike, and even their anger is usually tinged with deep concern.

Denmark has a bilateral kinship system whose basic unit is the nuclear family of mother *(moder, mor)*, father *(fader, far)*, and children *(børn)*. While childbirth out of wedlock is not uncommon on Mors, most parents are married, and those who are not usually plan to be. A nuclear family normally lives in a home by itself; children who have not left their parents' homes before marriage generally do so afterward. Relatives are considered equally close on both the mother's and father's side, and grandparents *(bedsteforældre)* usually assist with childcare and support of all of their grandchildren.

A Morsingbo's family is an important social group throughout his or her life. Siblings and cousins are playmates and confidants in childhood, and most remain important social contacts throughout life. Their value is material as well as emotional. A young man seeking an apprenticeship, for example, looks first to uncles and cousins in the trades; when he establishes his own firm later on, he may well enter a partnership with a brother or a cousin. And as he founds and raises a family of his own, he will repeatedly look to his parents, uncles, aunts and siblings for emotional and material support. The increasing mobility of young families in recent decades has somewhat stretched this support network. Unlike their parents, whose entire families usually lived within a few kilometers of their homes, young Morsingboer today may live on a different part of the island, or even in a city hundreds of kilometers away. Nonetheless, families come together fairly frequently for various celebrations, and few Morsingboer really lose touch with their relatives.

Rituals and the Seasons

On Mors, the physical world changes as the seasons change. The cold, dark, misty nighttime of January seems a world away from the endless sunlight and blossoming fields of midsummer. So too, the social world follows the seasons, with changing activities, festivals, and emotions for the different times of year. Winter and summer are not just different seasons for Morsingboer; they are different frames of mind, different ways of seeing and living in the world. The rituals of the annual cycle mark and express these times, and Morsingboer celebrate them with vigor and enthusiasm.

General Structure of Rituals

Each seasonal ritual on Mors involves a distinct set of observances, stories, and attitudes. Most of them, however, include a number of standard elements. Before discussing them individually, therefore, let us briefly review the general format of rituals on the island.

For rituals with a religious connection, a church service ordinarily precedes private celebrations.[1] This service often takes place at an unusual time, in the evening or on a weekday. It follows the broad format of an ordinary Sunday service, with hymns, scriptural readings, and a sermon from the priest; communion is ordinarily omitted, however, and the entire service is foreshortened. Hymns reflect the occasion; at Christmas, for example, most recount the birth of Christ. The church is decorated for the season with the appropriate flowers or evergreens, and candles may light the aisle if the service takes place at night. Attendance is very high, particularly at Christmas and Easter, when the normally roomy churches are crammed, bursting with parishioners. The combination of the crowd and the familiar texts gives the hymns a rare energy and fullness, leading to a cathartic effect seldom found in weekly services.

Most important rituals, church oriented or not, also involve a dinner party *(fest)*. For seasonal rituals, the party usually takes place in a private home; for life-cycle rituals, which are often attended by dozens of guests, the host usually rents a meeting hall or restaurant. Soon after the guests arrive, they are seated on either side of one or more long tables. Tables are set with tablecloths, dishes, silverware, candles, flowers, bottles of wine or soft drinks, and elaborately folded napkins. Small Danish flags often stand on the table, as well as elsewhere in the house. The flag symbolizes the festive nature of the occasion, and houses with flagpoles fly it outside on most holidays. The table setting is intentionally elaborate; a festively decorated table is an indispensable part of any celebration, and is often photographed more carefully than the guests. Once the guests are seated, the host serves a large meal. The size of the meal depends on

---

1. For detailed descriptions of religious services, see Part II.

the means of the host and the importance of the occasion, but it ordinarily includes at least an appetizer course, a large meat course, dessert, and coffee with pastries. Most parties include numerous toasts with wine or schnapps; Inner Mission and Pentecostal homes usually substitute soft drinks. For seasonal rituals, dinner may begin or end with the singing of a familiar hymn or song. Life-cycle rituals include many such songs, scattered through the meal fairly randomly, and often written by friends or relatives of the person being honored.

The party is often followed by a ritual observance, such as the distribution of gifts at Christmas or the setting of a bonfire at midsummer. Afterward, guests gather inside again for more coffee and pastries, and then go home. Parties usually last late into the night, especially for rites of passage. They tend to be expensive; even smaller holidays involve the purchase of special food, and the larger ones mean feeding a dozen or so relatives. For major life-cycle rituals, the cost of a party may easily exceed the household's monthly income. Morsingboer love to host them, though, and they accept the cost as a natural part of social life. Moreover, costs even out over time. An average Morsingbo hosts a major transition ritual only a few times in his or her life, but attends several every year.

Attendance at parties varies with the occasion. On minor holidays, such as St. Morten's Eve, guests generally include only close family members, such as grandparents or unmarried siblings. On larger seasonal occasions, such as Christmas and Easter, as much of the extended family as possible gathers together, including married siblings, aunts, uncles, and close cousins. For a major transition ritual, like a wedding, virtually any relative or friend may attend.

The Seasons

Autumn

Autumn on Mors begins in September, when the long days of summer have definitely ended, and cool breezes and rain of begin to intimate the arrival of winter. Summer vacation ends for schoolchildren and workers. Farmers begin to take in their harvest and tourism begins to ebb, as the days of outdoor activities draw to a close. Soon the leaves will turn brown and fall, gardens will die, days will grow dark. All over the island, people turn from the leisure and bounty of summer to prepare, physically and morally, for the long winter to come.

They do so in part by reviving the association life that has lain quiet over the summer. Most voluntary associations close from May to September, leaving each family free to pursue its social life and recreation individually. They open again in the autumn and begin to plan activities for the winter season. Churches recommence their parish meetings as well, and evening classes begin at the adult education center in Nykøbing. In many ways, the end of summer marks the beginning of community social life on Mors. It has less effect on work. Farming slows down considerably, since livestock comes in from pasture and winter crops require less daily work; businesses catering to tourism also slow down, since most of their customers leave. Fishermen too must adjust to winter conditions, although they continue to go out. But beyond the extravagant shopping that accompanies certain holidays, changes in season have little effect on how most workers do their jobs.

Like community life, the ritual cycle recommences in autumn after a fairly dormant summer. The biggest occasion of the season is St. Morten's Eve *(Skt. Mortens Aften)*, which comes at the beginning of November. The holiday commemorates a Protestant martyr who met his end at the hands of some ducks. According to local tradition, he had attempted to hide from his Catholic persecutors in their pen, and they gave him away by pointing to him with their wings. Danes avenge him symbolically by gathering their families together for a meal of roast duck.

Winter

By the end of November, the cold and dark of winter have arrived on Mors. People bustle through the damp, windy streets in thick wool coats and knit hats, sometimes contending with heavy mists or brief hailstorms. Darkness falls by three o'clock, and even during the day the sun never rises very high. Morsingboer do not generally like the "dark days," and many suffer from mild depression as the nights grow longer and longer. Even so, the onset of winter finds the island's residents in generally high spirits. For on the first day of December, the countdown begins to Christmas *(Jul)*, the biggest single event in the Danish annual calendar.

Most Morsingboer love Christmas, and they celebrate it lavishly. They begin decorating their homes in the beginning of December. Cut paper pictures *(papirklip)* of elves and Christmas trees fill the windows; homemade figurines of elves and goats ornament windowsills and shelves; arrangements of evergreens and candles appear on tables. The Walking Street Association strings wreaths across the shopping district in Nykøbing, and merchants all over the island market and use huge quantities of decorations. Merchants also promote gift items in their stores with colorful red and white displays, as families begin buying the necessary supplies for the Christmas celebration. Families light Advent candles, and churches hold Advent services. Candles in windows line the streets at night. Shortly before Christmas, every family sets up a small evergreen tree on a stand inside the house, and decorates it with elaborate homemade paper ornaments and candles. Wrapped gifts are placed at its foot. While Christmas itself only lasts a few days, preparations for it last the entire month.

Christmas begins on *Juleaften*, Christmas Eve, on December 24. Most families attend the church service, which features a tree in the church decorated with lighted candles.[2] Afterward, they return home or to a relative's house for a large dinner, featuring a large ham or pork roast. When dinner is over, the candles on the tree are lit, and the assembled family gathers around it in a circle. There they join hands and dance in a ring while singing Christmas songs. The dancing is not formal; while some families know folk dance steps, most simply walk or run while holding hands. Dances range from boisterous, breathless romps to slow, meditative walks, depending on the age and inclination of the assembled family. Regardless of the style, though, the dancing marks a high point of the occasion. The glowing tree, the family circle, the familiar songs about winter and spiritual redemption, all combine for perhaps the most moving moment in the Danish year. The entire family dances through at least four or five songs, and in some cases the children may dance for an hour or more. Afterward, everyone sits down near the tree, and a designated child hands out the gifts at its foot. Normally, every person in attendance brings a gift for every other, so a flurry of unwrapping ensues. Gift recipients thank givers profusely as they open each present, generating a cacophony of tearing paper and shouts of "a thousand thanks!" *(tusind tak!)*. When all of the packages are opened, and the thanks and admiration completed, the assembled family moves to another room for a final round of coffee and pastries, after which the guests depart.

Christmas itself lasts two days, called *Juledag* (Christmas Day) and *Anden Juledag* (Second Day of Christmas). The churches hold special

2. Danish village churches usually have a single public entrance near the back of the church; during the intensely crowded Christmas service, getting out in a hurry would be next to impossible. It therefore amazed me that churches would light real candles on the large, dry Jul tree. If a tree caught fire, most of the congregation might well die. The people I asked about it agreed that the practice was dangerous, but none could imagine electric lights on a church tree, and none could recall any fires resulting.

services on both days, and most families hold special dinner parties. These dinners are much less formal, however, and carry much less meaning than the festival on Juleaften. Church attendance is lower as well, especially on Anden Juledag. Adults take the opportunity to relax after the whirlwind of preparation for Juleaften, and children begin the long countdown to the festival next year.[3]

The festive atmosphere returns a few days later for New Year's Eve *(Nytårsaften)*. Unlike Christmas, this holiday has hardly any association with the church, and involves no special service. Many families, and some groups of older children, hold parties for the occasion in the late evening. At midnight, virtually every family walks out into the street or garden to set off fireworks and watch those set off by neighbors. Morsingboer use an extraordinary volume and variety of fireworks, all purchased from local stores; in Nykøbing, the litter covers the streets for days. Afterward, adults toast the new year with schnapps or soft drinks, and then go to sleep. For teenage children, however, especially boys, the business of New Year's Eve mischief remains. They roam the village or town playing such pranks as ringing doorbells, covering cars with confetti, writing on windows with toothpaste or shaving cream, tying doors shut from the outside, and running large objects up flagpoles. Serious property damage seldom results, and bodily assaults are unknown. Locally unpopular or anomalous residents, however, may be singled out for particularly concentrated attention.

A holiday atmosphere continues to reign until Epiphany *(Hellige tre kongers dag)*, the final day of the Christmas season. Many families mark Epiphany by lighting special three-branched candles, representing both the holy kings and the Trinity.[4] Afterward, winter sets in earnest. Anticipation of Christmas no longer brightens the winter darkness; with six or fewer hours of weak sunlight per day, with sleet, hail, and occasional snow, with withering winds and damp cold, the natural world feels bleak and oppressive. The public world seems to lose some of its warmth too, as curtains drawn against the weather replace the window displays that lined village streets during Christmas. Association life provides a welcome exception; most associations work actively during this period, and a variety of meetings, lectures and games break up the monotony of the long nights.

3. Iørn Piø (1977) provides an exhaustive description of Danish Jul customs and symbols.
4. Epiphany is not a major holiday on Mors. In some areas of Denmark, though, it involves some dramatic masking rituals.

Relief comes in February, with the celebration of *Fastelavn*, the last Sunday before Lent. On the Monday after Fastelavn, children dress up in homemade or purchased costumes, then go from door to door throughout the villages and towns. At each door they sing a two-verse song, an equivalent of the American "trick or treat";[5] in return, they receive either special pastries or small coins. Before the last war, the fishermen of Nykøbing added a festive custom to this primarily children's holiday. Dressed as sailors, a group of them would pull a boat on wheels down all the streets of the town; residents would gather along the streets to watch and throw in money to support the families of lost sailors. The town still holds this ritual every other year, although it now serves more to nourish nostalgia than orphans.

Spring

March begins much like February, dark and cold. By the middle of the month, however, some signs of spring are appearing. The first flowers bloom, for example; girls pick them and place them in specially decorated letters (*gækkebreve*), to be sent with riddles to their friends. Days begin to lengthen noticeably, and the wind and cold begin to ease. In April, summer planting begins as leaves start to appear on trees. By mid-May, fields of wheat, oats, and rye wave in the countryside, interspersed with brilliant yellow swaths of blooming rape. Temperatures remain cool, but the mist and driving rains of winter have ended, leaving sunny skies for the return of the tourists in June.

Spring brings a palpable sense of renewal to Mors, as islanders delight in the lengthening days and the blue skies. Nothing captures this feeling more than Easter (*Påske*) and the observances that surround it. Morsingboer decorate their houses with cut paper ornaments of chicks, ducklings, rabbits, and flowers; they raise daffodils (*Påskelilier*) in their

5.   For those interested, the song goes as follows:

Fastelavn er mit navn.	Fastelavn is my name
Boller vil jeg have.	I would like some pastries
Hvis jeg ingen boller får.	If I do not get any
Så laver jeg ballade.	I will make trouble
Boller op, boller ned.	Pastries up, pastries down
Boller i min mave.	Pastries in my tummy
Hvis jeg ingen boller får.	If I do not get any
Så laver jeg ballade.	I will make trouble

Despite the threat implied, I never heard of any trouble being made, perhaps because virtually every home gives something.

gardens and display them everywhere; they partake liberally of the potent Easter beer *(påskebryg)* put out annually by the breweries. Lenten abstinence is rarely practiced. Easter involves far fewer ritual observances than Christmas, and on the day itself, the celebration involves only a special church service and a large family dinner. Like Christmas, however, its anticipation in the preceding weeks creates a festive mood that permeates daily life.

Several other days also mark the passage of spring. Inner Mission and Pentecostal groups mark Great Prayer Day *(Store Bededag)* in late April with prayer and revival meetings. Others take advantage of the holiday to hold a dinner for the extended family. Flags fly at half mast on April 9, the date of the German invasion in 1940; they are hoisted high again on May 5, when Danes burn candles in their windows to mark the German retreat. Pentecost *(Pinsedag)* in May holds great significance for the churches, particularly the free churches, although it occasions little secular celebration. More festivities accompany May 1, which commemorates the establishment of organized labor. A small parade snakes through the streets of Nykøbing, followed by speeches before the town hall by local Socialist and Social Democratic leaders.

Summer

Summer begins with the Constitution Festivals, held by various political parties to celebrate Constitution Day *(Grundlovsdag)* on June 5. Each festival features a speech by a party leader relating the party's platform to the Constitution; pointed questions and lively debate from the audience often follow the speech. Two weeks later Nykøbing holds a festival of its own: the Pearl Festival *(Perlefesten)*, named for the oyster fishery that once flourished in this area of the Limfjord. Sponsored by local associations, the Festival brings singers, speakers, and a traveling circus into town for several days. It culminates with a parade of brass bands and decorated floats that draws thousands of spectators from around the island.

The season's biggest ritual, though, is the ancient celebration of Midsummer Night's Eve, or St. Hans's Eve *(Skt. Hans Aften)*. The days have grown steadily longer since winter, and by midsummer the sun hardly sets at all. On St. Hans's Eve, Morsingboer gather with friends or family in the early evening for an informal dinner party. Afterward, each group goes out onto the fields or to a beach, where the host has already erected a large pile of sticks and straw. In its center, a straw figure of a witch with a black cape stands tied to a tall post. When midnight approaches, the bonfire is lit, and the group cheers as the rising flames consume the witch and send her "back to Bloksbjerg." In Nykøbing, where residents cannot light their own fires, the town erects a huge bonfire on the north coast. Folk dancers and musicians perform for the hundreds of families in attendance. The crowd remains long after the last embers have died, drinking and talking in the pale light of the summer's largest festival.

It is also the summer's last, at least for the island as a whole. As the sunshine and mild weather of the summer return, community activities gradually wind down. Associations suspend their activities, churches end their parish meetings, schools finish their classes. Morsingboer look less to their neighbors for companionship, and more to their nuclear families. Many take vacations and travel; others move to summer houses along the island's coast to enjoy the salt air and solitude. On the farms, the press of summer tasks keeps workers in the fields and out of association work. In the town, the influx of tourists in July and August means long and busy days for business workers. All over the island, people turn their attention to individual and family matters. The community and the seasonal rituals that it observes fade into the background until the chill breezes of September blow them in again.

Local Identity

A long time ago, the story goes, a man from Salling set out on foot across the frozen Limfjord. It was a harsh winter day, with blinding fog and driving wind, and he soon lost sight of land. He trudged on through the featureless gloom, hoping that he was still going in the right direction. Suddenly, a towering figure appeared out of the fog. The man from Salling froze in terror – was it a traveler, like himself, or had a wandering demon found him alone and helpless on the ice? In a quavering voice, he shouted, "Are you a man, or a devil?" Neither, replied the figure: "I am a Morsingbo."

Denmark is a small country, with a long history, and its inhabitants have a strong sense of their own distinctiveness. Most Danes can rattle off a list of national stereotypes that distinguish them from each of their European neighbors: the Germans are militaristic, the Swedes repressed, the Norwegians lighthearted, the British snobbish, and the Danes the reverse of each. At the same time, Danes also recognize a surprisingly varied cultural landscape within the country. They draw sharp distinctions between Copenhagen and southern Sjælland, between Sjælland and Fyn, between both islands and Jutland, and between dozens of regions within each. As an island, Mors has a particularly well-defined border, and a correspondingly well-defined local identity. To finish my description of the island, I will mention a few ways of thinking and acting that are central to that identity.

One of these is the Jante Law. In 1933, the Norwegian author Aksel Sandemose published a semi-autobiographical novel entitled *A Refugee Crosses His Tracks*, in which he issued a scathing indictment of narrow-mindedness and provincialism in the Danish countryside. The setting is a town called Jante, which is very clearly patterned on Nykøbing; Sandemose was born and raised here before he emigrated to Norway. Its creed is expressed in the Jante Law *(Janteloven)*, a set of unspoken social rules that most Danes have come to identify with West Jutland and Mors:

1. Thou shalt not believe thou art something.
2. Thou shalt not believe thou art as good as we.
3. Thou shalt not believe thou art more wise than we.
4. Thou shalt not fancy thyself better than we.
5. Thou shalt not believe thou knowest more than we.
6. Thou shalt not believe thou art greater than we.
7. Thou shalt not believe thou amountest to anything.
8. Thou shalt not laugh at us.
9. Thou shalt not believe that anyone is concerned with thee.
10. Thou shalt not believe thou canst teach us anything.

(Sandemose 1936: 77-78)

The Jante Law clearly reflects Sandemose's own frustration as an ambitious child in a poor family, and many Morsingboer resent its application to the whole society. All agree, however, that something like the Jante Law does exist on the island. Morsingboer dislike self-importance and the expression of extravagant ambitions, particularly if they imply a superiority over other people on the island. Islanders do admire achievement, and they are quick and effusive in their praise of others' abilities. But the individual who offers or implies such praise of himself invites scathing ridicule. Morsingboer therefore avoid drawing public attention to themselves whenever possible. Those who find themselves in the public eye affect a slight embarrassment, and imply by their tone that their current visibility stems from chance, not from any special qualities they possess.[6] The Jante Law certainly exaggerates the repressiveness of the

---

6. The Jante Law is not exclusive to Mors; it characterizes much of rural Denmark, and even certain aspects of urban life. A brief glimpse can be found in Danish books describing the country for foreigners, many of which begin with a sort of apology for taking the reader's time with so tiny and flawed a land (e.g., Lauring 1963).

social climate on Mors, but it does describe something important about the rules for individual conduct.

At a broader level, Morsingboer identify heavily with the Danish stereotype of the Jutlander *(jyder)*. To be from Jutland is to be strong and silent, plain in manners, and reserved in expression. The archetypal Jutlander has little regard for the transient styles and pretensions of the urban east; he holds to the land and the traditions of his ancestors, certain of their enduring value. He says little, especially in matters of affection, which exists all the more securely for not being expressed. His temper is even, not given to extremes of anger, sadness, or joy. Ridiculed by city folk, ignored by politicians, he remains the backbone of a Danish society that would crumble without him. This image stands somewhat at odds with the Mors of today, whose inhabitants participate actively and proudly in the national culture of modern Denmark. Nonetheless, it underlies much of the literature and poetry of Jutland, and Morsingboer use it to distinguish themselves from eastern Danes.

True to the dictates of the Jante Law and the Jutlandish ideal, open expression of emotion is rare on Mors. This does not mean, however, that its inhabitants are cold or severe people. Quite the contrary: Morsingboer consider it important to enjoy life, and grim humorlessness meets with more disapproval than boisterous frivolity. Humor permeates life on Mors, as it does most places in Denmark. Almost every conversation contains the subtle ironies and teasing of Morsingbo humor, while no public speaker would consider opening a lecture without a joke. Emotional bonds among families and friends are seldom discussed openly, but the warmth that pervades them is unmistakable. It is particularly visible in the interaction between children and adults; men and women alike treat children tenderly and solicitously in public with no trace of embarrassment.

That warmth is expressed in the untranslatable term *hygge,* a state whose realization is one of the most valued products of social gatherings in Denmark (see Hansen 1970). Hygge involves a relaxed coziness, a sense of security and connection to others. It is experienced by a family gathered around candlelight and coffee on a blustery winter night; by old friends talking in a quiet corner of a pub; by a knot of women knitting and gossiping at a parish meeting; by two lovers talking over wine in a restaurant. Morsingboer set great store by hygge, and they try to create it in most of their social gatherings. More often than not, they succeed.

Their doing so stems largely from the closeness most Morsingboer feel to the island. Relatively few newcomers have moved to Mors since the Vikings settled it over a thousand years ago; most of its inhabitants have had ancestors here for as long as records have been kept. Most are related to one another at some level, a fact made evident by their general similarity of face and form. And while circumstances force some of them to leave, most regard the island as the only true home they could ever have. Morsingboer who have left the island can join an association to keep them in contact with it; that association is the largest of its kind in Denmark. Mors has plenty of economic and social problems, and true to the requirements of the Jante Law, Morsingboer admit them readily. But for all its drawbacks, Mors remains the center of the world for those who live on it, a Pearl of great price in the quiet waters of the fjord.

Part II

RELIGION ON MORS

4. A Brief History of the Danish Church

～ ～ ～

"Gammel ven og gammel vej"	"Old friends and old ways"
Siger folket, "sviger ej."	"Never fail," folk say
Og hvad man fra slægt til slægt	And that which is passed with myriad voices
Siger højt med alle munde	From generation to generation
Det har grund og det har vægt	That has reason and gravity
Må forglemmes ingenlunde	And must never be forgotten.

Grundtvig (1894)

*R*eligion on Mors, like everything else, derives from a stream of history that flows back to the days of myth. Its beliefs, its structures, and its internal conflicts build on a millennium of doctrinal and organizational evolution. For Morsingboer, this history forms a living part of their religious life; islanders of all faiths perceive and describe their beliefs as the fulfillment of, the retur1n to, or the triumph over the traditions of ages past. I will begin, therefore, by briefly discussing the history of Christianity in Denmark. I will concentrate on the time after the Protestant Reformation in 1537, and on those events that most directly affected the people of Mors, to sketch the general historical framework within which Morsingboer understand their faiths and themselves.[1]

---

1. Readers interested in a full history of the Danish Church have dozens of excellent studies to turn to. Among the best-known are Kornerup et al. (1950-66), Fabricius

Danish Religion before the Reformation

This history begins before Christianity's arrival, with the Norse polytheism that dominated Scandinavia for most of the first millennium. Much of the information on this religion comes from Christian historians, whose biases make reconstruction difficult. It seems clear, however, that it involved the worship of a myriad of deities and sacred places, as well as an active ancestor cult. The major gods included Odin, Thor, and Freja; in addition, an array of minor gods, water spirits, elves, trolls, gnomes, and other beings populated the supernatural landscape. All of these beings could bring success or ruin to various aspects of human life, and much of the religious practice involved seeking their favor. Kings, chieftains, and family heads conducted most of the rituals involved, without the aid of any special priest class. Public rituals included festivals for planting, harvest, midsummer, and midwinter, often highlighted by animal sacrifices; private rituals included sacrifices as well. Every nine years, according to some accounts, Norsemen held huge regional outdoor festivals, involving massive human and animal sacrifices. Beyond such rituals, the religion included an extensive mythology about the activities of the supernatural beings and their manifestation in the physical environment.

The most dramatic aspects of this religion disappeared after the establishment of Danish Christianity in the 10th century, and the major gods survive today only in such place names as Torshavn and Odense. Belief in the lesser beings held on much longer, however, especially in the countryside. Folklorists in the 19th century collected numerous legends of elves, gnomes, and trolls on farms all over Denmark. Even today, many rural people attach magical properties to certain springs and mounds, and some belief in gnomes endures. In some cases, Christian teachings have been mingled with older traditions; early missionaries, for example, retained certain pagan harvest rituals with an overlay of Christian symbolism, while annual festivals like Jul and Midsummer were connected to points in the

---

(1934, 1936), and Koch (1960), all lengthy and thorough scholarly works. A more accessible work is Martin Schwarz Lausten's (1987), which charts the church from its beginnings through the mid-20th century in concise and readable Danish. Works in English are much fewer, but Hartling (1964) and Hunter (1965) provide general treatments in the course of longer works. This chapter draws on primarily on Lausten (1987), Hartling (1964), and Hunter (1965) for the pre- Reformation era. Information on the Reformation comes from Lausten (1987) and Oakley (1972); post-Reformation material is drawn from Lausten (1987), Lindhardt (1959), Pontoppidan-Thyssen (1957), Iversen (1986), and others.

Christian calendar. On Mors, likewise, the legend of Harald Bluetooth's baptism was attached to a holy spring of pre-Christian origin. While Danish rural culture was indisputably Christian well before the Reformation, it retained elements of it earlier cosmology for centuries afterward.

The decline of this religion began around the year 700, when the English monk Willibrord ventured north from Holland to convert the "very wild people of the Danes" (Lausten 1987: 14). Willibrord's mission met no success, and he was lucky to escape with his life. Others followed, however, and in 823 a mission was established at Hedeby in Slesvig. Missionaries made headway very slowly; even the German monk Ansgar, the "Apostle of the North," won few converts in his tireless journeys through Denmark. The real impetus behind Danish conversion came from the German crown. Under pressure from Kaiser Otto, King Harald Bluetooth underwent baptism around 960, and in so doing imposed the new religion on the entire nation. By the end of the next century, Denmark had become a thoroughly integrated part of the church.

The structure of this church varied enormously during the pre-Reformation period; both Rome and the Danish crown exercised partial authority over it, and the changing fortunes of both put it under constant strain. In general, the church grew slowly and steadily both in terms of property and organizational complexity. Denmark became an independent archbishopric in 1104, and over the next two centuries the church acquired lands, tithes, and exemption from secular taxes and jurisdiction. Parishes all over the country erected stone church buildings, most of which are still in use. Religious orders established monasteries throughout the land, including the Knights of Malta's Dueholm Kloster on Mors. Mendicant orders began operation early in the 13th century. Throughout the Middle Ages, the Danish church increasingly took on the structure and trappings of the older churches in Europe.

It took on their problems as well. Early bishops fought unsuccessfully to establish their independence from the dictates of the crown; while they eventually achieved considerable autonomy, they were forced to acknowledge royal authority as superior to Rome's. Such bishops as Eskil and Absalon became close allies of the crown in the 13th century, leading crusades to Estonia and other Baltic lands.[2] As Denmark developed into a true

2. The crusade to Estonia is the scene for one of the most dramatic legends in Danish folklore. During a key battle, the story goes, the Danes knew that they could prevail so long as Bishop Absalon continued to pray for them. He finally collapsed of exhaustion, though, and the Danish crusaders seemed certain to be routed. In response to their need, God sent the Danish flag – called Dannebrog, "Strength of

nation-state during the 14th and 15th centuries, and as church wealth and properties increased, royal influence in church affairs grew pervasive. Bishoprics became political appointments, awarded as patronage to powerful nobles; corruption and clerical immorality undermined the church's moral authority, as they did throughout Europe. The church's wealth made it suspect to idealistic clerical reformers and appetizing to cash-strapped political leaders. By the close of the 15th century, in Denmark as in the rest of northern Europe, the conditions for the Reformation were in place.

State Protestantism in Denmark

The Reformation

The actual fall of the Danish Catholic Church grew out of a political crisis that began in 1523, when a coalition of Danish barons managed to drive King Christian II into exile. Christian had sought for a decade to undermine the power of the upper nobility, primarily by promoting the interests of the farmers and merchants in the market towns. He had also weakened the church, which at the time owned roughly a third of the nation's cultivated land. During the reign of his successor, Frederik I, the church's position eroded still further. Frederik refused to suppress the energetic Protestant movement that began in the market towns after Martin Luther's trial in 1523; in Slesvig and Holstein, the young Duke Christian became an avid Lutheran and actively promoted Lutheran priests. Slighted by the crown and under attack from the towns, the church became dependent on the support of the upper nobility for its continued existence.

When Frederik died in 1533, the barons on his council tried to assume control of the state themselves by putting off the choice of a successor. This action sparked revolts in the market towns, which demanded the restoration of Christian II. Civil war ensued, with the supporters of the exiled king winning impressive early victories. The barons found themselves in desperate straits; their only hope of survival lay in unifying around the Protestant Duke Christian of Slesvig-Holstein. When they did so, they effectively abandoned the church and placed it under the authority of its most avid and powerful detractor.

---

the Danes" – down through the air to them. They held it aloft and charged the Estonian forces, winning a total victory and making Estonia Christian. Dannebrog is thought to be the oldest national flag in existence.

Christian proceeded to win the war convincingly, and he ascended the throne as Christian III with an unprecedented degree of power. Shortly afterward, in 1537, he officially abolished the Catholic Church and instituted the Evangelical Lutheran Church of Denmark.

The new church retained the basic framework of its predecessor; parishes continued to be administered by priests, bishops continued to supervise dioceses, and tithing and priests' farms continued to support the enterprise financially. Christian imposed radical changes, however, both on the church's property and its theology. The constitution, approved personally by Martin Luther, withdrew the church from worldly affairs, restricting it to the promotion of salvation through personal belief in Christ's love. Bishops were no longer to be overseers of church property, but rather "superintendents" who ensured each priest's faithfulness to Luther's vision of Christianity. The church lost its great estates and monasteries to the crown, as well as the third of the tithe that had formerly gone to bishops. The bishops lost their relative independence from royal authority; in his rejection of the Holy Father in Rome, Christian asserted his own place as "the father of the superintendents." Virtually overnight, the church was transformed from a powerful and autonomous political actor to a powerless dependent of the king.

The Reformation probably tripled the property of the crown, and in doing so gave the monarchy an unprecedented independence from the upper nobility. Its financial effects on the church, by contrast, were devastating. Without the support of the estates and monasteries, local churches had only local resources to support their priests and buildings. Luther's rejection of clerical celibacy increased these costs; poor parishes that could barely support a single Catholic priest found themselves charged with feeding a whole Lutheran family. As a result, maintenance and improvement budgets shrank, and many churches fell into a state of disrepair that lasted for centuries.

The Reign of Lutheran Orthodoxy

The years after the Reformation saw a steady consolidation of the enormous political power that Christian III had established during the civil war. This power extended into the church as well; though Luther himself had advocated a sharp division between spiritual and temporal authority, Christian intervened freely in both administrative and doctrinal matters. He enforced a rigidly Lutheran view of Christianity among the clergy, warning against the polluting influences of Melancthon,

Calvin, and other rival Protestant theologians. He also manipulated appointments and church finances to promote his views and policies. His successors followed his example, and for the next 150 years a Lutheran orthodoxy reigned in the Danish church.[3]

This orthodoxy had explicit political motives; Christian and his followers felt that a devout population would provide a peaceable and productive foundation for the realm, as well as bring God's blessings to the kingdom. They therefore used their immense worldly authority to impose piety on their subjects. In 1629, for example, a royal decree authorized parish priests to monitor and punish immorality among their parishioners with the aid of local informers. Such directives intruded on personal conduct in ways the Catholic church never imagined. They mandated specific morning prayers in the home, and such sins as swearing, gambling, illicit sex, and fighting between spouses could bring punishments ranging from the stocks to exile. In 1645, the crown ordered priests to employ several men in the church "who can walk around with long poles, and hit them on the head, who sleep during the service" (Lausten 1987: 163). As the 17th century wore on, the government brought more and more of its authority to bear on individual morality.

Orthodoxy began to show some cracks in the late 17th century, when foreign and trade policies led the crown to introduce some limited religious freedom. Jews received permission to hold private religious observances in 1684, and in 1685 Huguenot refugees from France obtained religious freedom and a number of economic privileges.[4] Both exceptions came at the request of the commerce ministry, which wished to attract capable artisans and businessmen to the country. Catholics also gained some legitimacy in Copenhagen, where the French ambassador was permitted to hold services for his staff. The church, warning that

3. The introduction of absolute monarchy in Denmark in 1660 recognized this status formally; the king was "God's caretaker on earth," and as such merited absolute control over religion.
4. Some Huguenots made their way up to Jutland, and a number of their descendents now live on Mors. Many of them are quite conscious of their ancestry, and point proudly to their French names as evidence. I was unable to find evidence of Jewish settlement on Mors; persons of "Mosaic" faith crop up occasionally in censuses, but they were probably passing through on business trips. The largest Jewish settlement in Jutland appears to have been in the "free city" of Fredericia, an island of religious liberty in the south that also includes Calvinist, Catholic, and other non-Lutheran communities. The Huguenots and the Jews were by no means the only foreigners imported by the crown for their skills. Robert and Barbara Anderson (1964), for example, provide an excellent account of the history of imported Dutch dairy farmers on Amager Island near Copenhagen.

such dissidents could spread dangerous ideas, objected to any exceptions to the orthodox creed; by the end of the century, however, royal convenience had begun to outweigh Lutheran purity.

State Pietism

A new phase in church theology began in 1695 with the ascension of the pietistic Frederik IV to the throne. A pietist movement had been building in southern Jutland for several decades; inspired by the German theologians Spener and Francke, its followers sought a more personal and cathartic Christianity than the rigidly orthodox church provided. They urged Christians to turn away from the knowledge and company of the visible world, and focus instead on conversion and devotion to God. Laymen were to read the Bible assiduously, participate actively in church life, and gather the truly devout into special faith-building meetings. The church establishment had condemned the implicit anticlericalism in the movement, despite its popularity among many younger priests. Frederik and the devoutly pietistic Queen Sophie, however, began openly supporting it in the first decades of the 18th century.

Much of this patronage consisted in simply appointing pietist clergymen and bishops. But it also involved a number of projects that were new to the church. Pietism required active missionary work, for example, and in 1714 the king established a mission council to spread the Christian message in Greenland and Lapland. Social welfare projects began as well, such as the pietistic Vajsenhus orphanage in Copenhagen. Most importantly, the pietistic emphasis on Bible reading led to the construction of grammar schools all over the country. The king ordered construction of 240 schools for farm children in 1721, and various pietistic courtiers funded others. Though the education they provided was limited and often haphazard, these schools marked the beginning of widespread literacy in Denmark.

One of the most visible figures in the pietistic movement was Count Nikolaus von Zinzendorf, the German noble who founded the Moravian Church in Herrnhut. Von Zinzendorf persuaded Frederik's successor Christian VI to allow the Moravians to establish a colony near Fredericia in southern Jutland. From there, the "Herrnhutter" sent missionaries across the country to win converts and establish pietistic circles. While they never became a major movement, the Herrnhutter gained a sizable network of adherents in their voyages around Jutland. They even made their way to Mors, where they found a warm reception in some of the northwestern villages. Their influence was lasting; when the Grundtvigian awakening swept through Mors a century later, it found its greatest strength in the communities where the Herrnhutter had won their converts.

These converts sometimes espoused beliefs very different from mainstream pietism. Since pietist doctrine gave individuals primary responsibility for their own salvation, religious dissidents of many stripes used it to legitimate their views. On Mors, a small antichurch sect flourished briefly in the parishes of Ljørslev and Solbjerg in the mid-18th century (Jensen 1944). Led by a charismatic farmer named Jens Storgaard, the "Kissing Sect" *(kyssesekten)* disputed the inherent sinfulness of sexual contact; if Christ could kiss his followers without sin, said Storgaard, why couldn't good Christians do the same? Sect members boycotted their local churches and openly flouted church moral codes, creating some illegitimate pregnancies in the process. The movement dissipated shortly after Storgaard's death in 1741, and the clergy dealt leniently with its adherents. Kissing sects flared up elsewhere on the island later, though, led by other charismatic dissidents.[5]

The kissing sects had little long-term impact, but their existence reveals a growing discontent with the clergy among commoners on Mors. Pietism served as a vehicle for similar sentiments across the country, especially in Copenhagen. By 1734, the anticlericalism of radical pietism had become threatening enough to draw a severe reprimand from the king; the most vocal pietist critics of the church were exiled, and priests were admonished to adhere to the mild Hallensic pietism endorsed by the state. In 1741, the crown forbade religious meetings among laymen without the participation or approval of a parish priest. These measures successfully intimidated the radical pietists and silenced the church's most outspoken critics. They could not, however, stem the undercurrent of antichurch sentiment that was building throughout the 18th century.

The Enlightenment and Rationalism

The patronage of Christian VI had elevated pietism from theological movement to official doctrine; his death in 1746 dropped it back again. His son, Frederik V, rebelled against Christian's stern morality and embraced the enlightenment philosophy that was sweeping the courts of Europe. This philosophy contended that human reason, not revelation

---

5. It is difficult to gauge the size or influence of these sects, since information on them derives mainly from church legal records. See also Ejerslev (1970).

or emotion, should be the foundation of Christianity. Rational men could use logic and science to penetrate the mysteries of the universe, and even the dictates of scripture should be subject to the scrutiny of reason. "Rationalism" also supported freedom of expression and movement, education of the lower classes, and the improvement of rural living standards. These causes guided the policies of the Danish government for the rest of the 18th century, creating an economic and cultural renaissance in the nation. By the beginning of the next century, rationalism had become the new orthodoxy of the church and the state.[6]

To many of its adherents, rationalism implied a new role for the clergy, especially in rural society. Priests not only were the representatives of the church in the countryside; they were also the representatives of intellectual enlightenment, the only educated people whom most farmers would ever meet. They had a duty not only to proclaim the holy word, therefore, but also to bring the fruits of the new world that science was opening up. Priests should become expert farmers, leading their parishioners in the use of the most advanced methods. They should become fonts of practical information for improving the lives of their followers both spiritually and materially. Many priests took this obligation very seriously, and their farms became some of the most productive in Denmark. By becoming practical resources as well as spiritual ones, they also solidified their positions in the rural community.

Despite its practical strengths, however, rationalism found itself under fierce attack by the late 18th century. Inherent in enlightenment ideology was a tolerance of competing intellectual views; while it could dominate official doctrines and the appointment of priests, rationalism could not forcibly impose itself on its congregations. While pietism receded from the forefront of church policy after 1750, therefore, it retained considerable support among laymen. Moreover, with the introduction of press freedom in 1790, dissenting clergymen could voice their opinions to an extent previously unimaginable. Critiques of the

6. The rationalist period includes the reign of J.F. Struensee, one of the most remarkable figures in Danish history. As physician to the insane Christian VII, Struensee was able to exert an enormous influence on royal policy, ultimately making most of the king's decisions for him. In 1770, he arranged to have the king's authority transferred entirely to himself, and for two years he exercised absolute rule in Denmark. During that time, he worked ceaselessly to implement rationalist reforms in the country. He also carried on a very public affair with the queen, which eventually led to his undoing. His opponents unseated him in 1772; shortly afterward, he and his chief assistant were publicly executed, and most of his reforms were reversed.

church that would have once earned imprisonment began appearing regularly in newspapers, books, and privately published pamphlets. The rationalist church attracted the same anticlericalism that had dogged previous orthodoxies, but lacked the means to suppress it.

Most critics of rationalists charged that they had forgotten the Christian message in their enthusiasm for science and intellect. To back up their claims, these critics often cited flagrant abuses of the church service, such as a Christmas Eve sermon supposedly delivered by a rationalist priest on Fyn. The priest took as his text a passage noting the animals in the manger with the infant Christ; based upon this reference, he delivered a two-hour lecture on the proper methods for cleaning and supplying a cow stall. Whether or not this incident ever actually occurred, it encapsulated the pietists' objections to the church establishment, and it was recounted with outrage in pamphlets and speeches across the nation.

As the 19th century opened, then, the Danish church stood in a precarious position. It faced attack from outspoken pietist clergymen, rebellious pietist laymen, and a growing body of anticlerical parishioners. Its rationalist ideology allowed only a limited response to such threats; a government bent on promoting individual liberties provided little protection. And the rural masses from whom revolt would most likely come were gaining education, wealth, and political power unprecedented in their history. The road for the age of awakening had been laid.

The Awakenings

Prelude: The Strong Jutlanders

The awakening period began in southeastern Jutland, where a series of small pietistic laymen's movements spread through the countryside around Horsens and Vejle beginning in 1790. These movements preached a very emotional Christianity, involving a cathartic conversion and the renunciation of worldly pleasures; in some cases, believers claimed to receive inspiration and instructions directly from God. Led by men and women from various social classes, the movements differed in many respects. They agreed, however, in their disdain for the "false Christianity" of the local priests, and they lost no opportunity to castigate the church and its representatives as servants of the devil. They particularly objected to the new rationalist hymnals and confirmation texts that the church was beginning to introduce at the time.[7] Church authorities repeatedly tried to quell the uprisings with fines, jail terms, and even threats of child removal. The movements kept reviving, though, and ultimately the church gave in to most of their demands. Pietists were permitted to retain their old hymnals and build special schools for confirmation instruction; in some of the area's parishes, the old hymnals remained in use up to the 1960s. This awakening, whose members became known as the "strong Jutlanders" *(stærke jyder),* marked the first successful challenge of the state church's authority by a layman's group.

The Meeting Movement

A broader challenge soon developed further east, in the Kertiminde region of Fyn. This area had provided a fertile ground for the missionary activities of the Herrnhutter, and pietist sentiment remained strong among the farming and artisan classes. In 1819, a farm owner named Christen Madsen began assembling followers at his house for religious meetings on Sunday afternoons. There he preached the virtues of repentance and conversion, and inveighed against the teachings and private life of the local rationalist priest. Such meetings clearly violated the 1741 edict against religious meetings in private homes, and the church responded with criminal charges. In the resulting trial, Madsen became a well-known symbol of religious resistance. He ultimately lost – after nine years of proceedings – but his brand of "godly meetings" *(gudelige forsamlinger)* spread across Fyn and became the hallmark of a powerful pietist laymen's movement. By the beginning of the 1830s, despite the unyielding opposition of priests and church officials, the "meeting movement" *(forsamlingsbevægelsen)* had begun to reach into Jutland and Sjælland.

The godly meetings took place in private homes, usually those of farm owners or artisans who were local leaders of pietist circles. Their content was almost exclusively religious; the dozen or so participants sat around a table and sang hymns, read from the Bible, and talked about salvation. Some-

7. The Strong Jutlanders' concern about hymnals derives from the importance of hymnals in Danish life. The Danes sing from hymnals at occasions other than church services; many families sing a hymn before meals, for example, and hymns open and close many public meetings. Hymns are usually sung in their entirety from a hymnal, which contains the words but no music. Even the most casual churchgoers know a range of tunes by heart that is astonishing by American standards. Changing a hymnal is a serious matter, since it involves removing some old hymns as well as inserting new ones.

times a visiting lay preacher gave a sermon about the rewards of Christ's love and the perils of the sinful world. The tone of the meetings tended to be devout, but not severe, and later accounts by members convey an intense joy and feeling of community within the groups. The illegality of the enterprise intensified the communal feeling; leaders could be and sometimes were fined or jailed for their efforts. The lay preachers found themselves frequently in jail as they traveled across the country, and their willing acceptance of such punishment made them folk heroes to their followers.[8]

Clerical Awakening: N.F.S. Grundtvig

As the meeting movement spread across the countryside, a pietist revolution was brewing among the clergy as well. It found its leader in Nikolai Frederik Severin Grundtvig, a combative Copenhagen priest who was to become one of the most influential figures in modern Danish history. Beginning in 1810, Grundtvig began a fervent attack on the cold, impersonal institution that he felt the rationalist church had become. Denmark's priests, he said, devoted themselves to a comfortable worldly existence, amusing themselves with logical debates while the burning message of scripture went unpreached. Meanwhile, their congregations wended their way haplessly to perdition, detached and uninterested in a church that failed to touch their hearts. The word of the Lord, lamented Grundtvig, had disappeared from His house.

Grundtvig's life and influence defy quick summary, since both his occupation and his views changed repeatedly throughout his life. He was at various times Denmark's most celebrated theologian, its most influential folklorist, its leading educational reformer, and one of its most important politicians. At all times he was the nation's greatest hymnist, and even his bitterest critics admitted the beauty and elegance of his poetry. By the time of his death at age 89, he had become an object of near worship to followers across the nation. Even today his picture hangs in meeting halls and schools across Denmark, and his views on education and folk culture shape government policy.

8. See Holt (1961: 18-38) for a dramatic rendition of the beginnings of the meeting movement. Holt claims these meetings as the beginning of the Inner Mission movement; Grundtvigian authors such as Lau Jørgensen claim them with equal fervor as the beginning of their movement. Both are correct, inasmuch as both movements grew out of the Kerteminde awakening. The authors' viewpoint does affect their characterization of Christen Madsen's work, though, a fact which should be borne in mind when reading Holt.

Grundtvig's theological position changed dramatically at several points in his life, and it is impossible to distill a single message from it. Two themes, however, assumed special importance for the godly meetings and the awakenings that followed them. One was the central place of the congregation in Christian worship. Grundtvig argued that Christian congregations had existed before the writing of the New Testament, and that the essence of Christianity lay in the living faith of its members. Participation in the community of believers thus outweighed knowledge of scripture in importance. Surer than scripture was the Apostles' Creed, a formulation of the church's mission that derived from the days before the New Testament was written. This sense that Christianity required a living and active belief by the congregation echoed the thoughts of many organizers of the godly meetings.

A second theme emphasized the importance of folk culture to Christian belief. Real faith, said Grundtvig, comes only to those who understand their own natures; one must be "a human being first, and then a Christian" (Lausten 1987).[9] And to be human is to be particular, to be part of a certain people with a certain history.[10] Christians must begin by learning about and appreciating the cultures from which they are descended. Only then can they make a fully free and wholehearted decision to love and accept Christ. Grundtvig therefore exalted the folklore of rural society, which he believed had retained the traditions and beliefs of the ancients. He encouraged his followers to study Danish history, and he himself produced an imposing body of scholarship and poetry about Norse mythology. This attention to their own culture and history appealed strongly to many Danes, and it shaped the social activities of many Grundtvigian congregations.

Grundtvig's philosophy differed sharply from the pietism of the Herrnhutter and the Strong Jutlanders; indeed, as his positions became more clearly defined over the years, he became anathema to the nation's pietists. The awakening movement eventually split between those who embraced Grundtvig's folk-oriented views and those who adhered to the older pietist positions. In the first decades of the awakenings, though,

9. This formulation – "menneske først, og kristen så" – is for many Grundtvig's defining sentence, and Grundtvigian and Inner Mission members on Mors still use it to explain their relationship to one another.
10. This does not imply a superiority of certain peoples; one of the Grundtvigians' favorite lines was "Equal, but not the same" (*lige, men ikke ens*). Grundtvigians were among the most outspoken opponents of racist policies in Europe in the decade before World War II, and tenacious Grundtvigians like Frode Jakobsen have been leaders in Danish human rights movements.

Grundtvig's outspoken denunciations of the rationalists' dry faith made him the ideological leader of rebellious clergy and laymen. Young priests attended his sermons, read his pamphlets, and spread his message to congregations all across Denmark.

Awakening on Mors

By the middle of the 1830s, the meeting movement had spread throughout Jutland and Sjælland. Lay preachers traveled the old missionary routes of the Herrnhutter, holding meetings in sympathetic homes and generating local pietistic circles. One of the most successful of these preachers was Peter Larsen Skræppenborg, a farm owner from Fyn whose exuberant charisma and rural manners gave him a magnetic appeal to Jutland farmers.[11] Skræppenborg was a confirmed Grundtvigian; when he first read a Grundtvig pamphlet, according to one story, he immediately dashed out of his low-ceiling house so that he could freely jump for joy. The priest in Solbjerg parish on Mors was also sympathetic to Grundtvig, and in January of 1837 he invited Skræppenborg to hold a meeting in the Solbjerg parsonage.

It lasted only two hours, and consisted of singing hymns and a quiet sermon. Its effect, however, was electric. A young seminary student in attendance, Christen Kold, dashed afterward from farm to farm all around Solbjerg, shouting "Have you heard? God loves Man!" The farmers in attendance were also extremely moved, and over the course of the spring held twelve more meetings. The priest, J.C. Sørensen, approved of the new religious enthusiasm and participated in the meetings himself. In the ensuing decade, the meetings spread to most of the parishes in northern Mors, drawing regular crowds of up to 150 people.

The hostile division between laymen and clergy that characterized the meeting movement in most of Denmark never occurred on Mors. The dri-

11. His actual name was Ole Peter Holm Larsen; Skræppenborg was the name of his farm on Fyn, and he became generally known as Peter Larsen Skræppenborg. Grundtvigian folklore abounds with stories about this preacher, who personified the movement's ideal of Christian devotion combined with a love of life. One concerns his acquisition of Skræppenborg. According to the story, the original owner of Skræppenborg was an elderly Herrnhuttist widow with two daughters. Larsen worked as a hand on the farm, and eventually took over its management by dint of enormous aptitude. The widow then suggested he marry one of her daughters, and become the farm's actual owner. To decide which one, they followed Herrnhutter practice and cast lots; the lot fell on the older daughter, whom Skræppenborg dutifully married. For a comprehensive biography of Peter Larsen Skræppenborg, see Schrøder (1991).

ving forces behind the awakening were Kold and P.K. Algreen, both seminary students in Thy who had attended Skræppenborg's first meeting; they worked with the approval of Sørensen and other local priests, and painted the movement as strictly Lutheran. They often led meetings themselves, either reading from scripture or delivering energetic sermons on the need for repentance and conversion. They presented the meetings as an adjunct to the church, not an opponent, and their followers flocked to the services of the sympathetic priests. The pietist condemnations of clerical indolence thus fell on distant rationalists, not on local church officials.

A witness's description of one meeting gives a sense of the atmosphere:

> There were difficulties in the little farmhouses! Meeting houses were unknown at the time. Only the barns and the bedrooms were not pressed into service, and the last to arrive had to stand in the entrance or on the steps. It was certainly plenty warm! There was a man who wanted to leave right in the middle, but it took him fifteen minutes to make his way out. At a table in the big room sat the speakers with a pair of tallow candles in front of them. The audience sat in darkness, one had after all to be frugal. Even if they had had hymnals, they wouldn't have been able to use them. But the hymns one cared the most for were not in the "Evangelic-Christian Hymnal" in any case, for that was dry and rationalistic and very little liked.[12]
>
> So the songleader would sing or read two lines, which everyone would then sing. The came two more lines and so on until the end of the hymn. If there were 15-20 verses, this could take a long time. It was mostly Brorson's hymns, also Kingo's and some by unknown authors. After some hymns and one or more long, often heartfelt and ringing prayers, the speaker took over. If there was only one speaker, he would likely also read a sermon by Luther, Johan Arndt, Schriver or others. The Bible was never read from. The meeting ended with more prayers and hymn-singing. When most of the strangers had left, the inner circle remained behind for conversation or more singing.
> (translated from F. Nygaard 1883, in Fisker 1971: 13)

The awakening spread partly through Kold's and Algreen's preaching, but also through the social networks of the members. People were invited to meetings by relatives, by fellow farmworkers, and by neighbors; some of the awakened went so far as to proselytize, though such approaches met with a cold reception.[13] As a result, most of the members came from

12. This was the same hymnal that had roused the ire of the Strong Jutlanders.
13. They still do. During interviews, several older Morsingboer expressed irritation to me at the proselytizing methods that the Inner Mission used to use. The head of the local Pentecostal Church, likewise, said that he encountered very stiff resistance when he tried to proselytize on the island: "They think we are nice, friendly people,

a distinct set of lineages and farms. Movement leaders in Øster Jølby, Tøving, Bjergby, and Solbjerg, for example, all shared kinship ties to a single farm in Sundby. Most of these families and farms had participated in the Herrnhutter movement half a century earlier and many of them were later to play important roles in the development of the Free Congregation. This means of recruitment may explain the relatively small area within which the awakening took place; while it developed a large and avid following within its borders, the meeting movement never spread much beyond the western half of northern Mors (see map, p. ??).

The movement aroused some heated opposition by some of the island's clergy, including several whose parishioners were avid participants. The priest and the bailiff in Nykøbing showed particular outrage. Opponents derided the awakening as a machination of a fast-talking preacher and two self-important seminary students, a laughable attempt to create a cult among some gullible farmers. A teacher in Flade published the following description of a meeting in 1837:

> In a farm's outbuilding here on Mors was held at the beginning of February a great synod. A half-crazy seminarian, fresh from school, went around the parish and under various misrepresentations invited cripples, the lame, and the blind. They thought that a great communion awaited them, with a few drops of wine in the bargain, and not a few came, but instead of the wine they found the above-mentioned seminarian and a number of spiritual followers ... The president of the synod [Skræppenborg] and one of the overseers made an attempt to use the spice of faith to change wine into water, which succeeded beyond all expectations. At length they condemned a number of heretics, whose auto da fe will surely be discussed later. Around midnight the meeting broke up, but the farmers swore never again to waste a good night and strengthening sleep to wallow in these new prophets' spiritual mire. (translated from Poul Henrichsen, quoted in Fisker 1971: 10-11)

Critical priests reported meetings held without their permission to the authorities, and they ultimately succeeded in chasing Kold and Algreen off the island.[14] They had little success in quelling the awaken-

---

and they are very nice to us, but the moment we start to tell them about Jesus, they are not so happy with that." Perhaps as a result, I found the Pentecostalists and Inner Mission members on Mors much less forward in their witnessing than members of comparable churches in America.

14. While this opposition did succeed in getting Kold and Algreen off the island, it by no means ended their careers. Kold, in fact, went on to be a founder of the Danish folk high school movement, and became internationally famous for his revolutionary methods of teaching. Progressive educators in Denmark and elsewhere

ing, however, and by the late 1840s it had become an established part of the island's social life.

By that time, the awakening was changing its focus from private meetings to churches. The meeting movement represented something new in religion on Mors: its organization and membership were based on belief rather than locality, and spanned a number of parishes. The traditional church organization became increasingly constraining for the believers, who wanted a single church in which they could hear Grundtvigian sermons and conduct common rituals. They therefore began to push for the loosening of parish ties and the right to build a church of their own. I will discuss the consequences of their efforts in the next chapter.

The Church Movements

With the introduction of the new national constitution in 1849 (see p. 31), religion in Denmark changed dramatically. The state church's monopoly over religious expression disappeared, swept away by the enlightenment philosophy that had undermined the monarchy and transformed rural society. The old church had been an organ of the monarchy, commissioned to spread and enforce the word of God as interpreted by Martin Luther. The newly christened Folkekirke was a ministry of Parliament, with a mandate to administer religion as part of the nation's cultural heritage. No longer could the church dictate the beliefs of its parishioners, muzzle its critics, or suppress competing religions. While its organization remained essentially intact, the church lost its legal power over its congregations; in an instant, religious authority passed from the state to the individual.

For the first time since the Reformation, therefore, open divisions appeared in the theological positions of the church. Clergy split into several camps, called the Church Movements *(kirkelige retninger),* which became bitterly opposed to one another over the next half century.[15] They included

---

continue to revere him today. He eventually came to be grateful to the rationalists on Mors, since without their persecution, he said, he would have remained an obscure schoolteacher. Algreen went from Mors to Copenhagen, where he studied under Grundtvig and completed his theological degree; he later became an influential Grundtvigian priest.

15. A more exact translation of *kirkelige retninger* would be "churchly directions." Such a translation, though, suggests something more diffuse than the *retninger* are, hence the use of "church movements" here.

small groups such as the conservative Church Center *(Kirkeligt Centrum)* and the pietist Lutheran Missionary Society *(Luthersk Missionsforening);* the principal division, though, and the one that had the most significance for Mors, arose between the folklife-oriented Grundtvigians and the pietist Inner Mission. Both of these groups attracted enormous popular support, dividing regions, towns, and even villages along religious lines.

Grundtvigianism

Much of the laymen's movement in the first half of the century had taken Grundtvig as its theological leader. After 1849, therefore, Grundtvig's clerical allies found themselves at the head of a massive popular awakening. Followers flocked to the services of Grundtvigian priests, elated to hear the message proclaimed officially that they had been whispering clandestinely for a decade. Grundtvig's own church in Copenhagen became a magnet for clergy and students from across Denmark; its intense communal feeling and lively religious debates became models for Grundtvigian congregations around the country. By the end of the 1850s, Grundtvigianism had become the most active and powerful religious movement in the nation.

It received a considerable boost from the folk high school movement that began to blossom in the 1850s and 1860s. Folk high schools, developed by educators such as Kristen Kold and Ludvig Schrøder, built on Grundtvig's ideas about folk culture; they taught students about Norse folk traditions, language, history, and mythology. They became extremely popular after the war in 1864, drawing up to 13 percent of the nation's youth for a few months ever year. The students who attended, mostly from farm owner or smallholder families, returned to their homes brimming with Grundtvigian ideas and eager to apply those ideas in their own parishes. Attendance eventually became a standard rite of passage in Grundtvigian families, and the schools became regional centers for religious debate and theory.

As the awakening changed its focus from private meetings to church activities, though, a new set of organizational problems arose. Even under the new constitution, churches were organized geographically; members belonged to the parishes in which they lived, whether they accepted their priests' views or not. Grundtvigians who lived in rationalist parishes thus lost out on the congregational community, which lay at the heart of the movement. Accordingly, Grundtvigians pushed for the freedom to choose their own priests, either by switching parish affiliation *(sognebåndsløsning)* or by building their own churches within the Folkekirke. Both reforms eventually passed, and Grundtvigians built a number of their own churches around the countryside during the second half of the century. These "congregations of choice" *(valgmenigheder)* became avid and outspoken Grundtvigian strongholds; many remain so today, including the one on Mors.[16]

But the movement did not by any means remain within the confines of the churches. Grundtvig's celebration of folk culture inspired a myriad of secular organizations, mostly aimed at raising the consciousness and living standards of rural society. The Danish Society *(Det Danske Selskab)* held lectures and courses to educate farmers about their own history, culture, and political situation. Shooting clubs *(skytteforeninger)* promoted hunting and marksmanship, with an eye toward the formation of a peasant militia. Gymnastics associations encouraged "a sound mind in a sound body." Grundtvigians also provided critical support for the cooperative banks, stores, dairies, and slaughterhouses that bloomed around the country during the last part of the century. To house this secular side of the movement, Grundtvigians erected meeting houses *(forsamlingshuse)*. These buildings became the church's temporal counterpart in the Grundtvigian communities, drawing enthusiastic crowds to political, educational, athletic, and social events.

By the 1870s, the explosive growth of this side of Grundtvigianism was disturbing many of its older adherents. They felt that the original message of piety and redemption was being lost, forgotten in the flurry of political and cultural activity. They especially objected to the "new Grundtvigians'" active commitment to the Left party in the tumultuous parliamentary battles of the time. After Grundtvig died in 1872, a split developed between the religious and political wings of the movement, a split that grew wider and more bitter as time passed. By the beginning of the 20th century, the "old Grundtvigians" and the "new Grundtvigians" hardly recognized any link between themselves.

The Inner Mission

Grundtvig's ideas took a very different direction in the Inner Mission *(Indre Mission)*, a pietistic society founded by a group of Copenhagen lay-

16. The congregation on Mors is actually a "free congregation" *(frimenighed)*; it began as a *valgmenighed*, but split from the Folkekirke during a dispute in 1883. See next chapter.

men in 1853. Following Grundtvig's call to "awaken those who sleep in sin," the Mission's original members sought to fund a corps of traveling missionaries. Like the Herrnhutter of old, the missionaries were to crisscross the Danish countryside, holding religious meetings and bearing witness to the redemptive power of Christ's love. This layman's mission recalled the work of the itinerant preachers of the meeting movement, and it won the support of many Grundtvigian priests early on. Its work attracted a number of more radical pietist clergymen, however, and by 1860 priests had come to dominate the association's governing board. In 1861 they took control away from the laymen entirely; under the new name "Church Association for the Inner Mission in Denmark," they led the society in a direction that was to clash sharply with the Grundtvigians.

The Mission's new organization gave almost dictatorial control to the all-clergy governing board, which was dominated by a charismatic priest named Vilhelm Beck. Below the board stood a small corps of lay missionaries, each of whom organized and led meetings within a geographic region. In addition, a number of "coal porters" *(kolportører)* made circuits of the countryside, witnessing and selling religious tracts in house-to-house visits. Most of the movement consisted of local "circles" *(kredse),* which held both revival meetings and smaller "conversation meetings." Activity in the circles centered around "mission houses" *(missionshuse),* which became the Mission's equivalent of the Grundtvigian meeting houses. The governing board took care to keep this organization from competing with the official church; circles had no official members, for example, and were theoretically open to all members of the Folkekirke.

Participation in the local circles skyrocketed during the 1860s, turning the small association into a national movement in the course of a decade. The corps of missionaries grew from four in 1861 to forty-four in 1867; by 1900, 158 missionaries were each holding two hundred to three hundred meetings per year (Lausten 1987: 254). Much of the new membership grew out of missionary work among soldiers in the 1864 war. More came from Beck's missionary journeys in 1865 to Jutland, where anti-Grundtvigian elements of the meeting movement hailed him as something close to a savior. His riveting, sometimes terrifying sermons drew flocks of converts; "it was as though the apostles had returned," reported one witness, "and we wept with joy to hear [him]" (Lausten 1987: 254). The Mission met particular success among the fishing communities of Jutland's west coast, which later spread it to the coastal villages of the Limfjord. Such areas remain strongholds of the movement to this day.

The Mission's most striking feature was the sharp distinction it drew between its followers, "God's children," and the "children of the world." Beck urged converts to renounce the pleasures, fashions, and company of the sinful world from which the mission had saved them. The "holy ones" dressed in simple and severe clothing; they abstained from liquor, tobacco, card playing, dancing, and the theater; they studiously avoided any political involvement; and above all, they shunned social contact with the unconverted. Except for proselytizing, said Beck, any contact with the unconverted could only draw believers away from the true faith. The holy must keep their thoughts on heaven, not on the sinful and ephemeral world from which they came.

This view of the world contrasted sharply with the Grundtvigian love of the earthly community and folk culture, and over the next few decades the two movements came to oppose one another. People all over the country divided themselves into Grundtvigian and Mission camps; the bitter feelings between the groups often split regions and villages, setting up enmities between the "mission house people" and the "meeting house people" that have lasted to the present. These divisions often ran along occupational or geographical lines. While numerous exceptions existed, on the whole smallholders and fishermen tended to join the mission, while farm owners and artisans favored the Grundtvigians.

A key to the Mission's strength was its work among youth, both through Sunday schools and through the Young Men's and Young Women's Christian Association (*Kirkelig Forening for Unge Mænd/Unge Kvinder*, referred to as KFUM/K). Founded in 1878, the KFUM/K provided athletic, recreational, and social activities for children of Mission members. All of the activities took place under the leadership of Mission adults, and all attempted to incorporate elements of Mission teachings; summer camps, for example, included religious instruction, while social events carefully excluded dancing and drinking. The youth groups extended the tight communities of the mission to the children as well as the adults, making the movement self-sustaining. Children grew up in Mission families with Mission friends participating in Mission activities. They met their future spouses, neighbors, trading partners and business associates through the KFUM/K, and failure to join the Mission as an adult meant separation from their social world. Together with the charismatic appeal of preachers like Vilhelm Beck, the youth activities made the Mission a durable and powerful religious force in the first half of the 20th century.

Danish Religion in the 20th Century

The democratization of the state church, which the 1849 constitution had begun, reached its completion in the first decades of the 20th century. Danish law and public sentiment gradually accepted religion as a private matter, allowing such avowed atheists as Edvard and Georg Brandes entry into the highest political and literary circles. Private citizens gained increasing power over their churches, with the introduction of elective parish councils (1903), choice congregations (1868), and free congregations. Alternative churches gained legitimacy and began building congregations around the country. Even the medieval system of church funding underwent reform; a law of 1903 abolished the tithe and began funding the church as an ordinary state institution. By the end of World War I, the official and unofficial monopoly that the Evangelical Lutheran Church had held over religious expression in Denmark was effectively dismantled.

The end of this monopoly did not mean the end of the church; the vast majority of Danes retained their membership, and nine in ten still do today. The new circumstances did usher in several new trends, however, which have dramatically altered the nation's religious climate. I will briefly discuss two of them.

The Free Churches

Before 1849, alternatives to the state church existed only for a few enclaves of specially skilled workers, such as the Huguenots and the Jews. With the passage of the new constitution, a number of entirely new religious groups – the "free churches" *(frikirker)* – quickly appeared in Denmark. Most of them came from outside, brought by missionaries from England or Germany; a few, such as the Baptists, had already been conducting illegal services for decades.[17] These churches never gained great numbers of converts, but some of them became very visible, and a few made a significant impact on Danish culture. The Mormons, for example, proselytized extensively in Denmark during the late 19th century, persuading approximately 16,800 Danes to emigrate to Utah and join the church (Hvidt 1971: 295). Likewise, the brass bands and uniformed believers of the Salvation Army became fixtures around the

17. The rather heavy-handed suppression of the Baptists in 1839 aroused a storm of debate in Denmark, and inspired many people to join the drive for religious freedom that culminated in the new Constitution.

country in the early 20th century, and their charitable work remains widespread and important today. Pentecostal churches have also gained national attention with their dramatic baptisms and aggressive proselytizing. Regardless of their numbers, such movements provide vivid and public reminders that alternatives to the Folkekirke exist.

Free churches in contemporary Denmark span a wide range of doctrines. The largest is the Catholic Church, with about 25,000 Danish members and sizable congregations among guest workers. Non-Lutheran Protestant churches include the Baptists, with 20,000 members and a variety of religious and educational institutions; two Pentecostal churches, with a combined membership of about 7,000; the Salvation Army, with 8,500 officers and soldiers; the Seventh Day Adventists, with about 6,000 members; and the Methodists, with about 5,000. The Dutch Reform Church retains a tiny congregation, as do the Greek and Russian Orthodox Churches. About 7,000 Jews live in the country, almost all in Copenhagen. The Jehovah's Witnesses claim a large following, including 22,000 members spread over 190 kingdom halls. The Mormons also have a significant presence, with about 4,000 members (Nygaard 1982).[18] Another religious group has recently established itself in Copenhagen, where the burgeoning population of Turkish guest workers has created a large Muslim community. About 60,000 Muslims now live in Denmark; their attempts to build a large mosque in the capital have recently sparked a nationwide debate over their position.

Many members of the free churches say that their numbers are swelling today, particularly in Copenhagen and northern Jutland. Faith healers have drawn large audiences around the country, and many Pentecostal congregations appear to have grown significantly over the past decade. The evidence for this new "awakening" is largely anecdotal, though; moreover, the small size of the churches tends to exaggerate the impact of small fluctuations in membership. Whether this trend will continue remains to be seen.[19]

18. Judaism is not generally referred to as a free church, but as a "community of faith" *(trossamfund)*. The Jewish population in Denmark has remained fairly stable since the last century; while most of its members were evacuated during the Second World War, most of them returned afterward.

19. For doctrinal reasons, proselytizing religions have a strong incentive to portray themselves as growing, and their leaders have often exaggerated their size. See my article on the overestimation of American fundamentalist strength around 1980 (Buckser 1989).

Decline in Church Participation

Over the past several decades, an apparent decline in commitment to the Folkekirke has alarmed many of Denmark's priests and theologians. While church membership has remained high, attendance at Sunday services has fallen dramatically since the turn of the century. In a 1982 survey by Danmarks Statistik, only 2 percent of respondents claimed to attend church every week, while 37 percent said that they never went at all. Participation in such church life-cycle rituals as marriage and confirmation has also fallen, especially since the 1960s. According to many Danes, this decline has coincided with a number of less quantifiable trends, including a decreasing respect for church values and clergy, a general lack of interest in religious issues, and the loss of religious authority in moral and sexual matters. The core of Christian theology has lost plausibility with many Danes, and its most ardent defenders, the Inner Mission, have all but disappeared. The church, fear many, has become irrelevant in contemporary Denmark. People belong to it out of inertia, preserving its outer form, but no longer think or care about the doctrines at its core. Clearly, this perception derives partly from rosy views of the nation's piety at the turn of the century; nonetheless, both the church's moral authority and public participation in church activities appear to have ebbed considerably over the past fifty years.

Different parts of the country have experienced this decline in varying degrees. In general, Copenhagen has had the swiftest and deepest drop, while western Jutland has had the mildest. Between 1975 and 1985, for example, the percentage of children confirmed at age 15 fell from 98.2 to 93.6 in Jutland; from 93.3 to 89.6 in on Fyn, Falster, Lolland, and rural Sjælland; and from 72.4 to 58.0 in Copenhagen (Munck 1984: 80). Jutland also remains the stronghold of the highly committed Inner Mission and Pentecostal movements, as well as the doctrinally conservative Christian People's Party.

Some of this decline is nothing new. To a certain extent, it constitutes a continuation of traditional Danish anticlericalism. Opposition to and disgust with the state church is a recurrent theme in Danish religious history, and such events as the Lutheran Reformation and the pietist awakening owed much of their strength to it. Even in 18th-century Mors, Jens Storgaard's kissing sect stemmed more from a feud with the local priest than from any theological disagreement. Before 1849, legal sanctions against atheism required all such opposition to take the form of alternative Christian theologies. After the introduction of religious freedom, though, anticlericalism could attack Christianity and the church as a whole. Calls to abolish the Folkekirke rang through many early socialist programs, and still crop up occasionally among radical politicians. The impetus that once created church reform movements now tends to promote disaffection.

Some of the decline in church participation may also reflect the end of religious monopoly. Before the new Constitution's adoption, Danish law mandated church attendance. Failure to attend could bring severe penalties, including fines, corporal punishment, and even exile. Participation in baptism, confirmation, and other church rituals was a condition of citizenship. Even these draconian measures failed to ensure universal attendance at church; indeed, much of the appeal of Grundtvigianism for the clergy was that it brought people into their services. Without the laws, attendance would surely have dropped further. To a certain extent, then, today's decline in church participation may build on a tradition of apathy that earlier legal sanctions concealed.

Nonetheless, this trend clearly represents something new. The state church, for centuries a central institution in town and village life, is increasingly peripheral to Danish society. Its priests have lost much of their influence, its rituals have lost much of their appeal, its ideas have lost much of their importance. Individuals can ignore the church in a way that they have not been able to since Harald Bluetooth created it a thousand years ago.

And yet it lives. Despite all of their disaffection, the overwhelming majority of Danes remain members of the church, supporting it with their taxes and according it their respect. They baptize their infants, confirm their adolescents, marry their spouses, and bury their dead within the church's ritual structure. They mark the passage of the year with the church's ritual celebrations. All of these rituals require time, effort, and a lot of money. Clearly, Danes still see something in their church; not what they used to see, perhaps, but still something meaningful enough to associate it with the most important moments of their lives.

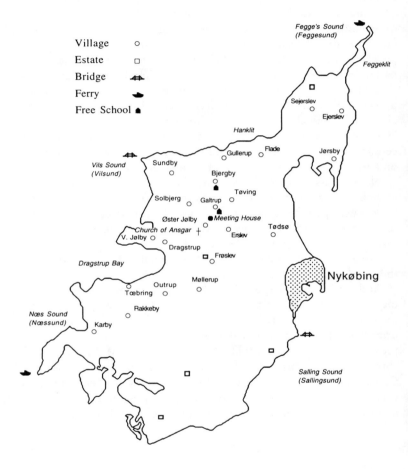

Map 3: Mors Island Free Congregation
Important Sites

5. The Mors Island Free Congregation

Frihed bedre er end guld,
var end verden deraf fuld,
og vor frihed af Guds nåde,
den for verden er en gåde,
er dog af al frihed bedst.

Frihed følger med Guds ånd;
brister alle trællebånd!
Hvad med Gud os frit forbinder
som med venner og veninder
det er tro og kærlighed.

Folket frit som fugl i sky
fristes ej til udflugt ny;
ej til ørken, ej til heden
stunder folket fra Guds Eden,
frydes ved at blive der.

Freedom is better than gold,
though the world were full of it,
and our freedom in God's grace,
though the world laughs at it,
is still the best freedom of all.

Freedom follows with God's spirit,
Bursting every chain!
What freely unites us with God,
as with fellow men and women,
that is faith and love.

A folk free as a bird in the clouds
Longs not for new voyages;
neither to desert nor heath
do they go from God's Eden,
but rejoice to remain at home.

– Grundtvig (1894)

*T*he staccato clangs of a churchbell cut through the wet morning air of the northern Mors countryside, ringing across the muddy fields and down the rutted lanes, echoing in the empty cobbled courtyards of a thousand scattered farms. From a red brick steeple in Øster Jølby, it rang out over the villages of Erslev, Bjergby, Galtrup, and Solbjerg. In

107

answer came streams of people, on foot and in carts, choking the narrow streets that led to Ansgar's Church and the Mors Island Choice Congregation. Wrapped in somber coats against the driving February wind, they came from as far as Nykøbing and Thy; they traveled in groups, usually entire families, saying little or nothing during the journey. The streams met in a corner of the Øster Jølby parish, where the Congregation's spartan brick church stood amid fields of winter wheat. Inside, early risers already packed the wooden pews.

It was February 2, 1883, and the congregation was coming to decide its future. A week earlier, the Folkekirke's bishop in Ålborg had formally dismissed its pastor, Rasmus Lund, from the priesthood, and ordered its members to choose a replacement from the recognized clergy. Lund now stood in the wings of the church, dressed in his black clerical robes, preparing to lead a Lutheran Sunday service. As a layman, he had no right to do so in a state church; as members of the Folkekirke, the parishioners had no right to join him. Anyone participating in this service would in doing so leave the Folkekirke, and the bishop had warned the congregation against such a step. If the congregation followed Lund, he had written, it would become a party outside the church. "And such a party," he had said, "can turn into a sect, one-sided and arrogant, wayward and fanatical" (Lindberg 1883: 2).

Anna Lillelund, wife of a sympathetic neighboring priest, describes the events of the day in her memoirs:

> The service in the Ansgarskirke, which was full to bursting, began as it almost always did with communion. Lund had had serious and moving hours in the days that had come before. [My husband] had visited him a number of times, and the congregational council had been assembled, but in the last night he had found a certain peace, and could lay all of his and the congregation's problems in the hands of God, and it was a sublimely serious and gripping communion. There was no sermon, but Lund gave a mild and humble homily over the scripture, and prayed our Lord to cast his blessing upon the events that this day would bring. Every one of us took communion, which took time, and it was nearly two o'clock before we left the church and walked over to the meeting house. [Lund himself, against all tradition, knelt down at the end and took communion himself, together with the congregation.]
>
> At that time Pastor Lillelund and Teacher Vestergaard arrived from Ovtrup, and the moment they entered the meeting house, they felt a mild and good atmosphere over the whole assembly. The speakers alternated with hymns, not that I can remember any in particular, but I will never forget the impression they made – especially when Lund asked the congregation's membership, whether they wished to keep him as priest, and how they wanted to situate

themselves? To which Povlsen Dahl, the wheelwright from Nykøbing, replied for us all, "That question we have answered already, over there in the church, when we all knelt at the altar together with you." (Lillelund 1921: 3-4)

The creation of the Free Congregation in 1883 culminated a half century of religious agitation in northwestern Mors. The unrest had begun in 1837, when Peter Larsen Skræppenborg sparked the pietistic Meeting Movement in Solbjerg (see pp. 94-97). Unlike most such groups in Denmark, the Mors pietists never developed strong anticlerical feelings; indeed, they flocked to the services of Grundtvigian priests, endearing themselves to the pietistic clergy in the area. Beginning in the 1850s, priests in Dragstrup, Erslev, Tødsø, and Øster Jølby found their churches bursting every week with "the awakened" from neighboring parishes. One Sunday in the mid-1860s, for example, a visitor to the village of Erslev observed a woman trying vainly to squeeze through the crowd at the doorway of the church. She eventually gave up and left, shouting behind her, "This is a disgrace, that I can't get into our own church, when after all I only come once or twice a year!" (Fisker 1971: 16).

These services, however, left most members of the movement dissatisfied. The Folkekirke organized its congregations along parish lines, and a faith-based group spread out over several parishes met inevitable problems. In the beginning, church law forbade laymen to receive sacraments in parishes other than their own; while the awakened could listen to Grundtvigian sermons, therefore, they could not take communion. The church relaxed this rule in 1855, allowing members to change their parish affiliations, but even so the awakened were outsiders in the church services. Local residents resented the presence of strangers in what had long been a strictly local ritual. Moreover, many disliked the meeting movement's ideology and actively tried to make the newcomers uncomfortable. In Frøslev, local women actually hid needles in their kerchiefs and stuck the "foreigners" with them during the service. And even if the congregation had been sympathetic, a new parish offered little long-term security. The priest might leave at any time, and his replacement might well be a rationalist. As time went by, the movement's members longed increasingly for a congregation of their own, a church analogous to a parish church that would enable them to worship as a Grundtvigian community. They embodied this longing in the idea of a shared holy communion, which became the primary concern of the awakening's leaders by the end of the 1860s.

Two events in 1868, one national and one local, spurred them to act on the problem. At the national level, the church bowed to Grundtvigian pressure and legalized "choice congregations" *(valgmenigheder)*, churches built and organized by members of particular movements within the church. Two such congregations sprang up immediately in Ryslinge and Kerteminde. Both centered around charismatic Grundtvigian priests, and both drew members from across a number of parishes. Back on Mors, meanwhile, the retirement of the Grundtvigian priest in Erslev prompted a frustrating administrative disappointment for the awakening. Erslev lay in the heart of the movement's territory, and adherents from across northern Mors had shifted their parish affiliations there. An overwhelming majority of the congregation favored a Grundtvigian from Tødsø as the new priest. Despite their pleas, however, the church hierarchy appointed a rationalist from off the island for the replacement. It seemed clear to the movement's leaders that they would never have a spiritual center unless they could choose their own priest. And for the first time in church history, the choice congregations gave them the means to do so.

In 1869, therefore, members of the movement voted to form a choice congregation on the island. The awakening had no formal organization at the time, and it is unclear how the decision was made. It involved a series of meetings, sometimes angry ones, in which the most active members of the movement gave their opinions. One participant, when asked much later who was there, replied "Everyone that counted for anything" (Fisker 1971: 19). It also involved considerable indecision and hesitation. At the final meeting, the leading men sat around a table and discussed the problem so interminably that one of their wives finally pounded on the table and demanded a decision.[1] Most importantly, the decision seems to have created a serious split in the awakening. Forty families favored the new congregation, while ten opposed it.[2] The leader of the opposition, a free school teacher in Galtrup, left the island shortly

1. Anecdotes like this one come up frequently on Mors, in which a sensible and outspoken woman reproves weak-willed men for vacillating on a decision. While the leaders of the congregation were mainly men, women seem to have had an important voice in most decisions, and they do not appear to have been shy about stating their opinions. It is worth noting on this subject that during my entire time on Mors, I never heard a man describe a woman as silly or flighty; nor did I ever hear it said that women were insufficiently intelligent for any tasks or decisions. Descriptions of gender differences tended to focus on physical strength, nurturing abilities, sexuality, temper, and interests.
2. This figure is cited from J.P. Wammen in Fisker (1971). The movement at the time probably involved more than fifty families, though, so the reliability of this figure is uncertain.

afterward, and bitterness between the two sides remained for decades. Some of those who opposed the new congregation later joined the Inner Mission movement.

About a quarter of the supporters came from villages in Thy, on the other side of the Vildsund. Of the members from Mors, all but a handful lived in the parishes of Erslev, Øster Jølby, Galtrup, Tødsø, and Skallerup. Most of the men were farm owners, smallholders, farmhands, small- scale artisans, or schoolteachers; none had major capital resources beyond their lands.[3] Their leader was Anders Christian Povlsen Dal, an associate of Christen Kold, who had built a Grundtvigian high school in Galtrup in 1864. The 40-year-old Povlsen Dal had combined fervent Grundtvigian activism with financial and organizational acumen, and the school had soon become the center of the awakening on the island. After the movement's final vote in May, he became the dominant figure in the establishment of the choice congregation.

Povlsen Dal and several of the movement's larger farmers quickly bought a plot of land for the new church, using his school and their farms as security for the loan. The site lay at a crossroads in the northeastern corner of Øster Jølby, easily accessible for most of the movement's members. Many members contributed money or building materials toward the project; in some cases, even smallholders took out loans on their properties. The congregation wanted a big church, large enough to hold the many converts they expected as well as the throngs of curious visitors who would surely assemble. They therefore economized as much as possible on labor and design, using virtually all the money for building materials. They did almost all the work themselves, under the direction of a Grundtvigian mason from Thy. Men worked in shifts after their farmwork was done, and women set up kitchens and

3. See statistics in Fisker (1971: 38). A number of authors (e.g., Lindhardt 1959) have suggested that Grundtvigianism was a movement of well-off farm owners, as opposed to the poorer rural classes; Fisker convincingly refutes this idea for Mors, pointing out that farm owners and teachers constituted only 24.9 percent of the original choice congregation, whereas smallholders and small-scale artisans made up 50.6 percent. Moreover, as he and others point out, "farm owner" was a term used fairly loosely in 19th century West Jutland. Whereas in Sjælland it clearly denoted a man of means, in Jutland it might well mean a smallholder with big ambitions. Erik Lau Jørgensen (pers. comm.) notes further that Grundtvigianism and wealth were not independent variables, since the Grundtvigian farmer's organizations tended to promote their members' living standards. The increasing percentage of Farm owners in the Free Congregation derives in great part from smallholders who increased their holdings.

cooked meals on the premises. In doing so, they cemented the community to an unprecedented degree. What had been a scattered network of common faith became a tangible project, visible in the brick walls that rose steadily out of the empty field in Øster Jølby. "Never," wrote Grundtvigian historian Holger Begtrup later, "has any church been built in a more folkly way" (Begtrup 1934). Grundtvigian hymns resounded constantly through the site, and even passersby who had no love for the awakening were impressed with the scene. In a sense, just as the community created the church, the church created the community.

Few outsiders believed that the church could be completed, since the materials and labor needed far exceeded the resources of the awakening's members. Povlsen Dal later wrote that he never would have begun the project if he had known what it would finally cost. But by dint of heavy mortgages and dangerously parsimonious building methods, the congregation completed the church's exterior by the spring of 1871. Their success astonished observers on the island, and confirmed the congregation's belief that God's will supported their actions.[4] Perhaps as a result, the construction of the building became an important symbol of the movement on Mors, and a corpus of folktales and legends sprang up around it. Years later, people in Øster Jølby would tell stories of ghostly lights that they had seen in the field where the church would later be built. One man reported seeing a castle tower rising from the mist there, another said he had heard voices singing hymns; one man riding to get the midwife in the middle of the night could not convince his horses to ride through the field (Schmidt 1957). Under the name Ansgarskirken, The Church of Ansgar, the new building became both the physical and symbolic center of the new community.

Finding a priest posed a problem at first, since none of the local Grundtvigian clergy wished to leave their tenured posts for the experimental congregation. The leaders finally settled on Rasmus Lund, the 43-year-old priest of a village near Ålborg. Taciturn and plain spoken, Lund fit well into the social world of Mors; while only a mediocre preacher, he was inspiring in rituals and discussions, and his fervent Grundtvigianism suited the congregation well. His wife Laura, the sister

4. God may also have supported the walls, which were built to only a third of the thickness necessary for a building of that height. Jens Laursen, the mason in charge of construction, learned of his mistake from a book only after the walls had been built. When he found out, he said later, "I threw the book far away. But that didn't actually improve the walls" (Fisker 1971: 26). When the building was restored some decades later, workers found it hard to understand why the building had not collapsed.

of socialist revolutionary Louis Pio, also took an active role in the community. The Folkekirke approved Lund as priest in November of 1871, and the following month a special service formally established the Mors Island Choice Congregation. The event attracted national interest. The Mors church was only Denmark's third choice congregation, and the first to be built without a noted priest as leader. Grundtvigian newspapers heralded it as a triumph of the folk spirit, while anti-Grundtvigians decried it as the beginning of clerical anarchy. The aging Peter Larsen Skræppenborg was jubilant; he shouted and danced in his carriage when he first saw the Ansgarskirke, and he donated a costly painting for the altar.[5] The attention brought droves of the curious into Sunday services, and many of them joined the congregation. The congregation grew rapidly, tripling in size by 1880, and soon became the recognized leader of the awakening in northern Jutland.

As their religious community grew, the congregation's members became increasingly interested in the cultural and political issues associated with the New Grundtvigianism (see pp. 98-99). Povlsen Dal, having established the church as the center for religious affairs, turned his high school meetings into political events. Guest speakers from around the country called for democratization of the parliament, mobilization of rural voting power, and freedom of expression. The audiences for their events routinely numbered in the hundreds. Most orators belonged to the Left Party, which the congregation overwhelmingly supported. On the cultural front, local groups studied history, folk culture, and agricultural technique, seeking to raise the self-awareness and living standards of the rural population. Members of the congregation founded a newspaper, the *Morsø Folkeblad*, to champion their political and cultural

5. The painting, by Christen Dalsgaard, depicts Ansgar conducting the first baptism in Denmark. It is a striking work, by one of Denmark's finest artists, and it contrasts sharply with the unremarkable altar paintings in most village churches. Skræppenborg may have written the motto beneath the painting, which reads: "Over daabens pagt med troens ord/ Helligaanden spredte lys i nord" ("Over baptism's pact with the word of faith/ The Holy Spirit spread light in the North"). Skræppenborg was initially skeptical of the choice congregation, evidently doubting its feasibility. On a journey to Thy in 1870, however, he passed through Øster Jølby, and upon seeing the nearly completed church tower rising above the fields, he stood up in his wagon, waved his hat, and shouted a booming hurrah. Subsequent meetings with the church council and with Lund convinced him that he had underestimated the Morsingboer. His complete change of heart about the congregation mirrored that of many of Denmark's Grundtvigians.

concerns.[6] Free schools and gymnastics societies sprang up around the island, promoting "a sound mind in a sound body." In 1874, members of the awakening unified these concerns in the Mors Danish Society *(Morslands Danske Samfund),* a political and cultural analog to the choice congregation. The Society built a large, eight-sided meeting house in Galtrup two years later; the house, which is still in active use, soon became a favorite stop on the Grundtvigian lecture circuit.

In addition to these ideological activities, the Grundtvigians developed a distinct sense of community, visibly separate from their neighbors in the countryside. They called themselves "the free," echoing Grundtvigianism's call for religious and cultural freedom. They patronized merchants from within the congregation; "free doctors," "free midwives," "free butchers," "free millers," and a "free bank" became institutions on the island. Attendance at the free schools became a standard part of childhood in the congregation, while children and adults alike flocked to gymnastics classes. When possible, women and girls dressed in the Grundtvigian costume of white dress and red sash, their hair pinned back with a silver arrow. Grundtvig's Songs of Celebration *(Festsalmer)* replaced traditional hymnals in private homes. Even naming practices reflected the new community; although first children were still named after relatives, younger children often received named like Christen Kold Smed, Rasmus Lund Overgaard, and Peter Larsen Skræppenborg Jepsen (see Balle-Petersen 1977).[7]

This boisterous growth posed a serious challenge to religious authority on the island. For centuries, religious authority had operated on a strictly local basis; each priest ruled within his own parish, and only the provst exercised a regional control. Now, however, individuals from all over northern Mors began to affiliate with the choice congregation, and many more sympathized with it.[8] Non-Grundtvigian priests resented

6. Most newspapers in Denmark today were originally established as organs for particular political groups, and their editorial policies generally reflect their orientation. The Morsø Folkeblad was for most of its history a typical *venstreblad,* or Left paper, with a strongly pro-Left and pro-farmer slant. Since the decline of its competitors, the socialist Morsø Social-Demokrat and the conservative Morsø Avis, the paper has attempted to be more evenhanded in its coverage. My own impression was that its coverage was quite fair, and I heard no complaints about it from non-Left Morsingboer.

7. Peter Larsen Skræppenborg Jepsen, born in Bjergby in 1874, emigrated to America around the turn of the century. His descendents never knew the origin of his name until 1990, when his great-grandson spent a year doing anthropological fieldwork on Mors.

8. Actual changing of church affiliation was a serious matter, involving a slight to the local priest and a break with the local community that many Grundtvigians were

this incursion into their territory, and even the provst fe lt challenged by Rasmus Lund's growing influence. As Lund became a recognized leader in the national awakening, Grundtvigian priests on the island looked to him more than the provst for theological leadership. In the early 1870s, the provst's own Grundtvigian sympathies forestalled any conflict; in the long run, however, a confrontation became inevitable.

It finally came in 1878, when Carl Sophus Cederfeld de Simonsen arrived as the new provst on Mors. Courtly and aristocratic, enchanted by rules and ceremony, Cederfeld de Simonsen embodied the empty formality that had originally sparked the Mors awakening. He saw the choice congregation as a challenge from the outset, and he publicly stated his intention to rein it in. Soon after he arrived on the island, therefore, he began a series of maneuvers to establish his authority over the congregation. He contacted Lund about several trivial matters in which the congregation had violated church rules; the Ansgarskirke had not had an official inspection, for example, and Lund had improperly held confirmation and first communion on the same day. By ordering a stop to these irregularities, Cederfeld intended to remind the congregation of its subordinate status. His interference annoyed Lund, who refused to comply with any of the directives, and an administrative battle ensued. For the next five years, the two men engaged in a flurry of charges, rebuttals, and appeals to the bishop. The congregation supported Lund vigorously, and he won most of the cases; when he lost, they helped him pay his fines. By opposing the provst, however, and sometimes deliberately provoking him, Lund flirted dangerously with dismissal.

In 1882, he went too far. As a Grundtvigian, Lund had little regard for confirmation; he considered it an empty formality, instituted by church administrators for reasons that had little to do with Christian faith. He especially objected to the denial of communion to unconfirmed children. As a central sacrament in Christian worship, he argued,

unwilling to make. Since a family ordinarily changed affiliation as a unit, moreover, a married person required his or her spouse's agreement to make the change. The membership of the new congregation was likely only a fraction of the number of sympathetic Morsingboer. An example is Karen Kortbek Sejersdatter, wife of a miller in Jørsby in the 1870s. She kept regular contact with members of the choice congregation, and hosted its traveling missionary Ole Overgaard once a year. Her husband, however, Simon Andreas Jepsen, disliked the congregation's members, going so far as to stay out of the house for the day when Overgaard visited. His opposition made a change of affiliation impossible for Karen. She remained in touch with the Grundtvigians, though, and named her fifth son Peter Larsen Skræppenborg Jepsen.

communion should be available to all who sincerely desired it, whether or not they had reached the arbitrary confirmation age of 14 years. In September of 1881, a 9-year-old girl in the congregation became mortally ill, and she asked Lund to give her communion. He granted her request, and she died soon afterward. The bishop approved Lund's action as an act of mercy. But when Lund requested permission to do the same for a healthy 11-year-old a few months later, the bishop turned him down, warning him that granting the request would clearly violate church law. When Lund went ahead anyway, the church ministry imposed a heavy fine and nearly defrocked him for insubordination.

By this time, the congregation had grown bitter over the provst's continual meddling in their affairs, and they pressed Lund strongly not to yield. In November of 1882, therefore, he informed the bishop that he intended to serve communion to a 13-year-old girl, even if it meant the loss of his priesthood. The bishop was still angry over the last instance, and Lund's outspoken criticism of the church had made him unpopular with the church ministry.[9] On January 17 of 1883, therefore, after a lengthy hearing, the bishopric of Aalborg officially stripped Rasmus Lund of his title as priest, forbidding him to hold services or sacraments in any state church, and ordering the Mors Choice Congregation to dismiss him as its priest. The bishop sent official notice of the decision to the congregation, and the stage for the meeting in February was set.

On February 17, 1883, the church council officially established the Mors Island Free Congregation. Their action created a separate entity

9. Among other things, Lund had been one of the organizers of a Grundtvigian meeting in Askov a few years earlier. The meeting had drawn Grundtvigian leaders from around the country, many of whom had spoken strongly against the restrictions of the current church authorities. Lund himself had given an energetic address decrying the importance that the church laid on confirmation. The church ministry assessed him a stiff fine for his participation; Grundtvigians all over Denmark sent donations to help him pay it, and the Danish Supreme Court later reversed the judgment. Danish church historians consider the Askov meetings one of the most important events in the history of the Grundtvigian movement, and the Grundtvigian newspapers of the day reported it as a milestone in the battle for religious freedom. Lund had not intended it to have any such significance; he and the priest from Frøslev had simply wanted to gather some friends to discuss issues of church freedom. Lund's prominence in the national movement came almost in spite of his own intentions. Likewise, while he clearly disagreed with Cederfeld de Simonsen on many issues, Lund does not appear to have desired the bitter quarrel that led to his own dismissal. A peculiar chain of circumstances, rather than personal drive, appears to explain why this quiet and unprepossessing country priest should have become one of the most embattled and celebrated churchmen of his day.

from the Folkekirke, a religious association without support, recognition, or supervision from the state. The congregation's organization remained substantially the same, as did much of its membership. The act of leaving the Folkekirke was a grave one, however, and some of the group's most active supporters could not bring themselves to do it. The membership from Thy, for example, who had always spoken vociferously for religious freedom, balked at joining the new church. So did Anders Kristian Povlsen Dal, who had led the choice congregation since 1871.[10] The congregation saw their refusals as a betrayal, and bitter feelings remained long afterward. Parents pulled their children from Povlsen Dal's school; the loss of revenue left him destitute, and he eventually emigrated to America to earn the money to pay his creditors.[11] As with the decision to form a choice congregation in 1879, the break with the Folkekirke created a significant split in the Grundtvigian awakening on Mors.

The members of the new Free Congregation had no desire to form a new religion; they regarded the break as a necessary administrative decision, not a theological rift. Indeed, they still saw themselves as members of the Folkekirke, whether the bishop acknowledged it or not. Over the next twenty years, therefore, with the exception of confirmation rules, the congregation adhered meticulously to the rules of the national church. Their new status made it difficult; Lund could no longer perform legal marriages, for example, and the Ansgarskirke's cemetery reverted to the jurisdiction of the parish priest in Galtrup. Yet with the cooperation of sympathetic local priests, the Free Congregation managed to approximate most Folkekirke sacraments. Lund remained friendly with local Grundtvigian clergy, who frequently petitioned the bishop on his behalf.[12] Members were sensitive to any suggestion that

10. Povlsen Dal's refusal to join stunned his many friends in the community, and it has puzzled local historians as well. The consensus among the Congregation's chroniclers is that Povlsen Dal had fallen under the influence of a controversial and charismatic pietist priest from Himmerland.

11. Povlsen Dal did well in America, earning enough to pay his creditors and return to the country. He eventually bought a medium-sized farm in the village of Jørsby in northeastern Mors. The break with the church was a terrible emotional blow, however, which he mourned throughout his life. By the time of his death, the congregation's hard feelings had eased, and at his request he was buried in the Ansgarskirke cemetery. His stone stands there today, and his picture adorns the wall of the meeting room in the priest's residence. His great-grandson, Peder Dal, is now the chairman of the congregation's church council; his descendents expanded the farm, and the Dals are now the largest landowning family in Jørsby.

12. Some suffered as a result. Vilhelm Hansen, the assistant priest in Nykøbing, maintained strong ties with Lund and the Free Congregation during his twelve years in

they were acting heretically, and they policed themselves against radical statements about religion and church law. Paradoxically, the achievement of religious autonomy brought the congregation into harmony with the church authorities for the first time in its history.

On a secular level, the congregation continued to be an active and tightly knit community. The cultural and political activity continued unabated in the eight-sided meeting house, with one member winning a seat in Parliament. Congregation members participated avidly in farming improvement and education programs, resulting in a general rise in the community's living standards. After an initial drop, membership began a steady rise, and by 1895 the congregation numbered over three hundred. The governing board, anxious to maintain respectability, carefully investigated applicants for moral uprightness. Members kept watch on one another as well, maintaining a mutual moral supervision that bordered on the oppressive. A Grundtvigian teacher named Ole Jakobsen founded a free school to replace Povlsen Dal's, and he soon became a leading figure in the community. On the whole, in the years between 1883 and 1900, the Grundtvigian movement on Mors established itself as a permanent, lively, and growing community, combining a religious mission with a rich and active cultural life.

A crisis came when Rasmus Lund died in 1889. The community had never been particularly focused around Lund, but his presence had assured its continuity. He had given up his official priesthood for the congregation, after all, and to desert him would have been a personal betrayal. After his death, many members suggested that the congregation return to the Folkekirke. The state church had become much more liberal in the past seven years, they argued, largely because of Grundtvigian activism; had the events of 1882 occurred in 1890, Lund might never have been defrocked. Moreover, the congregation was abiding by Folkekirke rules anyway. A return to the status of choice congregation would make it easier to find priests, and it would eliminate such annoyances as civil marriages. Lund's successor, Christian Nissen, favored a return, and sporadic negotiations with the bishop took place for the next fifteen years. Nothing ever came of them, though. The hard-line Grundtvigians in the congregation, led by Ole Jakobsen, refused to cede

the post. When the senior priest retired, Hansen should have replaced him; 650 citizens of Nykøbing petitioned the bishop on his behalf. Instead, Hansen was sent off the island entirely, not to return until he was finally appointed provst there twelve years later.

final authority over the church to the Folkekirke, and as time went by, it became increasingly clear that the congregation could survive on its own. After Thorvald Balslev replaced Nissen in 1905, the question of a return to the Folkekirke disappeared for good.

The Free Congregation in the 20th Century

When Morsingboer discuss the history of the Free Congregation, they talk mainly about the years from 1837 to 1883; about the 20th century, they usually say little or nothing. Compared with the tumultuous events that led to the congregation's independence, the later years seem rather mundane, the uneventful and unremarkable round of an ordinary church community. As Asger Højmark put it in his 1944 article, "Happy people have no history." And in some respects, he was right. While the Free Congregation has had its share of minor dramas during this century, its central ideas, organization, and geographical scope have remained largely the same. It still takes a traditional Grundtvigian approach to religious and cultural affairs, it still adheres to most rules and rituals of the national church, and its membership still lives primarily in northwestern Mors.

From 1905 to 1925, the imposing presence of Thorvald Balslev ensured a unified community. Forceful in conversation and inspiring in the pulpit, Balslev provided a firm leadership for the community, which Lund and Nissen had not. He dismissed all talk of a return to the Folkekirke, and steadfastly maintained a traditional Grundtvigian outlook in the congregation's religious and cultural life. He quickly attracted a devoted following among the congregation's members, some of whose admiration verged on worship; sixty-five years later, the mention of his name still puts stars in eyes of some older members. When he turned down an attractive position in Copenhagen in 1919, the congregation bought him a car in gratitude. When he finally did leave, the church was so packed for his final service that some bricks had to be knocked out of the wall to provide air. By that time, his leadership had so forcefully cemented the congregation's views and independence that their permanence seemed unquestionable.[13]

13. Balslev went on to be priest of Vartov Church in Copenhagen, where Grundtvig had been priest for many years. It was perhaps the most prestigious position a Grundtvigian cleric could have, and Balslev filled it with distinction.

His successor, Svend Kroigaard, had none of Balslev's charisma. A quiet man from nearby Tæbring, he put most of his energy into the social and counseling duties of the priesthood. While his sermons lacked Balslev's fire, his manner sorted well with the society of rural Mors, and Kroigaard headed the congregation peaceably for thirty-eight years. In some ways, his presence came as a relief. The congregational council, which Balslev had dominated, reasserted itself in running the church; as in the days of Lund and Nissen, the members rather than the priest set church policy. Kroigaard's diplomacy also mended many fences with the Folkekirke, which by the 1960s regarded the Free Congregation as an ally. The sanctions enacted against its members gradually fell away, ending with the resumption of weddings in the Ansgarskirke in 1970. The community that Balslev had cemented became normalized under Kroigaard.[14]

This period saw two new developments in the life of the congregation. One was an increasing commitment to provide social services for the members. The congregation had been making provisions for its poor for some time; as early as 1875, a fund had taken donations during services and distributed them among the neediest members. From 1904 to 1909, the congregation had employed a full-time nurse as well. In 1946, however, it took a much larger step, building a nursing home in Øster Jølby called The Ansgar Home *(Ansgarshjemmet)*. The Home, which was expanded in 1957, marked the congregation's first permanent, ongoing social service project. It employed nurses, caretakers, and various assistants, and it required a large capital investment. The congregation's ability to mount such a project demonstrated both the material success and the community solidarity of its members.

Another development concerned the Inner Mission religious movement, which had been building on the island since the late 1890s (see

14. This uneventful period in the congregation's history contrasts surprisingly with the wrenching effects that the time had for Denmark as a whole. When discussing the congregation's history with its older members, I initially expected to hear a lot about the Free Congregation's role during the war, and the effect of the German occupation on the life of the community. To my surprise, none of them brought the subject up; when I asked them, they shrugged and said that the war hadn't affected the church very much. This despite the fact that one of the most important leaders of the national resistance came from the congregation, and that the local resistance newspaper was published in Øster Jølby. The seeming irrelevance of the church may reflect the near unanimity of sentiment on the German occupation at the time. Free Congregation members joined the resistance in droves, and they bitterly resented the Germans; on the other hand, so did virtually everyone on the island. The war did little to distinguish the Congregation from the rest of Mors.

next chapter). The Mission had long had an antipathy to the Grundtvigians, both on a national and a local level. Many of the Mission's first converts on Mors were Grundtvigians who had been disenchanted with the Free Congregation. During the 20th century, the ill feeling between the two groups grew into a bitter opposition. Congregation members saw the Mission as misanthropic and judgmental, opposed to partaking of the world with which God had provided it, unwilling to respect the beliefs of those with whom it disagreed. Mission members saw the Congregation as a perversion of the pietistic message; its followers reveled in the delights of the sinful world and ignored the Word that they claimed to uphold. The Mission had its strongholds in southeastern and northeastern Mors, and members of the two groups avoided each other whenever possible. If they coexisted in the same village, they ignored each other in the streets and competed with each other in village politics.

The Free Congregation in Recent Years

During the late 1960s and early 1970s, the Free Congregation experienced its first loss of membership and community interest. Part of the decline appears to have resulted from the social changes that were sweeping Mors at the time. As in the rest of Denmark, modernization was transforming rural communities. The rise of industry in Nykøbing drew youths and smallholders away from the farms, just as mechanization was making them unnecessary there. Improvements in communication and education brought the world directly to villagers' homes, even as improvements in transportation made those homes easy to leave. And the imposition of a state welfare system obviated the social services that the kin networks of the villages had long provided. For a rurally based group like the Free Congregation, such a revolution in the rural community was inevitably disruptive. As the local community became less central, so did the local church; over the course of the ten years from 1965 to 1975, the religious and cultural activities of the Free Congregation became significantly less important to its members. Membership dipped as well, though not by more than 10 percent.

Much of the blame for this decline fell on the priest, Per Fisker, a noted theologian from Fjaltring who had replaced Kroigaard in 1965. Fisker faced a difficult task, despite his recognized gifts as a speaker and administrator; after nearly forty years under a well-liked local priest, the congregation looked on a newcomer from off the island with some suspicion. His confident and sometimes imperious manner added to their misapprehensions. Some voiced resentment at his air of intellectual and moral authority; in this church, they said, it had always been the congregation and not the priest who led the way.[15] As attendance at services fell during his tenure, a general dissatisfaction with the new priest rose.

Fisker's personal life did not help his case. As a condition of his appointment in 1965, the congregation had required his wife, Bodil, to give up her career as a schoolteacher. Although the council raised Fisker's salary to compensate for the lost income, Bodil never felt comfortable as a full-time priest's wife, and her unhappiness strained their marriage. In 1970, the Fiskers divorced – an unthinkable action for a Danish priest at the time.[16] In addition to creating a scandal, the divorce left the congregation without its primary organizer of social activities. Several years later, Fisker compounded the problem by engaging in a romance with a young woman from the congregation. The age difference scandalized the congregation, particularly since Fisker himself had confirmed the girl a few years earlier. In 1973, she even moved into the priest's residence with him. The council decided Fisker had gone too far, and finally fired him.

The dismissal came as a relief to most of the congregation, who had been uncomfortable with Fisker for some time. It left them without a priest, however, and finding a replacement could take several months. In the interim, the council asked Erik Lau Jørgensen, editor of the *Folkeblad*, to officiate at the Sunday services. Lau Jørgensen turned out to be a captivating speaker, whose sermons reflected an energetic and very old-fashioned Grundtvigian vision of Christianity. Moreover, the administrative talents with which he had rescued the *Folkeblad* from near bankruptcy proved equally applicable to salvaging the faltering Free Congregation. In 1974, therefore, by general agreement, the congregation's council offered Lau Jørgensen the position of priest, despite his lack of any of the normal credentials for the post.

They did not regret their choice. Lau Jørgensen and his wife quickly restored the vitality of the Free Congregation, and within a few years the pews were again filled for Sunday services. Much of the return to the

---

15. This sentiment was expressed by a number of members I spoke with, although only one suggested it as a primary motivation for Fisker's dismissal.
16. After the divorce, Bodil Fisker undertook theological studies, and is today the priest of a choice congregation on Sjælland. I spoke with her briefly when she returned to the island for the first time in 1990. Her recollections had a bittersweet quality; while she had obviously had a difficult time on Mors, she still held considerable affection for its inhabitants, whose attachment to their home had greatly impressed her.

church stemmed from the absence of Fisker, whose scandals had created an uncomfortable atmosphere for the rituals; a significant number were newcomers, however, some even from the Inner Mission, who were drawn to the congregation by Lau Jørgensen's preaching. A new priest could not erase the changes that had occurred in rural Mors, of course, and the Free Congregation in the 1980s lacked much of the intensity of community and culture that had characterized it before the 1960s. Many of the new members had a relatively casual attitude toward the church, far different from the avid converts of the 19th century. Yet they did join, they did contribute, they did take some part in the religious community, and by the end of the 1980s, the congregation was again an active and growing organization.

In 1988, Lau Jørgensen retired. He was succeeded by Erik Overgaard, previously headmaster of the prestigious Rodding High School in southern Jutland. In his first years as priest, Overgaard has continued Lau Jørgensen's traditional Grundtvigian theology, despite a marked difference in personal and speaking style. The church has continued to gain members, and its associated cultural and educational activities have held their ground. The Ansgar's Home has been expanded and modernized, the enrollment at the free schools is rising, and the eight-sided meeting house bustles with activity almost every day. The Free Congregation in 1991 is not the same community that it was in the days of Rasmus Lund and Cederfeld de Simonsen, just as Mors is not the same island. But Lund and Cederfeld would find much there that they recognized – including an avid Grundtvigian theology, an active study of folk culture, a commitment to Grundtvigian education, and a fierce attachment to the island and the history of Mors.

Free Congregation Theology

Basic Tenets

The Free Congregation follows the strain of Danish Lutheran Protestantism known as "old Grundtvigianism" (*gammelgrundtvigianism*). As mentioned above, this movement builds on the theology developed by N.S.F. Grundtvig during the early and middle 19th century. Grundtvig led the pietist revolt against rationalism in the early 19th century, and he later connected pietism with an appreciation of folk traditions and culture. Grundtvigianism stresses the importance of Christianity as an emo-

123

tional force within the community of believers; it argues that individuals must freely, consciously, and joyously accept Christ's gifts of eternal life and atonement for their sins. In order to make such a decision, it says, a person must first understand his or her own nature as a member of a particular tradition and community. Accordingly, Grundtvigianism encourages education about folk customs and beliefs, and it stresses the importance of the congregation as a community of believers. It also advocates freedom of thought, both because Christianity must be voluntary and because rules tend to stifle living faith. The Mors congregation has largely avoided the revisions of Grundtvigianism that have cropped up during the 20th century, and a sermon delivered by Rasmus Lund in 1875 could be used today with only a few revisions. [17]

Despite this apparent conservatism, the congregation's religious views are far from rigid. In the early 1980s, for example, the congregation shocked many of the nation's Grundtvigians by changing their baptismal ritual. The change concerned the Nicean Creed, a set of three questions that lay out the basic tenets of Christian belief. In the Folkekirke, as in the Catholic and many Protestant churches, the priest asks these questions at the baptism ceremony; the godparent must answer "yes" to each of them. Grundtvig laid great weight on this creed. Since its words predate the writing of the Gospels, he said, they provide a link with the earliest Christian congregations, and thus they connect us with the purest form of Christianity. Grundtvig celebrated the creed in sermon and song, and most Grundtvigians regard it as a foundation of the faith. Soon after Lau Jørgensen's appointment as priest in 1975, however, he discovered serious opposition to the creed among members of the Free Congregation. Many felt that such questioning violated Grundtvig's principles of free thought, since it required a specific answer to a question of belief. Moreover, some argued that willingness to belong to the community, not a preformed set of beliefs, was the proper prerequisite for baptism.

After researching the origins and meaning of the creed, therefore, the congregation made a subtle change in the wording of the baptismal ritual. Instead of presenting the creed as three questions for the initiate, the priest was to present it as a statement of the congregation's beliefs. The initiate was then to be asked if he or she wished to accept baptism into

17. Grundtvigianism is a large and complex theological and political movement. Readers interested in learning more about the theology should begin by consulting Lausten (1987) and Munck (1984).

the congregation. This change created a considerable controversy in Denmark at the time, since it specifically contradicted Grundtvig's writings on the subject. Lau Jørgensen defended the action, though, as consistent with the overall thrust of Grundtvig's views. As a free congregation, the Mors Grundtvigians were not bound even by Grundtvig's writings, but only by the spirit that those writings evoked.

Conceptions of This world and the Next

Members of the Free Congregation speak very little about any world other than the one in which they live; while most of them acknowledge an afterlife of some sort, few of them seem to think about it very concretely. Their iconography reflects this vagueness, concentrating instead on the historical figures and events that have shaped their community. The altar painting in the church depicts not Jesus but Ansgar, who stands in a wood baptizing the first Christian child in Denmark. In the meeting room at the parsonage, the gallery of pictures on the walls includes the founders of the Grundtvigian movement and the past priests of the church, but not a single portrait of Jesus or prospect of heaven. A favorite hymn expresses the prevailing attitude:

Jeg elsker den brogede verden	I love the varied world
Trods al dens nod og strid	Despite all its need and strife
For mig er jorden skøn endnu	To me, the world is as beautiful still
Som i skabelsens ungdomstid	As in the first days of creation
(H.V. Kolund, 1877)	

While the Free Congregation's members certainly have ideas about the next world, they devote most of their thought to this one.

Conceptions of the world vary among the members, as they do within any group of people, but Grundtvig's worldview forms a core on which virtually all can agree. This view sees the world as a collection of peoples, divided from one another by geography and cultural heritage. The peoples are inseparable from their homelands and heritage; while all are equally worthy in the eyes of God, their different traditions imply qualitative differences between them. Each is on a separate track of historical development, and each can only become Christian in its own context. The task of earthly life, therefore, is the creation within each people of a Christian congregation, a community that understands and believes in Christ in a way appropriate to itself. This congregation is a joy in the eyes of God, who wants His children to understand themselves, to appreciate their cultures, and to enjoy and celebrate the world that He has granted them.[18] Above all, He wants them to be part of their historically evolved community, outside of which the individual can neither thrive nor understand himself.

Insofar as people in the Free Congregation express it, the afterlife is a sort of continuation of the success or failure of this worldly task.[19] Heaven is an extension of the earthly congregation into the realm of the ideal, stripped of the impediments of disease, pain, hardship, and time that make it difficult to achieve in this world. The membership of heaven is the same as that of the Christian community on earth, with the exception that time no longer separates the living from the dead. Free Congregation members seldom discuss what goes on in heaven, and the subject seems relatively unimportant. The place will be happy, certainly, even lively; but the essence of heaven is to be together, as a community, in the presence of God, and all else is secondary.

Members of the congregation discuss hell even less than heaven, and many of them refuse outright to believe in its existence. The idea of God punishing sinners with fire and torment does not square with the loving creator that Grundtvigianism imagines. The most concrete description I received of hell was that of an existence out of the sight of God, and out

18. I follow here the convention of using capitalized, masculine pronouns to refer to the Christian deity. I do so only for the sake of clarity, not for the purpose of any sort of religious statement. Danish religious writings generally refer to God as masculine, and Morsingboer almost always use masculine pronouns when discussing God. They capitalize the word God *(Gud)*, but not the pronouns.

19. I have abstracted this picture of the afterlife, like most of the material in this section, from discussions with Free Congregation members. These discussions covered a broad range of issues, not limited to religious topics. This method of research allows an ethnographer to learn about a culture in a very broad way, providing a sense of the relation of subjects like the afterlife to the rest of the life in the society. At the same time, however, it is vulnerable to the biases and preconceptions of the ethnographer. I believe that the construction of the Free Congregation's theology presented here is accurate for most members of the group; I believe it is also consistent with the memoirs and other written sources available on the subject. Readers might do well, however, to compare my description with other accounts of religious belief on Mors and in Denmark as a whole. Useful sources in this connection would include Frode Jakobsen's memoirs of life on Mors (esp. 1976); Margareta Balle-Petersen's studies of Grundtvigian cultural milieux (1987, 1983); Jakob Rod's studies of Danish folk religion (1961, 1972); Per Salmonsen's sociological examination of Danish religion (1975); Anders Pontoppidan Thyssen's collection of studies on Danish religion (1967, 1970); and Herbert Hendin's revealing examination of suicide in Scandinavia (1964).

of touch with the heavenly community. Hell in the next world, as in this one, is to be alone and outside of the congregation.

In any case, the issue of hell is irrelevant for members of the Congregation. By virtue of their membership and baptism, they belong to the Christian community, and they can firmly expect to enter heaven. They make no predictions about nonmembers, whose traditions and ways may be right for them. But as surely as they belong to God's congregation in this world, the Free Congregation's members will not be left out of whatever community God has ordained for the next one.

Conceptions of God and Other Deities

God, like heaven, seldom enters the conversations of the Free Congregation. All members agree that God exists, and most have a more or less defined image of Him, but they shy away from discussing Him directly. This reticence has long distinguished them from the other religious movements on the island. In his memoirs, Congregation member Frode Jakobsen notes that the subject of God and Jesus separated the Grundtvigians and Inner Mission adherents even at the beginning of this century. On market days, when groups from around the island met in Nykøbing, he could readily tell the Mission members by their constant reference to Jesus; when a man asked a cousin of his whether he believed in Jesus, the cousin responded, "Well, I come from Northern Mors!" It is worth remembering that Jakobsen, as the son of the deeply devout free school teacher Ole Jakobsen, might if anything have been more prone than most of the congregation to discuss religion.

On the fringes of their conversations, however, a distinct picture of God does tend to appear. People disagree about His appearance; some picture him as a formless cloud, others as an old man with a white beard.[20] But they generally agree on His personality and actions. This God is a benevolent creator, who has given mankind a rich and bountiful world in which to grow and thrive. He values that world, and wants His people to enjoy it. Yet he does not intervene in it, except to inspire individuals to act morally. While God may provide the fire that animates a person to fight an injustice, for example, He will not blight the crops or the offspring of the injustice's perpetrator. Humans

---

20. Per Thomsen, a priest in Nykøbing, regularly asks his confirmation students to draw pictures of their idea of God. While his collection includes some very interesting exceptions, the old man with a white beard predominates.

are free to act on the earth as they will. It is only their own moral sense, and the joy of Christian belief, which cause them to love God and follow His dictates.

To an extent, the Congregation's God is a personification of its community – a source of moral guidance and inspiration, the creator of the culturally specific individual, an agency that can offer but not impose the love and happiness of belonging. As with the community, people know that God is there, even if they cannot describe His form. Like the community, He offers a world and asks only allegiance in return. Like the community, it is only through Him that human beings can fully and happily live.

The Christian trinity divides God into three parts, but Congregation members rarely discuss Him as such. They do acknowledge Jesus's sacrifice as a great gift, and they cite his teachings as guides to moral action. Likewise, they acknowledge the Holy Spirit's work in inspiring awakenings and moral courage. Yet divisions within the Trinity do not figure much in their conversation. Jesus and the Holy Spirit are less separate figures than aspects of a single being, a guiding essence which has been manifest in different forms at different times.

The other prominent figure in Christian worship, Satan, plays almost no role in the Congregation's worldview. The Apostolic Creed proclaims his existence, and members do not specifically deny it. Never in my time among them, however, did I hear a Congregation member attribute any evil event or action to the Devil. The evil that men do comes from within themselves, not from any external fiend.

Conceptions of the Individual and Society

The members of the Free Congregation see an extremely close connection between the individual and society. Their Grundtvigian individual is unique, with a constellation of abilities, desires, and weaknesses specific to himself. Yet he draws these features from a particular tradition, a particular culture with a particular history. In order to develop them fully, he needs the help of his community. The community has the customs, the folk knowledge, and the fellowship that the individual needs to realize his nature. Society, properly conceived, is a community that fosters the lifelong maturation and fulfillment of its members.

This relationship between the individual and society underlies the Grundtvigian notion of freedom *(frihed)*. Grundtvig's poetry and prose exalt freedom as "the best gold," the key to proper faith, expression, and education. His followers established free schools, free congregations, free banks, and free barbers; free institutions continue to form the backbone of the movement today. But this freedom is not the negative freedom of libertarians, the mere absence of any external controlling agency. It is the freedom to become a Grundtvigian individual, to fully develop the potential that one's history and culture have bequeathed. Free schools, for example, foster creativity, not anarchy. They use storytelling, art, and history to guide their students to an understanding of themselves and their culture. Likewise, the free adult is not a heroic loner, but an active participant in the life of his community. To be free is to know oneself; and since ones culture is an integral part of one's self, freedom is inseparable from the community. [21]

The relationship has important consequences for worship as well. A person who struggles against his nature becomes emotionally stunted and embittered. Such a person cannot truly feel God's love or understand His grace. In fostering individual development, therefore, society fosters the love and worship of God. The entire complex of Grundtvigian secular institutions – historical societies, community houses, gymnastics clubs, political parties – serves a vital function in the religious community. By promoting community solidarity and individual self-awareness, it enables members to become fully conscious and appreciative Christians.

Free Congregation Organization

The Free Congregation is a voluntary association that functions as a church. Although it has ties of tradition and belief with the Folkekirke, its members have full control over its structure and operation. Its organization therefore differs significantly from that of a local state church.

21. This Grundtvigian notion of freedom is very widely accepted in Denmark, and I suspect that it accounts for some of the differences between the Danish and American welfare states. The American credo that the individual should not depend on society makes no sense in Denmark; the individual there depends on society by definition, and is inseparable from it. The disdain with which Americans regard dependents on the state falls in Denmark on those who fail to contribute their fair share to the society. The reprehensible thing is not to receive support from the society, but to withhold support for it. Tax rates that Americans would consider grounds for revolt are consequently accepted as just by the Danes; while they might (and usually do) think that the government is taking too much in taxes, they do not dispute the government's claim to a portion of their income.

Authority Structure

Ultimate authority in the Free Congregation resides with the adult members, who each have one vote in the Congregation Meeting, which takes place every May. At this meeting, they may change the church's constitution, approve or reject proposed uses of church funds, and elect or remove church officials. Some of them take this responsibility very seriously, and the annual meetings involve lively and occasionally heated debates. Overall, however, only about a tenth of the members actually exercise this authority. At the 1991 meeting, around ninety of the thousand or so adult members attended the meeting.[22]

During the rest of the year, a congregational council *(menighedsråd)* oversees the operation of the church and its attendant institutions. The council consists of nine elected officers and the priest; a foreman, elected by the council members, officially heads the body. The council drafts the church budget and policies, organizes and oversees committees, and arranges the hiring of priests. Members may be male or female, young or old, and from any social background. In practice they tend to be middle aged, predominantly male, and either farmers or artisans from northwestern Mors. Most run for election after participating actively in church affairs for several years; two or three candidates usually run for vacant seats, while incumbents are routinely reelected if they wish to be.

The priest runs the operation of the church itself; while the council may overrule him, he ordinarily organizes church services, festivals, and confirmation instruction at his own discretion. He keeps records of the church sacraments, and reports such information as births, deaths, and marriages to the state. In addition, as the church's most important full-time officer, he works closely with the council and committees on virtually all church projects. The congregation may select anyone it wishes as priest, though the requirements of the position ordinarily restrict it to Folkekirke priests. The only two exceptions have been Erik Overgaard and Erik Lau Jørgensen, the last two occupants of the post; both possessed unusual qualifications, however, and both were subsequently recognized as priests by the Folkekirke. The priest receives an unusually high salary for a country priest, but he has no tenure. As Per Fisker's experience illustrates, the council may fire him at any time.

22. This low figure does not imply that only a tenth of the members care about the church; many members find it difficult to attend a five-hour meeting on a weeknight, while others find it difficult to give up the pleasant weather that arrives in May after a Danish winter.

Below the council and priest stand a number of committees, which oversee the operation of church projects. One committee oversees the Ansgarshjem retirement home, for example, while another organizes improvements to the church grounds. Committees consist of one or more council members and several interested members of the congregation. They usually have broad day-to-day authority, though the council must approve any large or costly projects.

Financing

The money for the Free Congregation comes almost entirely from its members, in the form of dues and bequests. Since members do not belong to the Folkekirke, they do not pay the normal church tax *(kirkeskat)* to the Danish state; instead, they pay annual dues to the Free Congregation. Many also leave substantial bequests to the church in their wills. Together with such minor activities as selling Christmas wreaths, these sources provide amply for the church and its subsidiary activities.

All members over the age of 18 must pay dues to the congregation. The amount of the dues is fixed by a committee, which assesses them according to each member's income. The average contribution is about 900 kroner (US$ 150) per year, slightly higher than the state church tax for a working adult. A member may appeal the assessment if he considers it unfair, but such appeals rarely succeed. Unlike taxes, dues do not automatically go down if a member retires or becomes unemployed; for retirees, dues are often significantly higher than taxes would be. Members do not consider the amount burdensome, however, and dues occasion little or no resentment.

In 1990, about 1,400 members contributed just under 1.1 million kroner (about US$ 180,000) in dues to the Free Congregation. An additional 230,000 kroner came in from bequests and other sources.[23] Over half of this income went to the salaries of church employees, and most of the rest paid for church maintenance and ritual expenses. The council also set aside 185,000 kroner toward future building expenses and a fund for a new organ. Even with these savings programs, the Congregation's budget reported a small surplus for the year. Financially, the Free Congregation appears to be quite secure. [24]

23. Other sources include interest, burial fees, sales of wreaths, and rent on a church-owned house.
24. These figures come from the congregation's 1990 annual financial report, which the treasurer distributed to all members at the annual meeting in May 1991.

Associated Organizations

As mentioned above, the founding of the Ansgarskirke in 1870 sparked a wave of Grundtvigian secular institutions on Mors. Free schools, free banks, free artisans, and free merchants sprang up all around northern Mors, owned by and catering to the members of the awakening. Many of these enterprises disappeared as the Congregation became established on the island; free butchers and bakers, for example, reverted to serving the general public. Some of the larger institutions gradually loosened their affiliation with the movement for business reasons. The *Morsø Folkeblad*, originally the movement's newspaper, adopted a more impartial and independent orientation after the other newspapers on the island folded in the 1950s. During the 1980s, the People's Bank of Mors merged with another island bank to survive the encroachment of the national banking companies. Such institutions, while still sentimentally attached to the Grundtvigian movement, no longer have formal ties or exclusive business arrangements with it.

The Congregation still has very close ties with several secular organizations, however. Just south of the church lies the Ansgarshjem nursing home, which the church owns and operates as a community service (see p. ??). The home consists of a complex of very modern buildings, built in the 1970s, which house twenty-six elderly and infirm residents. It employs several full-time nurses and a number of assistants. Most of the residents belong to the Free Congregation, as do many of the employees; residents pay fees according to their income. A committee of the Congregational Council oversees operations.

The church does not own the nearby free schools, but it does maintain very close ties with them. The free schools in Bjergby and Galtrup together teach hundreds of students, most of whose parents belong to or sympathize with the Free Congregation. The schools use the techniques of storytelling and liberal instruction pioneered in the 1840s by Christen Kold; parents I spoke to particularly appreciated the schools' stress on art and creative expression. The schools receive some support from the state, since they relieve the workload of the public schools, but they also require tuition from the parents. Tuition ranges around 500 kroner per month, with financial aid available for very poor families. Galtrup also has an Efterskole, a Grundtvigian boarding school for students who want a year or two of extra instruction after the nine years of standard schooling. With 126 students and nineteen teachers, the school constitutes one of the most prominent institutions in northwestern Mors.

The connection between the Congregation and the schools shows itself most vividly in the Eight-Sided Meeting House, the historic brick octagon that stands next to the Galtrup Efterskole (see pp. 59). In 1979, the congregation donated the meeting house to the Efterskole, on the condition that the church would retain the right to use it. The school rents out the building for meetings, gymnastics competitions, receptions, and concerts; the church uses it for the annual meeting. The joint operation of one of northern Jutland's best-known symbols of Grundtvigian culture dramatized the close relationship between the educational and religious projects of the awakening.

The Danish Society of Mors, originally founded to promote the worldly activities of the Grundtvigian movement, also remains close to the Free Congregation. Its members organize night courses in history and folk culture, as well as folk dances and other cultural events in the meeting house. Its leaders belong to the congregation, and most of its activities reflect the Grundtvigian orientation of the community. About three hundred people belong to the society, and many more attend its activities.

Membership

The demographic structure of Mors has changed radically over the past century. Villages and farms have shrunk and sometimes disappeared, while Nykøbing and its factories have steadily expanded. The Free Congregation, in contrast, has changed its membership remarkably little. A hundred years after its inception, the congregation has neither grown nor declined dramatically. Its members live in about the same areas, and pursue roughly the same occupations, that they did at the turn of the century. The transformation of the island has affected the congregation, of course, bringing several significant demographic changes. But overall, the persistence of the church's membership structure is striking.[25]

Geographically, the congregation remains centered in the northwestern quarter of the island. The villages of Øster Jølby, Bjergby, Erslev, Toving, Galtrup and Solbjerg account for over half of the members on Mors (see Map 135); Øster Jølby alone has 223 members, almost 20 percent of the island's total. The villages bordering these contain most of the rest of the members. The southern half of the island contains less than a tenth of the congregation, the northeastern peninsula less than a fiftieth. Many of the scattered members in these areas have either moved

---

25. See Appendix for an explanation of the sources of the statistics cited here.

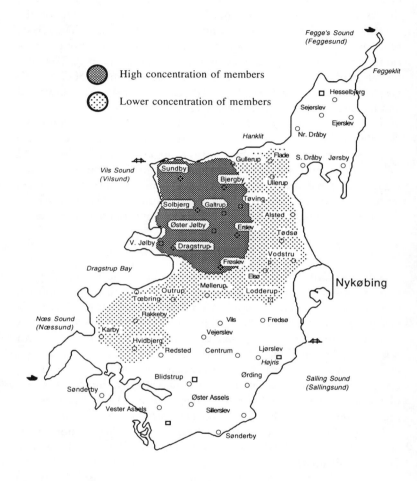

Map 4: Mors Island Free Congregation
Distribution of Members, ca. 1885

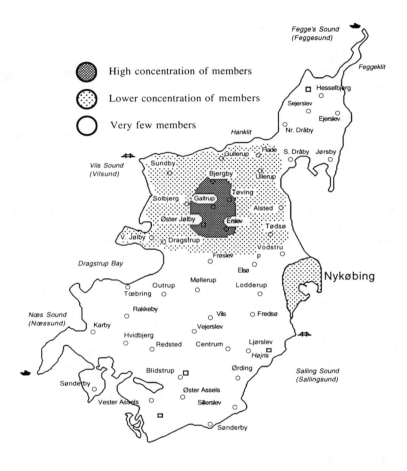

Map 5: Mors Island Free Congregation
Distribution of Members, 1990

there from the northwest, or else have strong family ties to the congregation. The members in Jorsby, for example, all trace their descent from the exiled founder of the congregation, Anders Kristian Povlsen Dal (see p. ??). Likewise, two of the three members in Ljorslev come from a large Free Congregation family. While the group's membership extends across the entire island, its center remains firmly fixed in the northwest.

Almost two hundred members, incidentally, live outside of Mors altogether. Many live in Thy, where the roads provide easy access to Øster Jølby, but others are spread across Jutland and even as far as Copenhagen. Most of these members come from families that have had to leave Mors for employment. While their participation in community life is limited, these families often set great store by their membership, and they usually return to the Ansgarskirke for important life-cycle rituals.

Occupationally, the congregation has maintained a surprisingly strong agricultural component. The mechanization of farms and the decline of crop prices have decimated the agricultural labor force of Mors; whereas nine in ten Morsingboer worked on farms in 1900, only one in ten do so today. In the Free Congregation, however, about 35 percent of the working population are farmers, and 42 percent of the households contain at least one full-time farmer. This figure represents a considerable decline, certainly. At its establishment in 1871, nearly three quarters of the congregation were farm workers. As late as 1950, the figure ranged around 60 percent for the countryside. But even at 40 percent, the Free Congregation's farming members constitute its largest occupational group, and by far its most influential. Farmers have usually presided over the congregational council, while their enthusiastic participation has given them a commanding voice in church policies.[26]

The remaining membership falls into several occupational categories. The three main groups are professionals (15 percent), artisans (15 percent), and laborers (14 percent). Clerical workers make up another 7 percent, and medical workers 6 percent. These members are distributed rather erratically around the island. While professionals have predictably strong (22 percent) representation in Nykøbing, for instance, their distribution in the countryside ranges from 20 percent in Sundby to none

26. These figures represents the proportion of farm workers among those for whom an occupation is listed in the Mors Island Kommune address book. It does not include housewives, who do not ordinarily list an occupation. Most housewives on farms, however, contribute greatly to the farm's maintenance, through cleaning, vegetable gardening, and the feeding of livestock. If one were to include them as farm workers, the percentage of the congregation in agriculture would rise to about 46 percent.

at all in Sindbjerg. Retirees also make up a considerable proportion of the congregation, possibly as much as 35 percent. Employment categories are difficult to ascertain for retirees, but the majority appear to have worked in agriculture. A sexual division runs through most of these figures. At least 129 of the congregation's women are full-time housewives *(hjemmegående husmødre)*, for example, a strictly feminine occupation. The other working women are concentrated in clerical work (26 percent), the professions (23 percent), and nursing (20 percent). Men are almost absent from clerical work and nursing; they fall mainly into the classes of farm workers (47 percent), artisans (18 percent), laborers (16 percent), and professionals (11 percent).

Like the geographical and occupational distributions, the total membership of the congregation has stayed largely stable over the past century. While membership rose rapidly in the first few decades, it reached a plateau in the early 20th century of about 1,500 members. Since then, the rolls have never risen much above 1,700 members or much below 1200. In 1990, the congregation listed 1,394 members, and all accounts suggest that the number has increased slightly since then.

Considering the changes that have hit Mors in the 20th century, this relative stability of numbers, occupations, and residences in the Free Congregation is remarkable. It is not, however, complete. The changing rural society has changed the church as well, and the effects are significant. Three changes have had especially noticeable effects on the life of the congregation.

One is the rising affluence of its members. While historians have often painted Grundtvigianism as a movement of the rural upper class, its origins on Mors were fairly humble (Balle-Petersen 1977: 111). Smallholders made up the largest occupational group, followed by farmhands and serving girls; farm owners, so dominant in many choice congregations, made up only 19 percent of the one on Mors. The financial struggle of building the Ansgarskirke reflected the complete lack of major landowners to back the enterprise. The congregation's farmers and smallholders gradually increased their assets, however, thanks at least in part to the aggressive education efforts of the movement's secular wing. By the middle of the 20th century, Free Congregation farm owners outnumbered smallholders in a typical parish by two to one.[27] Today, the vast majority of agricultural workers in the congregation are farm owners, with only a handful of smallholders remaining. Moreover, the farms are doing fairly

27. The parish referred to is Frøslev; see Appendix for details.

well. In an area where most farms require an income from the wife to remain solvent, at least 40 percent of the congregation's farms have full-time housewives. Together with the rise of the well-paid professional and artisan categories, the increasing affluence of farmers marks an important change of fortune for the Free Congregation.

The swelling ranks of professionals constitute another important change. While artisans and laborers have long made up important parts of the Free Congregation, professionals have come quite recently; even thirty years ago, only a handful belonged to the church. Their numbers have grown quickly, though, and in 1990 they were tied with artisans as the second-largest occupational category. They are the congregation's largest occupation in Nykøbing, where over a quarter of the member households include at least one professional. Their rise stems partly from a general increase in professional jobs on Mors, as industry and government have required increasingly educated and specialized workers; it also derives partly from the increasing educational opportunities that have opened up to youth in the Mors countryside. The Free Congregation has had unusual success in attracting the members of this class of workers, many of whom express a deep cynicism about and distrust of religious institutions. Even those who do not belong tend to look at least mildly favorably on the group. As one told me, "I refuse to belong to any church, but if I did join one, it would probably be the Free Congregation."

A third major change in the congregation's demographic structure involves its increasing concentration around a few centers. The movement that built the Ansgarskirke had its roots in northern Mors, but it was widely dispersed around the island. Most villages in the northern half of Mors had Grundtvigian followings, which tended to shift their focus with the comings and goings of Grundtvigian priests. When the movement finally built its own church, they chose a remote corner of Øster Jølby that had the sole advantage of being near the intersection of four heavily Grundtvigian parishes. At the time, the movement's members were spread out fairly evenly among Sundby, Solbjerg, Øster Jølby, Erslev, Bjergby, and Tøving, with sizable circles in other villages. Very few lived in Nykøbing; the factory workers and merchants of the market town had little use for the rustic romanticism of the Grundtvigians.

After the building of the Ansgarskirke, the movement became more focused. The church's presence attracted members from nearby, swelling the membership in its immediate area. At the same time, it thinned out the adherents in the more distant areas, the less ardent of whom declined to make the long journey on Sundays. Local rivalries also came into play. The firm location of the congregation in the northern herred put off some southern Grundtvigians; similarly, a long-standing antipathy between the residents of Øster Jølby and Solbjerg made some Solbjerg Grundtvigians reluctant to join.[28] The very act of building a geographically fixed church tended to concentrate the movement in a specific area.

In the second half of the 20th century, the depopulation of villages on Mors reinforced the trend toward concentration. As smallholdings became untenable and farm machinery made farmhands superfluous, the island's population moved increasingly to Nykøbing and the larger villages. As populations dipped below the level needed to sustain shops and voluntary associations, the smaller villages tended to disappear almost entirely, remaining only as clusters of half-empty houses around little-used roads. The Free Congregation's circles in such villages inevitably declined. The substantial member circles in places like Gullerup, Ovtrup, and Mellem Jølby dropped to handfuls of stalwarts, while even functioning villages like Sundby, Frøslev, and Flade declined by half. At the same time, membership burgeoned in Nykøbing and Øster Jølby, where many of the villagers went. In 1990, Nykøbing had twice as many members as in 1950, and claimed the largest group of Free Congregation members outside of Øster Jølby.

Leaders

The structure and ideology of the Free Congregation place the priest in a paradoxical situation. On one hand, as the spiritual leader of the church, he holds enormous moral authority. Every Sunday he stands in a pulpit high above his parishioners, proclaiming the Holy Word and instructing the congregation in the meaning and duties of Christian worship. At baptisms, weddings, and funerals, his homilies connect the lives of the members to their community and to the divine. He instructs them in confirmation classes, and presides over them at parish meetings. In his every official capacity, he represents the authority of God and the community. On the other hand, he serves at the congregation's pleasure, and the insecurity of his tenure stands clearly in the minds of his followers. While his authority over them is wide ranging, theirs over him is

28. The rivalry is still felt today; a Solbjerg woman, whose parents were active members of the Free Congregation, told me that she had nonetheless not attended the Free School because it lay so close to Øster Jølby.

final; they have dismissed a priest once, and they can certainly do so again. The priest's job thus comes with a certain tension, a requirement to lead a flock decisively, but only in the direction it wants to go.

Accordingly, most Free Congregation priests have approached their authority rather warily. Rasmus Lund, for example, though his daring challenges to Folkekirke authority earned him a national reputation as a maverick, never made a major change in the church on his own initiative. His admittance of unconfirmed children to communion came only upon the insistence of the congregation's leaders; he agreed to begin very reluctantly, though he pushed the issue vigorously later. When the congregation split from the Folkekirke, he himself gave no sermon or polemical address on the matter, instead letting the congregation decide for itself by acclamation. Most other pastors have followed a similar approach. When discussing the recent changes in the baptism ritual, for example, Erik Lau Jørgensen emphasizes that it was not he, but a perplexed parishioner, who initiated discussions on the matter. Erik Overgaard illustrates his position by recalling the words of welcome he received on his installation. The head of the council thanked him not for coming to lead the flock, but for "coming to help us celebrate our services." Free Congregation priests do not thunder from the pulpit, nor do they shame their parishioners for lax morals. They must exercise their authority discreetly, ever mindful of a congregation conscious and jealous of its ultimate command.

The only priest to violate this rule successfully was Thorvald Balslev, who ruled the congregation with an iron hand from 1905 to 1925. Balslev gave fiery sermons in the Ansgarskirke, dominated the congregational council, and demanded an almost military respect from the members. Members writing memoirs in the 1960s recall their childhood awe of Balslev, and the stern reproofs he gave boys who failed to stand at attention and remove their hats when he passed (Fisker 1971). When he declined a position in Copenhagen to remain with the congregation, its members thanked him with the gift of a car; when he finally did leave, a procession of grieving members followed him to the ferry in Nykøbing. Balslev's ability to maintain this status stemmed partly from his stunning gifts as an orator.[29] In addition, though, he came to the

29. In an interview with an elderly man in Bjergby, I once asked what Balslev was like. The memory seemed to animate the frail old man, who immediately sat up at the edge of his chair and began describing Balslev as "one of the most fantastic Grundtvigian preachers in Denmark." Bodil Fisker told me of similar episodes when she first arrived as a priest's wife on Mors. She said that she asked women what had

congregation at a very uncertain time, when the membership was divided and seriously considering a return to the Folkekirke. The firm vision that he gave the church must have come as a welcome relief, and his departure must have seemed very threatening. Even so, a number of members expressed relief when he eventually left. The "cult" which had developed around him, they said, was "a danger to the healthy life of the congregation" (Fisker 1971: 82).

Per Fisker's dismissal stemmed at least in part from his disregard for the peculiar status of the Free Congregation priest. His personal scandals not only violated the norms of priestly behavior, they also implied a certain arrogance, a disregard for the congregation's opinions of his conduct. According to several members, this arrogance extended to his religious teachings as well; he seemed to have come to Mors with the intent of educating its backward farmers, of leading the congregation to a proper understanding of the faith. Such a goal would be normal for an average priest, and even his opponents acknowledged Fisker's unusual intellectual and theological sophistication. But this approach clashed with the congregation's understanding of the priest's role, and it made them less inclined to forgive his trespasses. A council that might have worked out its problems with a humbler priest fired Fisker instead.

Ritual in the Free Congregation

Grundtvig himself laid great weight on the importance of rituals in Christian worship. The early Christian congregations were built around ritual, he said, and today ritual makes the Christian community tangible in a way that scripture alone never can. He especially emphasized baptism, which brought the individual into the community, and communion, which gathered the community into Christ's presence. He considered these two ceremonies, "the bath and the table [*badet og bordet*]," the most precious of God's gifts to His people. In this respect, the Free Congregation has followed Grundtvig faithfully. Baptism and communion remain its most valued rituals today; confirmation, in contrast, reviled by both Grundtvig and Lund as an imposition of the state, is all but ignored.

---

been so special about Balslev; they got stars in their eyes and a dreamy expression, and said "You just had to hear him *speak (du sku' bare høre ham* tale)." While Lau Jørgensen became famous for his sermons, I have never heard any Free Congregation priest described in the tones which are routinely used for Balslev.

The Free Congregation hold many rituals in the course of the year, from parish meetings in the winter to the Constitution Day celebration in June. In the next few pages, I will briefly describe the most important of those rituals, the ones that figure most vividly in the life of the congregation, and that define the congregation's distinctiveness in the minds of its members.

Communion

Communion takes place in the Ansgarskirke, during the course of the normal Sunday service. About halfway through the service, after his sermon, the priest descends from the pulpit and walks to the altar, where a silver chalice and a bowl of wafers stand on a marble table. At the same time, people in the congregation begin leaving their seats on the tall wooden pews and making their way down the center aisle toward the altar. The first ones to reach it kneel at the semi-circular rail that stands before the altar; in front of them, the priest has been joined by his wife, who is helping to ready the communion. Each communicant take a small silver cup from a ledge below the rail and holds it upright on the rail. When no more can fit at the rail, the priest's wife turns to the kneeling group and makes her way around the semi-circle, placing a wafer in the outstretched hand of each communicant. With each wafer, she looks at the recipient and softly says, "This is the body of Jesus Christ." The priest follows her, pouring a splash of wine into each upturned cup and saying "This is the blood of Jesus Christ." The kneeling members eat and drink their communion immediately, then return the cup to the ledge and clasp their hands atop the rail. When all are served, the priest stands at the center of the altar and pronounces a blessing; the words vary, but all end with "His peace be with you." He then makes a sign of the cross over the little group, and they rise and push through the waiting throng back to their seats. Another group kneels at the altar, and the process repeats itself until all of the communicants are served. At the end, the priest serves the wafers and wine first to his wife, and then to himself. He kneels at the altar, prays in silence, and then arises to continue the service. The communion closes with a single-verse hymn, which thanks Jesus for the sacrament and for salvation.

Unlike many Danish churches, the Ansgarskirke is nearly always full on Sundays, and about two-thirds of those attending usually take communion. In a typical service, about sixty come to the altar. Participation is voluntary, and no records of the service are kept. Most regular attendees take communion every week, and all members do so at least occasionally. No one is forbidden to participate; strangers, even non-Christians, may do so, and even the Folkekirke has abandoned the age limitations that so outraged Grundtvigians in the last century.

Baptism

Baptism also occurs during a regular Sunday service, though not as frequently as communion. The church newsletter announces upcoming baptisms in advance, and the church flies a Danish flag on days when a baptism is to take place. The church is unusually crowded on such days, since the entire extended family of the baptized child usually attends. They arrive early and take the pews in the front, to assure a good view; the parents and the child go to a waiting room outside the church sanctuary. At a designated point in the service, before the communion, the organ sounds an anthem, the congregation stands, and the parents enter through the back of the sanctuary, the child reclining in the mother's arms. Parents wear ordinary church clothing, but the baby wears a long white dress, fringed with lace, a long pink or blue ribbon around the waist indicating its sex. The parents walk slowly down the aisle as the parishioners smile and lean for a better look at the baby. They stop at the granite baptismal font, where the priest stands waiting. When they arrive, the music stop and the priest incants a blessing. As he does so, small children in the congregation leave their seats and approach the font, where they can get a clear view of the baptism.

After the congregation sings a hymn, the actual baptism takes place. The priest states the three conditions of the Apostolic Creed, and declares them the basis for the faith of the Free Congregation. He asks the child if it wishes to be baptized into this faith; the mother, on the baby's behalf, answers "yes." She then leans over the font, so that the baby's head is above the water. The priest addresses the child by name and scoops three handfuls of water onto its crown, while saying "I baptize you in the name of the Father, the Son, and the Holy Spirit." The baptism complete, the congregation sings a single-verse hymn as the parents sit down in the front pew with the baby, who by this time is usually in tears. The priest returns to the altar, and the service continues.

All members of the Free Congregation must be baptized, normally as infants. Adults and older children who convert to the faith may also undergo the ceremony, though they often choose to do it in private. Those who are to be baptized must have a godmother and a godfather (although the total number of godparents can be as high as five), who are recorded as such in the record of the event. These godparents have no official duties, although they are expected to take a special concern in the child's spiritual development; the tie has no connotations of patronage or political alliance. Parents normally choose either close friends or relatives of about the parents' age.

A small reception usually follows the baptism, attended by the child's close family. Relatives and friends of the parents bring gifts for the child, often keepsake jewelry with a religious theme.

Confirmation

As discussed above (p. 115), opposition to confirmation played a key role in the Free Congregation's break from the Folkekirke. The legacy of that dispute remains in the ritual today, which is simpler, smaller, and much less valued than the extravagant confirmation ceremonies of the Folkekirke. Unlike those in the Folkekirke, for example, the congregation's confirmations do not take place all at once; individual confirmants are confirmed when they wish to be, usually in groups of two or three spread out over the course of the spring. No special service is held for them, and the regular service is altered only mildly.

As with baptism, a confirmation brings most of the close relatives of the initiate into the church early; the confirmant sits with them in one of the front pews. Boys wear stylish shirts and ties, girls wear elaborate white dresses with red sashes. At a designated point in the service, the confirmants rise and approach the altar, where they stand in a line before the priest. He asks each if he or she wishes to be confirmed in the church, to which each responds "yes." Placing his hand upon each of their heads in turn, the priest then incants a prayer for each confirmant, welcoming them into the congregation and asking God to support them in their faith. When all are finished, he shakes their hands, and they return to their seats; the service then goes on as usual to the end. After the service, the children's relatives engage in a frenzy of picture-taking, posing the confimants with the priest, with the parents, with each other, and with all of the family members present. They then adjourn to the confirmants home, where a standard Danish confirmation party awaits.

While this service is very understated, the confirmation actually involves considerable preparation. Initiates must take confirmation classes for months in advance, to learn the theological and ritual bases of church participation. Confirmants learn to know the priest and their classmates well in the process, and confirmation groups often remain close for years afterward. Moreover, confirmation is an important transition in Danish society, and the party and gifts which accompany it hold great significance for the confirmant. Even so, the Congregation deliberately downplays the ritual, regarding it as important for the individual, but not for the community.

Other Rituals

The other life-cycle rituals in the Free Congregation follow standard Folkekirke forms. Weddings, like most Danish weddings, are held at a special service; both families attend, and the bride and groom are led by the priest through a series of vows. Funerals also follow standard forms, and like weddings are followed by a reception. I noticed no difference in form between these rituals at the Ansgarskirke and those performed elsewhere on Mors, nor could the Free Congregation members tell me of any.

Seasonal events follow Folkekirke forms as well; Christmas and Easter mark the highest points, with festive church services and lively family gatherings (see pp.69-70). Virtually all members of the congregation try to come to these events. On Christmas Eve, the Ansgarskirke like all Danish churches fills to bursting with excited members, many of whom seldom if ever attend regular Sunday services. Easter is somewhat less crowded, while services such as Pentecost and Fastelavn hardly exceed regular attendance.

Two special seasonal rituals deserve special mention, however. One is the Constitution Day celebration, which the Congregation holds in concert with the Galtrup Efterskole and the Danish Society. On the anniversary of the ratification of the Danish constitution, political and religious groups hold similar meetings all over Denmark. Each meeting invites a speaker to discuss the contemporary meaning of the constitution, and in the process to reaffirm the political views of the assembled crowd. The Mors Grundtvigians hold their meeting in the eight-sided meeting house in Galtrup; they almost always invite a speaker from the Left Party, the traditional political affiliate of Grundtvigianism. The reputation of the church enables it to attract fairly eminent speakers. In 1991, for example, the nation's finance minister discussed the complexities of Danish membership in the European Community. In its association with this meeting, and in the vigorous questioning its members direct at the speaker, the Congregation declares its place in the secular political system of the larger society.

Even more important is the annual meeting, held each May, at which the congregation discusses its activities and elects its officers. The meeting, which also takes place in the eight-sided meeting house, generally attracts between eighty and a hundred members. The participants sit at long tables set for coffee and pastry, with a raised podium at one end. The meeting opens with a hymn, which is followed by reports from the head of the Congregational Council and the chairmen of the various committees. Speakers discuss the projects they have pursued, the problems that have arisen, and the financial details of the work. The audience listens attentively between sips of coffee; after each speaker finishes, the members ask detailed questions about the presentation. The questions are sometimes harsh, and the discussion can become heated. After the reports, members offer nominations for vacant positions on the Congregational Council. The nominees must make speeches about their intentions, after which the congregation votes by secret ballot. The meeting often lasts well past midnight, punctuated by rounds of coffee, pastry, and hymns.

The events of this meeting resemble those at any Danish voluntary association, or indeed at a corporate annual meeting anywhere. For a Danish church, however, they are remarkable. They establish concretely that the congregation governs itself; it is not the provst or the bishop or the church ministry that audits the Ansgarskirke, but the individual members. Each member who questions an officer, votes on an issue, or nominates a candidate asserts a personal authority that no member of the Folkekirke ever possesses. In a way, the annual meeting is as significant a rite of renewal as Christmas or holy communion; it allows members once each year to see, feel, and use the power they command.

Living in the Free Congregation

To join the Free Congregation is to leave the Danish Folkekirke, an important and rather unsettling act that involves renouncing a half millennium of Danish national Christianity. Only firm believers tend to do it, and the Congregation therefore tends to have a very committed membership. Even those born into the Congregation are conscious of its traditions, and very few drop out. Yet the commitment of the Congregation's members takes different forms. For some, the Congregation is the church of their families, a religious tradition that expresses their heritage and their local culture. For others, often newcomers to the area, the church is a theological haven, a beacon of free religion and progressive thought. Both groups generally support the Congregation enthusiastically, but their degree of interaction with it differ markedly. A look at two representative members illustrates the difference.

Gudrun Bro was born Gudrun Krog, a member of one of the Free Congregation's original families. Her great-grandfather, a farm owner in Solbjerg, was among the "awakened" laymen who built the Ansgarskirke in 1870; most of her family still lives in the immediate area, and most of them belong to the Free Congregation. Her uncle, a sculptor, carved the granite baptismal font that stands in the center aisle of the church. Gudrun grew up on a small farm in Solbjerg, from which she traveled with her parents and siblings to Øster Jølby every Sunday in a horse cart. As a girl she bicycled frequently to the Galtrup meeting house for gymnastics classes, which she loved, and which she has continued throughout her life. She participated enthusiastically in the activities of the Free Congregation and the Danish Society, though the rivalry between Solbjerg and Øster Jølby kept her from ever attending the free school. After she finished her schooling, she worked for several years as a cook and serving girl at farms in the area. At age twenty she met Niels Bro, a fisherman's son from Agerø, at a gymnastics exhibition. The two of them loved gymnastics, music, and eventually each other, and a year later they were married in the Ansgarskirke. They moved to a small farm in Øster Jølby, which Niels operated while Gudrun raised their three children. Their youngest child, a daughter, is now 18 and studying for a driver's license; one son works for a mechanic in a neighboring village, the other is an apprentice carpenter. All speak, like their parents, in the rapid lilting dialect of northwestern Mors. At age 45, Gudrun now works as a nursing aide at the Ansgarshjem retirement home. Niels works the farm, in addition to serving as the church singer at the Ansgarskirke and a member of the congregational council. Both still practice gymnastics, and neither can imagine ever leaving northwestern Mors.

Gudrun regards the Free Congregation simply as her home church. It is no different to belong there, she says, than to belong anywhere else; if she lived somewhere else, she would surely feel the same way about the church there. It is where she was raised, where her family has come from, where she feels at home. She sees no major difference between the theological position of the Folkekirke and that of the Free Congregation, the Inner Mission excepted. While she understands the independent tradition of the church and appreciates her own voice in it, she does not consider her participation different from that of any Danish woman in her own home parish.

Gudrun does, however, participate much more in church activities than most Danes. She usually attends church at least twice a month, and always goes to holiday services. She enjoys evening coffee meetings in the winters, and she serves on the nursing home committee. Moreover, much of her everyday life takes place within the social world of the Congregation. Most of her family and friends belong, as do most of her co-workers and patients. The gymnastics classes she leads consciously promote Grundtvigian values, and most of her students come from Free Congregation families. Though Gudrun discounts the importance of the Congregation in her life, the Grundtvigian movement largely defines the social world within which she moves, as well as the activities and relationships most important to her life.

Else Olesen came to the Free Congregation in a very different way. Born and raised in the city of Randers, she moved to Mors as a young woman, soon after finishing her education as a registered nurse. While at nursing school, she had met and married Peder Olesen, a machinist from Vester Jølby who was attending a nearby technical school. Afterward the couple moved to a house in Vester Jølby, where he worked for a machine shop and she for health ministry. She began as a mobile nurse, traveling from house to house to administer medicine to elderly invalids; her command of the Morsingbo dialect, which Peder had taught her, made her instantly popular among her rural patients. After a few years she found a staff position at the hospital in Nykøbing, and then finally received the coveted post of mobile pediatric nurse. Today she makes monthly visits to all of the infants in one section of Nykøbing, monitoring their development and advising their mothers on medical problems. She and Peder have two boys of their own, aged 14 and 17; both plan to attend gymnasium, and one has studied in America. The entire family belongs to the Free Congregation, Peder's childhood church. Else loves Mors, and hopes to spend the rest of her life on the island.

For Else, the difference between the Free Congregation and the Folkekirke is clear. The Free Congregation, she says, is a life-affirming place, relaxed and friendly, supportive of its members. Its theology gives the individual a freedom and opportunity for personal growth unheard of in the stifling state church. Moreover, the Congregation nourishes the values of the rural Mors culture she has learned to love. In keeping with these values, she has given her sons the old-fashioned names Frode and

Tor. She sends them to the free school in Galtrup, where she feels they get a more free and creative education than the state school system offers. Else speaks enthusiastically of the Grundtvigian movement, which she regards as a different and better world than the Folkekirke in which she grew up.

For all her sincere enthusiasm, though, Else's actual participation in congregational life is quite limited. She almost never enters the church except at holidays; she does not go to evening parish meetings, annual meetings, or church social occasions. Though their names echo those of the Congregation's founders, neither of her sons ever attends Sunday services. Neither her co-workers, her patients, nor the majority of her friends belong to the Congregation. Her political support goes not to the Grundtvigian Left Party, but to the Social Democrats who built the national medical system. Else likes belonging to the church, and she genuinely believes in the doctrines that it promotes; she also appreciates its importance to her husband's family. Yet it does little to shape her social world or her activities in daily life.

The Gudrun Bros outnumber the Else Olesens in the Free Congregation today, and they provide most of the manpower for the ongoing work of the church. The Elses are increasing, however, especially in the growing professional and medical sectors of the Congregation's membership. More and more members experience the church as a vehicle for religious and ritual concerns, rather than an encompassing community within which to live. With their relative wealth and influential positions, these members can provide important financial and political strength for the Congregation. The community on which the church is founded, however, will ultimately depend on the continuing commitment of active rural members like Gudrun Bro.

Future Prospects

The idea that Danish religion is dead has become so widespread as to be received wisdom; scholars and journalists in and out of Denmark regularly lament its demise, and wonder what will hold society together now that religion has disappeared. Active religious communities like the Free Congregation are generally viewed as rural holdouts, dregs of the old system that will wash slowly away as modern society extends its reach to all corners of the nation. A close look at the Free Congregation, however, reveals none of the cracks one would expect in a dying community. The church's financial base is robust; its membership is steady and even slightly growing; its relations with local institutions are friendly; its officers and employees are capable and experienced. Nor does its setting appear to be a enclave of the premodern era. While Øster Jølby is not Copenhagen – it is, after all, a rural area – its inhabitants are well educated, prosperous, and conscious of the world outside of their island. They own televisions, drive cars, send their children to good schools, and travel all over Europe. The Free Congregation is neither withering in the face of modernity, nor prospering on an island that time forgot.

Nor, from its tradition, should we expect it to be. For all its interest in folk customs and culture, the Free Congregation never based its existence on a denial of modernity. Its very creation violated the traditional village-based organization of Danish religion, substituting a regional structure based on shared ideology. Its founders railed against Folkekirke regulations that depended solely on tradition for validity. The Free Congregation took an active part in the struggle for rural empowerment in the national political system, and its members depended on education in scientific farming methods to lift themselves out of their initial poverty. Their alterations in ritual, from the admittance of children to communion to the modification of the baptism ceremony, have anticipated the actions of the national church. If anything, the Free Congregation has embraced the changes that Danish modernization has brought.

Its members consequently have few fears for its future. When I discussed the church's future with members, they talked mostly about capital improvements and other plans; they took the church's survival for granted, and dismissed suggestions that it might be endangered. They cited the vitality and growth of the membership as evidence for their belief. On the whole, I agree with them. The solid base of members in the northwest Mors area shows no sign of eroding, and a body of members and sympathizers is growing among the educated and professional classes in Nykøbing. The Congregation has changed, certainly, and the nature of affiliation and community among its members continues to evolve. Without such changes, though, the Congregation would become a fossilized and ultimately moribund relic of days gone by.

One danger does threaten its existence. The Free Congregation is deeply rooted in northwestern Mors, and it still draws most of its members from the area. Even those who live elsewhere value the culture and tradition of the island; part of the Congregation's appeal is the hard-boiled independence of the farmers who form its bedrock. But events of the last half century have threatened the very existence of those farmers.

Mechanized agriculture has depopulated many villages, while the centralization of administration and trade in Nykøbing has sapped the vitality of those that remain. If the society of the Mors countryside were to gradually disappear, the Free Congregation would find survival very difficult. Such a threat seems improbable; even if some villages were to disappear, the larger ones might well remain as local trade and community centers. Moreover, rural depopulation may well be approaching its limit. No one can predict the future, though, and the ultimate fate of the Free Congregation will follow that of the island on which it rests.

6. The Church Society
for the Inner Mission
in Denmark

Aldrig er jeg uden våde,
Aldrig dog foruden nåde,
Altid har jeg suk og ve,
Altid kan jeg Jesus se.

Altid trykker mine synder,
Altid Jesus hjælp tilskynder,
Altid er jeg udi tvang,
Altid er jeg fuld af sang.

Så er sorg til glæde lænket,
Så er drikken mig iskænket,
Besk og sød in livets skål,
Sådant er mit levneds mål.

Men, o Jesus, jeg vil græde,
Hjælp du til, at troens glæde
Over synd og sorrig må
Altid overvægten få!

Never am I free from blame,
Yet never beyond mercy,
I always have sighs and woes,
But I can always see Jesus.

My sins always press me,
Jesus always sends help,
I am always oppressed,
I am always full of song.

Thus is sorrow chained to joy,
Such is the drink which I have been given,
Bitter and sweet in the bowl of life,
Such is the measure of my existence.

But, O Jesus, when I weep,
Help ensure that the joys of faith
Over sin and sorrow
Shall always prevail!

— Kingo (1982)

*J*ens Bertelsen was dead, buried this very day in the cold, hard earth of Ejerslev churchyard. His relatives and neighbors had dutifully come to the funeral, listened to the priest's meandering sermon, sung hymns by the grave, and watched the coffin descend under the warm light of the June sun. They had returned to his widow's little house for dinner, coffee, and a few more tearful hymns; they had done their duty by the dead. Now night had fallen, and it was time for the living to continue. As the dishes disappeared from the long table, decks of playing cards came out of pockets, and men began the laborious process of puffing their long pipes into life. The women, holding knitting needles and yarn, slipped one by one into the kitchen to join the buzzing circle of conversation. Within minutes, the hum of gossip and the jingle of gambled coins filled the air.

At one end of the table, though, a growing fury radiated from the grim faces of three black-clad men. The men were fishermen from Harboøre on the North Sea, and they lodged with the Bertelsens while they fished in the Limfjord each summer. People did not play cards in Harboøre, nor did they let a few mild hymns suffice for the death of a Christian. Harboøre was a Mission town; people there believed in a caring but rigorous God, who punished sin as thoroughly as He rewarded righteousness. Such a God must surely weep at the sight of gambling and gossip at the funeral of one of His children. After a few minutes, the fishermen could bear it no more. Rising to their feet, they formed a line before the door, and began singing the stately hymns of the Harboøre Mission. Their massive forms towered over the men in the room, while their booming voices drowned out the busy conversation.

At the table, the men turned astonished from their cards. First they waited for the hymn to end; then, as one hymn led on to another, they put down their cards and exchanged baffled looks. Their discomfort grew as the fishermen began preaching, urging them to put away the instruments of sin and Satan, to think about the fiery perdition to which their ways must inevitably lead. Think about Jens Bertelsen, who might even now be standing before God, awaiting his judgment, the magnificent vista of heaven at one hand and the yawning chasm of hell at the other. Think about them now, tonight, while they had the chance, before an overturned boat or a runaway cart cut off their opportunity to change their ways. The room began to feel warm, and some began to look for a way out, but none dared challenge the three hulking fishermen blocking the door. Finally, the urge to escape became overpowering, and one by one men began clumsily squeezing through the tiny window at the other end of the room. Those who stayed felt an uncertainty and dread in the depths of their souls, and listened despite themselves to the thundering apostles from the western sea.

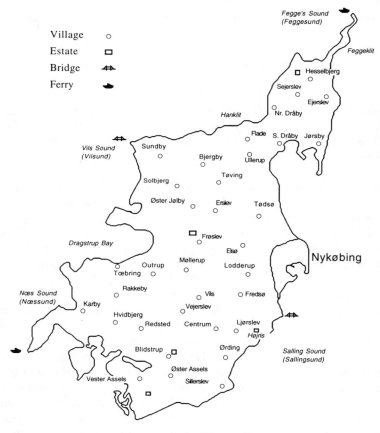

Map 6: Mors Island Inner Mission
Important Sites

Map 7: Mission Houses on Mors Island

It was 1888, and the Inner Mission had come to Mors. Over the next twenty years, the fishermen and their allies would spread their message to little groups of converts all over the island. In some villages, those converts would become pariahs, viewed by their neighbors as half-crazed zealots. In others, they would convert the neighbors as well, building a chain of devout religious communities that would rival those of the Grundtvigians. They would build mission houses and youth centers, seamen's homes and dry hotels, all observing and promoting the stringent moral codes of their demanding faith. A half century later, the Church Association for the Inner Mission in Denmark would stand as the Free Congregation's primary competitor for the souls of Morsingboer.[1]

The Mission awakening drew on the same stream of Lutheran pietism that had spawned the Free Congregation. As described above (pp. ??), a pietist awakening began on Mors in the late 1830s, sparked by the lay preacher Peter Larsen Skræppenborg and nourished by Christen Kold and P.K. Algreen. The movement was strongest in northwestern Mors, where both Kold and Algreen lived, but it attracted sympathizers from all over the island. By the 1850s it had taken on a Grundtvigian flavor, and it became associated with Grundtvigian schools and social views; when the members finally built the Ansgarskirke in 1871, they chose an avid and outspoken Grundtvigian as priest. To observers in the rest of Denmark, the awakening on Mors became synonymous with radical and separatist Grundtvigianism.

On the island itself, though, many of the awakened had no affection for the Ansgarskirke. Some rejected its philosophy, which they felt had strayed too far from standard pietism. Grundtvig's ideas about folk culture, education, and political reform had little to do with their

1. Most of the material in this section is drawn either from interviews, from Inner Mission papers in the Mors Island Historical Archive, or from Valdemar Pedersen's (1937) *Indre Mission paa Mors gennem 50 Aar (Inner Mission on Mors through 50 Years)*. Pedersen's account of the island's awakening is the only published source dealing directly with Mors, and is rich in anecdotal material. The scarcity of historical material on the Inner Mission has been noted elsewhere (Balle-Petersen 1977). In contrast to the Grundtvigians, whose consciousness of their communities and of folk history inspired a rich corpus of histories and memoirs, Inner Mission members have seldom written their own history. A project designed in the 1980s by the national Inner Mission Society has recently gathered a large number of contemporary memoirs, but such projects can shed little light on more distant events. The early history of the movement will have to be inferred from the few records that do remain, a monumental task that may never yield the rich data so easily available about the Grundtvigians.

understanding of the awakening; the central issues of sin and redemption, damnation and salvation, seemed to have been forgotten in the Grundtvigian mind. Other members objected to the church's location, which privileged the residents of a few neighboring towns. Still others disagreed with the entire notion of an independent congregation. The godly, they argued, should not forsake their parishes for an artificial community, but rather build communities of the faithful among their own neighbors. Even among the awakened in the Øster Jølby area, up to a fifth may have refused to join the Choice Congregation in 1871.

The Congregation's break with the Folkekirke in 1883 alienated even more. Within the Choice Congregation itself, a number of members refused to go along with the decision, including the group's foreman. Elsewhere, some previously sympathetic pietists withdrew their support. To form a new congregation had required imagination and daring; to actually leave the Folkekirke implied something else, a sort of arrogance that sat poorly with the keepers of the Jante Law. Folkekirke loyalists joined the ranks of disgruntled but unattached pietists dispersed around the island.

Some of these pietists had already found an alternative in the doctrines of the Inner Mission. Here and there across Mors, individual conversions had aroused the curiosity, annoyance, and ridicule of villagers and townspeople. A saddlemaker in Ejerslev, Peder Geneser, preached redemption and sang hymns to customers on his rounds; a woman of the village, Grethe Kong, was also known to "have conversations with the Lord." In Sundby, a pair of seamstresses witnessed their faith to farmer's wives as they went from house to house to sew. Before the late 1880s, such lone believers found little support from their neighbors. Their constant proselytizing lost its novelty very quickly, and irritated listeners concluded that "the holy ones" had lost their minds. Farmers greeted their arrival on business with sarcastic remarks, while neighbors avoided their company. Existence became lonely for the faithful. In his old age, Peder Geneser prayed impatiently, baffled that God could have forgotten His servant; he never made a convert, and the only answer to his calls for an awakening was the missionary who visited his deathbed (Pedersen 1937: 9).

At the end of the decade, however, two developments breathed life into the Mission movement. One was a series of small awakenings around the island, generally sparked by Mission proselytizers from outside the island. The fishermen in Ejerslev, a converted coppersmith in Nykøbing, and Mission-oriented priests in Frøslev and Galtrup developed small groups of converts, or *missionsfolk*. These converts were not numerous, but they did form communities of sorts. They met in one another's homes for religious "conversation meetings," they proselytized together, they invited missionaries to visit their villages, and they commiserated with one another over the scorn and mockery they met at the hands of their neighbors.

The other development was Vilhelm Beck's visit to Nykøbing in 1890. Beck, the fiery leader of the national Inner Mission Society, brought stirring rhetoric and organizational acumen to the scattered and disorganized Mors missionsfolk. He held revival meetings in the church in Nykøbing, where his thundering invocations of sin and damnation terrified many and converted some. Perhaps more importantly, he met privately with any missionsfolk who wanted his advice. He told them how to organize and lead meetings, how to approach hostile unbelievers, and where to reach the missionaries and booksellers of the national Inner Mission Society. Missionsfolk from around the island came to meet and hear him, and they came away enraptured. Not only had they received expert advice on their problems, they had spoken personally with God's foremost servant on earth. All of them had previously read Beck's sermons; for many, his writings had inspired their own conversions. To meet him in person, to hear him praise their work, was an experience they would treasure all their lives and tell to their grandchildren. They returned to their villages changed people, confirmed in their faith, clear about their tasks, and certain of their ultimate success.

Thus armed, the faithful threw themselves into the task of conversion. They brought in missionaries from Thy and Salling to hold revival meetings in the villages. They held conversation meetings themselves, inviting friends and neighbors to attend. In Nykøbing, missionsfolk in the giant iron foundry began preaching to their co-workers. As time went by, the converts came. In Nykøbing, a steadily rising crowd attended Bible readings held in the second-floor apartment of a believing coppersmith. When the apartment became too small, the leaders rented a meeting room; by 1895, they were drafting plans for their own building. Revival meetings in some villages found similar responses, quickly outgrowing the available meeting places. The previously tiny flocks grew into communities with up to several dozen member families. As they grew, they began instituting standard Inner Mission activities. The larger groups held "mission weeks" in the summer, during which outside priests and missionaries would hold revival meetings every night. They also began holding children's Sunday services *(børnegudstjeneste)*, where children could receive instruction in morals and the Bible. By the turn of the century, active Inner Mission communities thrived in villages around the island.

These communities were holy, but not particularly happy. Even by the standards of the Inner Mission, the Mors movement was a severe one; one Mission-oriented priest in Nykøbing, for example, a native of Copenhagen, found himself repeatedly offending the town's missionsfolk with his lighthearted manner (Pedersen 1937: 21).[2] Mission proselytizers spoke less of the joys of heaven than of the terrors of hell to their neighbors, and their own memoirs describe their constant consciousness and fear of damnation. Mission ideology demanded vigorous self-scrutiny, a perpetual watchfulness for the sin that forever threatened to arise from mortal nature. Mors missionsfolk took this obligation very seriously. They also adhered rigorously to the Mission's injunctions against drink, dance, card playing, and other pleasures of the sinful world. Abstention from dancing and cards, two of the liveliest diversions of rural life, came particularly hard for many believers.[3] Missionsfolk dressed in plain dark clothing, hung pictures of Jesus and scriptural texts on the walls, and found their social life in prayer groups and revival meetings.

Part of the power of this lifestyle came from its insularity. Vilhelm Beck advocated a doctrine called the Separation *(Skellet)*, a firm distinction between the community of the holy and that of the world. "God's children" had a duty to preach to and proselytize the "children of the world," but other contact was unwise; mixing with the ungodly could

2.   Danes often use the terms dark and light *(mørk* and *lys)* to contrast the mission and Grundtvigian views of life and the world. Darkness implies a focus on the sinfulness of mankind and the wages of evil, while lightness stresses the love of God for humanity and the joys of earthly existence. In Pedersen's (1937) work, he states that the temper of the Morsingboer, like that of most Jutlanders, tends toward the dark; he uses this fact to account for the severe attitudes of the Mors missionsfolk. The light attitude of the island's Grundtvigians, however, casts doubt on this characterization. The darkness that Pedersen ascribes to Morsingboer in general may apply best to the missionsfolk who constituted most of his own social circle.

3.   Pedersen's (1937) book recounts some poignant episodes regarding dancing. One man in the countryside found his greatest joy in the circle-steps of Mors folk dancing, and could never hear a fiddle play without jumping up to join the group. In all other ways he was the picture of a Mission Christian; he followed the moral codes, was scrupulous and generous in his business dealings, and wept with emotion every Sunday in church. His dancing separated him from the local missionsfolk, however, and they enjoined him constantly to give it up. Finally he did, reluctantly, and he became an active member of the mission community. One can picture him in his dark clothes later in life, overhearing fiddle music from the village inn, wistfully thinking of the dancers inside.

only tempt and corrupt the faithful. Missionsfolk therefore avoided social contact with nonbelievers whenever possible. They might have to buy their sugar from a nonbelieving grocer, but they did not have to exchange small talk with him, greet him on the street, attend his wedding, or permit their children to play with his. They could not cut off contacts with nonbelieving family members, but they could make every family meeting an occasion for proselytizing and prayer. To convert was to join a Mission world, to leave old friends and family members for a new and intense community. The walls around that community were high and tightly guarded.

Nonconverts took this insularity as an affront, and they often deeply resented the presence of missionsfolk in their communities. According to the accounts of the missionsfolk, unbelievers subjected them to ceaseless and bitter scorn and ridicule. In the countryside, villagers insulted missionsfolk who came to proselytize; in Nykøbing, foundry workers hurled endless mockery at the circle of converts there. Conversion occasioned its most painful strife when it occurred within families. When one spouse joined the Mission, the other felt excluded and resentful; such cases nearly always created marital strife and severe treatment of children, which ended only when the other spouse finally converted.[4] Missionsfolk returned the outsiders' hostility in good measure; they likened the "children of the world" to those who persecuted Jesus, and loudly pronounced their imminent damnation. Indeed, they sometimes seemed to revel in their antagonism, which placed them in the same despised but holy position as the prophets of old. Missionsfolk reserved a special contempt for the Grundtvigians, whom they regarded as little better than atheists. In areas with strong Grundtvigian communities, such as northwestern Mors, an open hostility characterized all social relations between members of the two movements.[5]

As Mission communities developed, they quickly outgrew the available facilities for holding revival meetings. During the 1890s and early

4. At least, that's how it goes in Mission annals. Mission stories, understandably, do not mention cases where the converted spouse finally left the Mission.
5. In most cases, the missionsfolk appear to have felt this hostility much more strongly than the Grundtvigians. Neither side liked the other, certainly. But whereas the few existing Inner Mission histories frequently discuss the rivalry with the Grundtvigians, the Frimenighed materials say virtually nothing about the Inner Mission. Indeed, one Grundtvigian priest in Nykøbing, Vilhelm Hansen, made a point of always hiring a mission priest as his assistant. It is difficult to imagine a mission priest on Mors returning the favor.

1900s, therefore, they began building mission houses in Nykøbing and around the Mors countryside (see Map 7), The buildings, usually red brick structures about the size of a small country church, quickly became the social and spiritual centers of the local Mission movements. They cost a lot to erect, so that the very existence of a mission house in a parish indicated a fairly strong awakening there. Local missionsfolk seldom had the resources to finance such a project; they typically sought donations from believers around the island, and sometimes from elsewhere in Jutland. Unlike the Free Congregation, they also drew support from major landowners. The owner of Ullerup Manor near Tøving, for example, provided substantial bequests for the mission houses in Øster Assels and Sundby.

By 1905, the Inner Mission had found its way to every region of Mors. Its strongholds lay in the northeastern and southeastern parts of the island, but strong circles also existed in Grundtvigian areas like Frøslev and Sundby. Over the next twenty-five years, these circles tried to establish themselves as viable ongoing communities. Some, such as Frøslev, Sejerslev, and Øster Assels, succeeded. They converted large percentages of the village populations; they maintained strict Mission rules for moral and social life; they instituted activities such as the children's Sunday services and the KFUM/K to socialize children; they crowded into revival meetings, Bible study circles, conversation meetings, and church services; they established dairies and groceries that kept the Sabbath; and they kept a strict separation between themselves and the children of the world. Other parishes, such as Hvidbjerg, Ljørslev, and Tøving, were unable to establish such a community. Inner Mission groups either died out or, more commonly, reverted to scattered groups of individual believers, without a separate community of their own.

The direction that a parish took seems to have depended on three main factors. The most important was the presence or absence of a charismatic priest or lay leader. In the northeastern peninsula, for example, the priests Dyekjær and Brostrøm actively proselytized for the Mission between 1893 and 1903; their authority gave legitimacy to the embryonic movement, and their feverish activity built it into a viable enterprise. In Frøslev, the priest P.J. Munch drove the movement in the critical years between 1896 and 1912. Even after these priests were replaced by less fervent Mission adherents, the local missionsfolk included lay leaders with sufficient presence to continue the movement. In Karby, in contrast, while a local smallholder managed to get a mission house built, a lack of strong leadership prevented a strong community from emerging.

A second factor seems to have been the presence or absence of large farm owners in the Mission community. A major landowner could provide the funding for building mission houses, holding meetings, and paying guest speakers. Perhaps more importantly, though, a landowner had standing within the rural community. His presence at a meeting gave it a certain legitimacy, insulating it from the scorn and catcalls of outsiders. Moreover, he could influence his servants and farmhands to join as well. In Frøslev, for example, a large portion of the missionsfolk either served on or had family connections to the Frøslevgaard and Betinasminde, the area's largest farms. Hvidbjerg, without such support, never managed to sustain a Mission community (Pedersen 1937).

A third and more complicated factor concerns the opposition of local Grundtvigians and other non-Mission residents. To a certain extent, such opposition helped the missionsfolk; it brought the community closer together, and provided a clear contrast to the community's values. Indeed, in places like Galtrup and Sundby, the anti-Grundtvigian rhetoric of the Mission made it popular among opponents of the Free Congregation. When the Grundtvigians actively tried to undermine the Inner Mission, however, they could be quite effective. Pastor J.B. Estrup inspired a Mission awakening in Ljørslev at the beginning of the century, for example, using particularly harsh condemnations of the Grundtvigian worldview. In response, the local Grundtvigians imported a long string of Grundtvigian priests to give speeches in the meeting house there. By the time Estrup left Mors in 1911, his opponents had gotten the upper hand. Likewise, the heavy presence of the Free Congregation in Tøving ultimately drowned out the Mission society there.

By about 1930, the Mission presence on Mors had reached a plateau. The awakenings had ended, and the marginal Mission circles had faded; remaining were a set of established, cohesive Inner Mission communities spread across the island (see Map 7). In these communities, the Mission had become part of the framework of daily life. Children grew up in a society of Mission children, attending Sunday schools, mission summer camps, and participating in the KFUM/K. After their confirmations, country youths usually worked for Mission farmers or artisans; in Nykøbing, they often sought positions in factories with strong Mission circles. They met their spouses through KFUM/K or at revival meetings, and they sought their friends in the same circles. They joined Bible study circles, they volunteered to lead Sunday school classes, they helped at the summer camp in Bjørneborg. They held positions on the cooperative market board, on the cooperative dairy board, and on the parish council. The Mission had become a world in which whole lives were lived, centered around the mission house and the church. These communities lasted through the depression of the 1930s, and through the German occupation of the 1940s. They provided their members with a sustaining faith, though a demanding one, and a supportive social network.

In the 1950s, however, these communities began to encounter troubles. As mentioned above, mechanization in Mors agriculture began in earnest after World War II. With the advent of large farms employing few laborers, farmhands and serving girls found their employment disappearing. They went instead to Nykøbing or beyond, to work in the growing factories of the towns and cities. Smallholders likewise turned to factory work, selling off or leasing their lands to the increasingly small number of farm owners. As they did so, the village communities within which the Inner Mission thrived began to erode. The young adults who had once flocked to the KFUM/K and to revival meetings, who had once produced children for the Sunday services, who had once grown into the leaders of the mission houses and parish councils, gradually began leaving the countryside. Those who remained no longer lived as totally within the framework of the village as they once had. With improved transportation networks, villagers could easily work and trade almost anywhere on the island. Buses, cars, and telephones let them maintain social circles outside the local community. At the same time, the spread of mass communications brought the ideas and images of the outside world increasingly to their homes. Even as they began to lose their populations, the villages lost the insularity that had made them such enveloping social units.

These changes shook the foundations of the Inner Mission in the Mors countryside. The movement's essence lay in the society of the village, with its own church, mission house, merchants, and farms. God's children had created a holy community there, independent both of the outside world and of the nonbelievers in the parish. That community had been the heart of the movement's success, guiding its members from birth to death within the structure of the godly.[6] But as the 1950s and 1960s wore on, its basis gradually fell away. Many members remained in the Mission, and they continued to hold revival meetings and proclaim the old doctrines of sin and redemption. But they could no longer

6. The Free Congregation, in contrast, was never organized around a village community; the movement was a regional one, spanning Mors, and specifically opposed to the ties of the old parish system. I will return to this issue below.

restrict their social contacts to each other as they once had. Their work, their families, and their entertainment became increasingly tied to the world outside the parish and outside the Mission. Moreover, even within the village, the dwindling population made the Separation hard to maintain. Many villages could not support a single baker anymore, let alone separate Mission and Grundtvigian merchants.

Mission customs reflected the decline of the Separation. The stern black clothing that had once made missionsfolk easily recognizable gave way to more ordinary clothes. Prohibitions on the theater relaxed somewhat, allowing missionsfolk to see motion pictures and television. Even the messages of preachers and proselytizers gradually softened; they began focusing less on the dangers of sin and more on the mercy of Jesus. Many members even began questioning the Separation, which often seemed to hinder proselytizing more than it helped. Missionsfolk saw in these changes not a weakening of their faith, but a reconsideration of overzealously interpreted rules. They were probably right. Still, the changes made the Mission community less distinguishable and less removed from the rest of the world. Bit by bit, they eroded the walls that had held God's children within the society of the holy.

In 1975, the separation of the KFUM/K from the national Inner Mission Society dealt a crippling blow to the Mission on Mors. Missionsfolk had depended on the youth group to guide children into Mission membership; through KFUM/K, the movement had received a steady stream of young adult participants. The effect stemmed not only from the KFUM/K's religious teachings, but also from the community of Mission children that it created, a community that maintained itself as the children grew into adulthood. The bitter 1975 split swept all that away. Many missionsfolk pulled their children from the organization, many others withdrew as teachers and counselors. The KFUM/K began seeking members among non-Mission children, and it began promoting a moral code quite different from that of the Mission. Inner Mission Sunday schools continued to operate, as did the summer youth camp at Bjørneborg, but they could not replace the organization and activities of the KFUM/K. The stream of young adults coming into the Mission slowed to a trickle, and the Mission on Mors went for over a decade without a youth organization.

By 1990, the Mission on Mors was clearly in decline. Most of its mission houses operated only rarely, and some had been sold to private use. Membership, once in the thousands, had fallen to less than three hundred, of whom few were younger than middle age. Bible study circles still operated in the remaining active mission houses, some groups still held revival meetings, and all groups cooperated for mission weeks in the summers. Attendance was sparse, however, compared with the throngs of days gone by, especially in the countryside. Even the Nykøbing chapter, less affected by the restructuring of the village communities, attracted fewer and older participants than it ever had before. Some members saw reasons for optimism about the future; the Mission had begun a youth program to replace the KFUM/K, and observers around Denmark noted an increased interest in religion among the general population. But the Mission community, the self-conscious, self-contained world of the children of God, the society that Vilhelm Beck and the Harboøre fishermen had dreamed of and helped create, that community had all but disappeared, and not even the most optimistic of the remaining faithful could imagine its return.

Unlike the Free Congregation, the Mission operated primarily on a village level, with very little regional structure to hold it together. Its history is thus the history of twenty-odd separate circles, each of which evolved in a different way. Before finishing the Mission's history, therefore, let us briefly sketch the histories of two of these village communities, to illustrate the courses which local circles tended to take. I will not do so in detail, but merely indicate the general development of the communities.[7]

Frøslev-Mollerup

The Mission's presence in Frøslev and Mollerup begins in 1883, when the Mission priest Jessen served in the allied parishes.[8] Jessen converted Marie Schade, the widowed owner of the large Betinasminde farm; along with her daughter, Schade began holding children's Sunday services as well as prayer meetings for the servant girls on the farm. Jessen's succes-

7. The two communities described here are chosen for two reasons. First, they exemplify two rather different styles of mission awakening, one developed early and slowly by priests, the other occurring later and more explosively, and initiated by a lay preacher. Second, histories of the Mission in both towns have been written in the last ten years by members. These histories are short and impressionistic, but they provide a historical perspective unavailable for most villages.
8. The information in this sketch comes from Pedersen 1937 and Jensen n.d.; the latter, a short history written by a member of the Frøslev Mission, appears to have been written in the mid-1980s.

sor, Pastor Faurskov, continued his Mission work, and succeeded in converting the local postman and merchant, together with their families. By the time he left the parish in 1896, the Mission flock in Frøslev had grown to around ten members.

P.J. Munch, who replaced Faurskov in 1896, turned this little circle into an awakening. He preached passionate Mission sermons in the church, and he personally participated in the conversation meetings and Bible study groups. He allowed revival meetings to be held in his own residence, where his speeches attracted listeners from around northwestern Mors. Together with the invigorated proselytizing of the lay members, his work produced a powerful awakening in the parish. A mission house was erected in Mollerup in 1900. The awakening involved powerful emotions for the converts; an account by one, who found the faith at a Munch church service, illustrates the strength of the feelings:

> I was the bell-ringer at the church, Pastor Munch had held an evening service, and I stood now by the church door and awaited the priest. The Word had struck me to the quick, my soul was in turmoil. Finally the priest came; he stopped before me, looked at me with his penetrating eyes, and quietly said: "Are you a believing man?" "Yes, I am trying to find my way," I answered, and broke out weeping. "The proud shall be punished," said the priest, "but the humble shall receive mercy; you stand on the threshold, one more step and you shall be in the Light." ... There came light, yes, and it was God's mercy that he found me. I was, after all, well into my sixties before it happened. (Pedersen 1937: 41-42)

The awakening also brought strife, even within families. Another account describes a family in a neighboring parish in which the father, but not the mother, converted:

> Father began to go to church in Mollerup with the new priest [Munch also served Mollerup church], and thereby he was awakened to his sin and became very uneasy in his mind. He had been severe with us before, and it got no better now. We had to obey, and his uneasy conscience made him completely mean and confused. Mother said, "That must be a horrible priest, since Father has become this way since he began to listen to him." Mother was a Grundtvigian, and preferred our own parish priest ... Father and Mother often went out the door at the same time, each on the way to his own church; but Father became a believing person. Missionaries were invited to visit us, which Mother didn't like, as she didn't like these missionaries. But she finally got to like one, missionary Kristensen; he could talk with her; they both loved a bowl of porridge and a drop of coffee; she therefore thought

him a man who appreciated the small things in life, who was not arrogant. She then began going frequently to meetings in the old school in Frøslev. One evening Pastor Brostrøm spoke, and she took hold of his words faithfully and realized, the she was a forgiven sinner. From that moment it was delightful in our home, and the visits from the missionaries are among my favorite childhood memories. (Pedersen 1937: 43-44)

Munch took a post on Sjælland in 1912, leaving behind him a large and active Mission community. Its lay leaders continued his work, expanding and consolidating the community of the faithful. They maintained close ties to Munch's successors; in the late 1920s, a priest actually served as foreman for the Mission chapter.

The Mission community stayed strong throughout the middle of the century, thanks largely to the active participation of the owner of the Frøslevgaard estate. Most of the members appear to have been agricultural workers, many with ties to Betinasminde or Frøslevgaard. Youth involvement through the KFUM/K persisted actively through the early 1970s.

Beginning in the 1960s, however, the Mission community in Frøslev began to lose members. The break with KFUM/K in 1975 cut off youth recruitment, and by the 1980s the community was in serious decline. Today Frøslev still has a small number of missionsfolk, and the mission house is used occasionally, but the days of the movement in the village appear numbered.

Tæbring

The awakening in Tæbring began in the winter of 1906, under the leadership of an American.[9] Karsten Kristensen, a native of the village, had previously emigrated to the United States to work in a missionary movement there; when he returned to visit his family in 1906, he held a series of revival meetings for the villagers. His sermons found an enthusiastic audience, who converted by the dozen. When he returned to America in the spring, missionaries from Nykøbing and Pastor Munch from nearby Frøslev kept the converts organized. They held children's services, Bible studies, revival meetings, and mission weeks, all despite angry opposition from the local priest. Lay members, some of them relatives of Kristensen,

---

9. The information about the Tæbring Inner Mission comes from Pedersen 1937 and Svane 1987. The latter is a brief history of the village's Mission community written by the daughter of one of its original members.

eventually took over the leadership of the group, and the Tæbring Mission became an active and self-sustaining community. The members built a mission house in 1917, on land donated by a farm owner who had converted. Children participated eagerly in youth activities, particularly Sunday school.

The Tæbring Mission community began to decline in the 1950s, as death began taking away the original members of the awakening. Sunday school classes became intermittent, and attendance at meetings dropped. By the end of the decade the flock had become too small to maintain the mission house; in 1965, the house was sold to a private buyer. A few people in the Tæbring area hold to Mission beliefs to this day, but nothing remains of the community of believers that flourished there in the first half of the century.

Inner Mission Theology

Basic Tenets

As mentioned above, the Church Association for the Inner Mission in Denmark adheres to a pietist interpretation of Lutheran Protestantism, formulated most explicitly in the writings of Vilhelm Beck (see pp. 100). The faith lays great stress on the gravity and inevitability of human sin, as well as the importance of cathartic personal conversion for salvation. Converted individuals must incorporate Christian teachings into their daily lives, preferably as part of exclusive pietist communities. Membership in the community of the holy involves a renunciation of worldliness; drinking, dancing, gambling, theater going, and fashionable dressing are generally forbidden, though the prohibitions have relaxed in recent years. Converts must also work to spread the faith, witnessing their experiences to nonbelievers and promoting moral lifestyles. All of their activities take place in cooperation with and under the guidance of the Danish Folkekirke.

The Inner Mission chapters on Mors follow the theological positions of the national Association, with no significant revision. A few of the Association's stands on social questions have provoked some disagreement; some members reject the Mission's opposition to female priests, and a few question its exclusion of homosexuals and its opposition to legal abortion. Overall, however, members around the island speak with striking unanimity on questions of religion, society, and moral values.

Conceptions of This World and the Next

The Inner Mission, in stark contrast to the Free Congregation, sets little store by earthly existence. It views life on earth as a temporary matter, whose importance pales next to that of the eternal life that follows it. While paintings and photographs of historical figures decorate the altar and meeting rooms of the Ansgarskirke, images of Jesus and the heavenly host line the walls of the Mors mission houses.

This mission sees this world as a trial of sorts, a period of hardship and want during which one has an opportunity to find either God or damnation. The hardships are partly physical, for life involves pain, sickness, hunger, and strife. But the worst pains are spiritual – separation from God, fear of death, and consciousness of the sin and inadequacy inherent in the human condition. The world does have its pleasures, which can distract people from the gravity of their situation. Those pleasures are hollow and short lived, though, ultimately unsatisfying, and always haunted by the spiritual emptiness that they try desperately to obscure. Such is the human condition, from which mankind could never escape of its own power.

God, however, out of pure good will, has given humanity a way out. He has sent His son, Jesus, to suffer horribly and die on the earth; in so doing, Jesus has accepted the punishment due a sinful mankind. Those who acknowledge this gift of mercy can have forgiveness, and thus be freed from the agony of sin and the fear of damnation. Moreover, for those who will accept it, the spirit of Jesus can enter the heart, establishing a permanent presence in the individual, and ending the person's separation from God. For such people, the painful nature of the physical world becomes irrelevant, its hardships as inconsequential and empty as its pleasures. The convert can cheerfully ignore the most grievous losses and misfortunes, which he recognizes as temporary effects of the mortal condition. The favorite anecdotes of the Mission often concern the calm with which devout members have endured painful illness or financial ruin. Their demeanor testifies both to the strength of their faith and to the power of their savior.

The existence of this gift divides the temporal world into two groups of people, those who have accepted Jesus and those who have not; missionsfolk refer to them as God's children and the children of the world (*Guds Børn og Verdens Børn*). Other distinctions among people, like those of nationality, class, or religious denomination, are illusory and irrelevant. Membership in the community of God's children involves certain duties, such as moral conduct and the spreading of the faith. It also inevitably involves the antagonism of the children of the world, who hate those who try to divert them from the only pleasures they understand.

Before long, though, such pleasures come to an end, as the death of the body sends the individual's soul to the plane of the afterlife. There each person is brought before God, to be judged for his conduct in the mortal world. He is, of course, found wanting, since by his nature he has committed acts abhorrent to God. He is therefore banished from God's sight, and given over to the eternal custody of Satan in hell. If the condemned is one of God's children, however, Jesus intercedes; He accepts the person's sins, forgives them, and allows the convert to enter heaven and the kingdom of God. Those who have known Jesus as mortals accept this intercession as the greatest of all possible kindnesses. For the children of the world, though, who have never called on Jesus before, it is too late to invoke His mercy now.

Mission members speak only vaguely about the actual conditions of the afterlife. They describe heaven simply as a place of bliss, a place where spiritual desires are filled and physical wants do not exist. Mortal distinctions of wealth and social group have no meaning, as all unite in the joyous celebration of their union with God. Its closest earthly counterpart is the undivided solidarity of the loving family, where a benevolent and affectionate father provides for the needs of all; indeed, when a Mission member dies, he is often said to have "departed for home."

Hell is the mortal world extended into the eternal, but without the presence or intervention of God. In hell, Satan has no more need of pleasures to distract men and women from Jesus; he can unleash his vicious cruelty upon them, with physical torments that dwarf the worst of earthly agonies. During the original Mission awakening on Mors, proselytizers constantly invoked the endless fire and torture endured by the damned. Even worse than such physical pain, however, is the spiritual void of hell. Its inhabitants must face eternal separation from the face of God, eternal banishment from the joys of his kingdom. And for all eternity, as they twist and scream in the cauldrons of Satan, they must remember that they spurned the gift of grace that the Inner Mission once begged them to accept.

Conceptions of God and Other Deities

The Inner Mission and the Free Congregation both derive their theology from a Lutheran base, which posits a tripartite God and a demonic Satan as its primary deities. They differ deeply, though, in their descriptions of these beings. While Grundtvigians tend to minimize the Trinity's divisions and almost ignore Satan, the Inner Mission assigns important roles to every member of the cosmology.

The notion of the Trinity divides the supreme deity into three parts, each of which has a separate form and personality. The senior is God the Father, creator of the universe and final judge of mankind. God rules the kingdom of heaven in the afterlife, and He takes a keen interest in earthly events; He does not, however, actively intervene in mortal affairs. He loves human beings, and wants them to join Him in His kingdom after death. Yet He holds them scrupulously accountable for their actions in life, and His judgments are severe. Jesus is God's son, whose life and gruesome death on earth have enabled Him to atone for the sins of mankind. He takes a more active role on earth than His Father; He provides strength, comfort, and occasional advice for those who believe in Him. He also sows doubt in the minds of overconfident unbelievers. He cannot, however, help anyone who does not freely and wholeheartedly invite Him to do so. The Holy Spirit, finally, is a formless agent of God and Jesus, which these deities use to communicate with the faithful. A convert to the Mission can feel the Holy Spirit's presence within him, giving him confidence in his faith and strength in his daily life. At times, It may even give him messages from Jesus. The conversations with Jesus that crop up occasionally in Mission memoirs take place through the agency of the Holy Spirit.

Satan is a fallen angel, a servant of God who turned away from him, and now seeks to turn away others as well. Satan intervenes actively in mortal affairs. He invents sinful pleasures such as gambling and dance to divert mankind from the contemplation of God. He inspires false prophets and leaders, who give false instructions for finding happiness and salvation. He also provides earthly misfortune, to dishearten human beings and to indulge his own sadism. He particularly hates God's children, who have thwarted his schemes, and he often targets them for particularly grievous suffering. In times of hardship, he may even appear to them in person, tempting them to leave God's fold. Satan has a far more active role in the physical world than the forces of God, who do not generally intervene on a physical level. He cannot, however, turn an unwilling soul away from God, any more than Jesus can force one to convert.

The Inner Mission deities intervene far more actively in the world than those of the Free Congregation, particularly Jesus and Satan. Indeed, missionsfolk often describe the earth as a battleground between these two beings, each of whom employs servants and tactics in an effort to win.

Satan seduces and torments the weaknesses of the flesh, while Jesus offers to fill the void of the spirit. In the long run, Jesus will win; His gifts of grace dwarf Satan's puny physical instruments, and His converts need fear no demonic assault. For now, though, the minds of men fall easily into Satan's snares, and his servants are many and wily. Only a pious few find their way past them to the narrow gates of the kingdom of God.

This competition gives a special importance to the moral conduct of God's children. If a convert transgresses the Mission's moral code, he has not merely committed a sin: he has deserted his post, failed in his duty, and given a small victory to the forces of Satan. Missionsfolk are Jesus's instruments on earth, and they must not disappoint Him. In the heyday of the Mission movement, parents often used this responsibility to discipline children. A child contemplating a sin, for example, was told that if he committed it, "Jesus would weep." Such statements place personal actions in an epic frame unknown to Grundtvigianism, one which confers a dramatic excitement on the mundane business of daily life. They also impose a burden, however, which many members find difficult; one must tread warily indeed, when the theft of a piece of candy can bring tears to the eyes of God.

Conceptions of the Individual and Society

Nowhere do the worldviews of the Inner Mission and the Free Congregation clash more than in their understanding of the individual's relationship to society. For the Mission, society and tradition are not the priceless resources that Grundtvigianism imagines. They are rather hindrances, distractions, ties to a world that is ultimately ephemeral and unimportant. Insofar as the individual pays attention to his society, immerses himself in its history, and attaches himself to its customs and rewards, he takes his mind away from matters of real and lasting value. Humans must keep their eyes on the world where they will spend eternity, not on the one where they live temporarily.

This outlook implies a very different construction of the individual from that of the Grundtvigians. The Mission individual has a divided nature, even a paradoxical one. On one hand, his nature is to sin; the pleasures of the world appeal to him, even as they offend and dismay God. His greed, lust, and ambition make him gamble, dance, and drink as naturally as the birds fly. He cannot change this part of him, much though he may try, and at his best he cannot pass a day without sinning. On the other hand, he has a spark of the divine in him; he hungers after spiritual fulfillment and feels lost when he does not find it. This side of him can bring him to Jesus, and it can give him the strength to overcome his darker self.

While ordinary society has its good sides and its good people, it cannot nourish the individual's spiritual side. It can provide for his animal nature, give him worldly pleasure and comfort, but it must always leave a spiritual void in his soul. By taking away his time and attention, it can even derail his effort to fill that void. Some of its members, like the false prophets of atheism, Islam, and Grundtvigianism, will actively misguide him, giving him a false belief that he need not seek Jesus. The temporal world can at best distract, and at worst mislead.

The Inner Mission awakening therefore sought to make society anew, to create a social world based on the contemplation of Jesus and the performance of His will. Vilhelm Beck argued that while such communities could not change their members' sinful natures, they could remove the most seductive distractions from the ways of God. Members could keep watch over one another, warning of the onset of sinful preoccupations, saving each other from Satan's ruses and temptations. The community could be a community of God, not the devil, of heaven, not of hell. The completeness of its isolation testified to the enormity of its difference from ordinary society.

The breakdown of Beck's communities in recent decades has undercut this approach to society. Mission members now live in non-Mission communities, with friends and co-workers who ignore or even ridicule Mission beliefs. Today's missionsfolk cannot shun secular society, and they no longer try to. Instead, they try to provide an example of their faith to the unconverted, to let the joy they find in Jesus influence others to join Him as well. This "mission by example" implies a greater interaction with and concern for the unconverted masses; many missionsfolk consider it a more effective and responsible approach than a retreat into their own communities. It does not provide the security of the old Mission villages, though, whose decline many members still mourn. They watch their children grow up in a sinful world, surrounded by the traps and temptations of a wily Satan, and fear for their souls.

Organization of the Inner Mission

Authority Structure

The Church Society for the Inner Mission in Denmark uses a very clearly defined authority structure, which extends from each individual local chapter to a national organizing body. Day-to-day responsibility for Mission activities rests almost entirely on the local level, while decisions about theology and social policy come almost entirely from the top. This system produces a remarkable uniformity in the message promoted by different chapters, even as it leaves the organization of activities free to reflect local circumstances.

At the top of the hierarchy stands the Inner Mission Head Council (*Indre Missions Hovedbestyrelse*), a committee of Folkekirke priests headed by a foreman. Members of the Council do not stand for election; when one retires, the remaining members elect a replacement from among the nation's most active Mission priests. The Council determines the Inner Mission's policies on theological, moral, and social issues. It also oversees a number of subcommittees, which oversee the implementation of those policies. One committee drafts and distributes teaching material for Sunday schools, for example, while another administers the society's finances. The Council also oversees the education and placement of missionaries, who spread the Word at revival meetings around the nation. A large corps of lay assistants helps manage these activities, but final authority lies with the priests in the Council.

Below the national organization, a regional Inner Mission Circle organizes affairs at the level of the *provsti* (see p. 55). The Circle is composed of the foremen of the local Mission chapters, and is headed by a Mission priest from the region. On Mors, Pastor Erik Bennetzen of Ljørslev chairs the committee. The regional circle has almost no real authority; policy decisions take place at a higher level, and organizational ones at a lower level. The regional circle essentially acts as a coordinating body, to allow contact between the different chapters and cooperation for such regional activities as mission weeks and the Mission camp at Bjørneborg.

At the local level, each pastorate with a Mission presence has its own Mission Association (*Missionsforening*). An elected council of five or six members usually oversees Mission activities in the pastorate, under the leadership of an elected foreman. Elections ordinarily take place at an annual meeting. The specifics of this structure vary between parishes, each of which has its own constitution. Subcommittees of volunteers administer the business of the chapter; they arrange meetings, maintain the mission house, collect and distribute funds, and work with other chapters on regional projects. They do so with almost no supervision from higher levels in the hierarchy, although missionaries and local Mission priests may advise them. Local chapters have no control over one another.

Strictly speaking, the Inner Mission has no actual members; its activities are open to all members of the Folkekirke, and the Association studiously avoids creating any formal subgroup unrecognized by the state church. In practical terms, however, membership in the organization is fairly clear. Virtually all people who participate regularly in Mission activities contribute money to it. In most chapters, only those who contribute money may vote at the annual meeting. Moreover, because missionsfolk have had so much friction with their neighbors in the past, only converts tend to have anything to do with the Mission. Through the elected council, this de facto membership has substantial control over the activities of the local council.

The structure of authority in the Inner Mission contains a striking discontinuity between the national and the local levels. The higher level consists entirely of priests, the lower entirely of laymen. The higher level controls the theory of the movement, the lower controls the practice. And interestingly, the higher level consists entirely of men, while the lower incorporates both sexes. The foremen for several chapters on Mors today are women, as have been many of its most prominent proselytizers. Social rules kept women out of leadership positions during the Mission's first years, but even then they often exerted a strong informal authority.[10] The national leadership, in contrast, has led a bitter fight to keep women out of the Danish priesthood. Despite these differences, the local chapters do not appear to resent the national leadership. During my time with them, missionsfolk on Mors invariably spoke in glowing terms of the priests in the Head Council. They read the Council members' writings with care and appreciation, and showed them to me with evident pride.

Financing

Each local chapter in the Inner Mission is financially independent, receiving no support from the national committee. The money for local activities comes entirely from the members, in one of three forms. First,

10. One example, related by a Frøslev farmer, involves the large, robust wife of a diminutive farmer. The wife clearly made the decisions in the family; even when walking along the road, she always went three steps before him. At Mission meetings, she made long, forceful speeches to advance her own opinions. At the end of her orations, though, she always turned to her husband and said, "Isn't that right, dear?" The farmer can never recall him doing anything but nodding his agreement. While formal authority lay with the husband, the wife clearly held the real power.

every member makes a regular contribution every three months. Members determine the amounts of these contributions themselves; a member of the local council collects and records the funds, using a list of pledges. Annual contributions average around 200 kroner, and they do not affect the amount of the contributors' church taxes. If an unusual financial problem arises, such as a large repair for the mission house, the chapter may also take up a special collection. Most members contribute to these collections, which sometimes ask for a standard sum from every adherent. Finally, some money comes in from gifts and bequests. All these revenue sources vary with the size and wealth of the local Mission community. For most of its history, for example, the Frøslev chapter could count on the support of at least one wealthy landowner; as a result, it escaped the financial crisis that hit many of the island's chapters during the 1950s.

The funds collected go to maintaining the mission house, paying and feeding visiting speakers, buying hymnals and instructional materials, making contributions to charitable causes, and contributing to the expenses of the national Association. Budgets are kept confidential, but a significant portion goes to the national Association. The decline in Mission membership has created severe financial problems for local chapters; some have had to sell their mission houses and close down, others teeter on the brink of doing the same.

Associated Activities

Unlike the Free Congregation, the Inner Mission movement on Mors has developed very few affiliated organizations. Social and cultural activities traditionally focused around the mission house and the conversation meetings; the Grundtvigians' historical societies, political associations, and athletic groups had no place in a community that deliberately disdained the pursuits of the temporal world. The main exception to this pattern has been youth work. The KFUM/K was affiliated with the Mission from the awakening's beginnings until 1975; every Mission chapter of any size had an affiliated chapter of KFUM/K, which was usually led by a member of the Mission community. KFUM/K offered Christian amusements and activities for children, who could attend Bible study groups, play games, and go on outings under the supervision of a Mission adult. For these children, the members of their KFUM/K classes became their entire peer social group; they would grow up, marry, and seek their livelihoods largely within the classes. The schism between KFUM/K and the Mission in 1975 ended this pattern, and in doing so crippled the Mission's recruitment of youth. In recent years, the national Mission Association has attempted to build a youth group of its own, called Youth of the Inner Mission (IMU). Some of the Mors chapters have begun the work of setting up IMU chapters, and they seem pleased with their progress; it seems unlikely, though, that IMU can ever duplicate the role once played by KFUM/K on Mors.

During the first part of this century, some Mission members established businesses oriented toward Mission values. The most prominent were cooperative dairies, which catered to Mission farmers and closed operations on Sundays. Several of these dairies operated on the island during the first half of the century. In addition, Mission members tried to influence local merchants to close on the sabbath. Except for the cooperative markets, where they could pack the governing board, missionsfolk had little success with these efforts even in their heyday. The cooperative dairies succumbed to consolidation in the 1960s, and little sign of Mission influence on the island's businesses remains today.

Two national political organizations have ties to the Inner Mission, and they draw some support from missionsfolk on Mors. In the 1970s, dissident elements of the Conservative and Left Parties seceded after the parties' endorsement of legalized abortion. They formed the Christian People's Party, which took several seats in the last national election. Many of the missionsfolk on Mors, perhaps more than half, support the party, although no formal tie with the Mors Mission exists. The other organization is the Christian Workers' Movement, an alternative to the standard labor unions established in the early 20th century. The Movement opposes strikes, and tries to settle labor disputes through arbitration with management. Its leader on Mors is a Mission adherent, as are many of its members. Its presence on the island is limited mainly to Nykøbing, however, and it has little membership in the countryside.

Inner Mission Membership

Since the Mission came to the Mors countryside in 1888, its roots have stood fast in the village community. The farmers, smallholders, and artisans who populated village society formed the core of the Mission awakening, and they still do so today. The Mission's decline has followed the erosion of those occupations. As villagers moved from agriculture and the trades to factory and office jobs, they passed out of both their old social system and the community of the holy. In Nykøbing, the mechanization of the Mission's factory strongholds has had similar effects. Roughly the same sorts of people belong to the Mission today as did a half century ago; but like the Mission itself, they have become harder and harder to find.

Chroniclers of the Mission have often painted it as a movement of the lower classes, of smallholders and fishermen and the landless country poor (cf. Lindhardt 1959, Kirk 1926, Lausten 1987). On Mors, though, the Mission attracted a broad cross-section of the rural community. Fishermen and smallholders did join in droves, but so did farm owners and artisans. Its original leaders included a saddlemaker in Øster Assels, a smallholder and his son in Karby, a farm owner's widow and a postman in Frøslev, a pair of seamstresses in Sundby, a coppersmith in Nykøbing, and the Harboøre fishermen in Ejerslev. Many of their occupations, such as postman and seamstress, involved regular travel within their parishes. The movement spread along kinship and economic lines; farmers invited their neighbors and relatives to revival meetings, while artisans and merchants preached the Word to their customers. Farm owners urged their employees to convert, sometimes holding prayer meetings for them on the farm. As the movement took hold, agricultural workers soon outnumbered fishermen and artisans. By the middle of the century, a large majority of members in the countryside either owned or worked on farms. A few of them came from the upper reaches of the rural community; the owners of the manor at Ullerup and the major estates in Frøslev were steadfast supporters of the Mission communities.

Geographically, the Mission worked best where the Free Congregation worked least. With the exception of Sundby and Galtrup-Tøving, where avid Mission priests waged a fierce battle with the Grundtvigians, the mission houses stand outside of Free Congregation territory. The dividing line runs along the old herred boundary, and many Morsingboer refer to the Mission as a phenomenon of the southern herred. Some of the Mission communities, such as those in Karby and Tøving, never grew very large. Those in the smaller villages, such as Ejerslev and Vester Assels, tended to decline in the 1950s. Today, the largest Mission communities exist in Sejerslev, Øster Assels, Frøslev, and Nykøbing.

The manor at Ullerup stands empty now, its moat choked with reeds, its lawns and gardens overgrown. Pollution and improved equipment have thinned the ranks of fishermen, while competition and loss of customer base have driven many rural merchants and artisans out of business. The ironworks in Nykøbing, once home to a thriving circle of God's children, has replaced most of its workers with machines. The communities of the Mission have declined accordingly, especially since the rift with KFUM/K crippled its youth work. Knud Grøn, a retired missionary in Ejerslev, estimates the total active membership at three hundred; in the 1930s, half that many might easily have attended a regular village revival meeting. Those who remain tend to be farmers and artisans, middle aged or older, mostly from Mission families. Few children participate actively, a source of concern for Mission leaders. During the Mission's heyday in Sejerslev, over 150 children attended the Sunday school each week; today, an average Sunday brings in three or four. The decline does not appear to stem from a loss of belief by the converted, but from the loss of the community from which the converts came.

The nature of Mission membership makes it difficult to document these changes precisely. As mentioned above, the Mission has no official members; as an ally of the Folkekirke, it avoids creating any formal party that could divide the Danish church. Unlike the Free Congregation, therefore, the Mors Mission chapters have no membership rolls or admission records that could help us trace its evolution. Written histories of the Mission tend to focus on its leading personalities, not on its size or structure (cf. Pedersen 1937, Balle-Petersen 1977). The best existing source for membership data lies in the contribution lists, the books where each community recorded contributions to the mission houses. Unfortunately, each chapter keeps separate lists, and none of the chapters on Mors has made a practice of storing old books. A detailed reconstruction of the Mission on Mors will require a major long-term research project.

We do, however, have data on the present composition of a representative chapter, that of the northern Mors village of Sejerslev. That chapter today has about sixty-five members in thirty households, each of which contribute money regularly to the upkeep of the mission house. The members fit squarely into the traditional economic structure of the Mors countryside. Over half the men are agricultural workers, and another third are artisans; the others include two postmen, a teacher, and a laborer. Most of the agricultural workers own their own farms. Two-thirds of the women are housewives, the rest either nursing aides or shop assistants. The chapter runs a small Sunday school and two classes of the new Inner Mission youth group. Its meetings alternate Bible study groups with sparsely attended revival meetings; it also holds a mission week every summer. (See Appendix for more detailed statistics.)

Leadership in the Inner Mission

Just as the national Mission Association puts its theology in the hands of a council of priests, the Mission on Mors vests ideological leadership in a corps of educated, salaried professionals. The island has one full-time missionary, located in Nykøbing, who has studied in a Mission seminary and receives a salary from the national Association. The missionary leads revival meetings in mission houses around the island, in addition to participating in conversation meetings and providing individual spiritual counseling. Priests can do the same, if they wish to; within their own parishes, Mission-oriented priests usually support and advise the work of the local missionsfolk. These leaders, especially the priests, have enormous prestige within the movement. Unlike the members of the Free Congregation, missionsfolk neither can nor wish to influence the theological positions of their leaders. They listen attentively to their leaders' sermons and value their counsel greatly. The teachings of the missionary and priests set the ideological tone for most activities of the local Mission communities.

Organizational leadership, on the other hand, comes almost entirely from the local lay community. Private missionsfolk arrange maintenance of the mission house, organize meetings, collect and administer funds, and proselytize among their neighbors. The foreman for the local mission takes on much of the workload, and he also speaks in some capacity at most meetings. Members elect the foreman on the basis of his or her strength of faith, zeal for the office, and talent for organization. Social rank and sex do not bar applicants; local leaders on Mors have included men and women from the smallholder, artisan, and farm owner classes. The most successful leaders, though, tend to have fairly high social standing. A large farm owner, for example, has a prestige that can attract missionsfolk to meetings and silence the opposition of local nonbelievers. In the first decades of the awakening, schoolteachers often provided the most forceful leadership. Their seminary educations and roles in religious instruction gave them some of the prestige of religious professionals, while their close involvement with the local community gave them important organizational resources. Like their clerical counterparts, local leaders enjoy high regard among their fellow missionsfolk; I never heard a Mission member express dislike for or disagreement with a local foreman. Unlike the priests, though, lay leaders are subject to removal by their constituents.

Leadership in the formal structure of the Mission Society rests with a very few individuals. In a broader sense, though, every convert to the

Mission has a responsibility to lead. Each must carry forth the gift of grace that he has received from Jesus, and light the path of moral and spiritual righteousness for the great mass of men who walk in darkness. Each must bear witness of his faith to his neighbors, must tell them of the importance of repentance, must do anything necessary to plant in them the seed of self-doubt that opens the door to conversion. Even the personal conduct of the faithful involves a leadership of sorts, since God's Children exemplify Christian behavior to the Children of the World. In this sense, every member of the Mission practices a leadership that no Free Congregation member would dare attempt: the guiding of his neighbor's soul to the one true understanding of God.

Ritual in the Inner Mission

The Inner Mission does not hold sacraments of its own. As a loyal adjunct to the Folkekirke, one that is governed by a council of priests, the Mission avoids any competition or overlap with church rituals. Even the family festivals associated with church sacraments differ little from those of non-Mission families; they do not include dancing or alcohol, and they might include a few extra hymns, but they use the same structure and most of the same activities. The one important ritual that clearly distinguishes them as a community takes place outside the church entirely, and has no family party or life cycle change associated with it: the mission revival meeting *(missionsmøde)*.

Most mission houses hold revival meetings either every other week or every month. The meetings take place in the evening, after dinner time, in the main hall of the local mission house. Members arrive as families, in groups of two or three; most are usually middle-aged or older, and only a few bring small children. They sit at tables set for coffee, which stand in rows down the length of the rectangular hall. When all of the members have arrived, the foreman for the local Mission Society takes his place at a podium at one end of the room. He leads the audience in one or two hymns, then introduces the evening's guest speaker. The speaker may be a missionary, a visiting priest, or a religious educator, but is not normally a member of the local Mission Society. After the introduction, the speaker takes over the podium and launches into a ringing revival sermon. He usually focuses on a particular text from the scriptures; he elaborates on the meaning of the text, and draws from it a message about the importance and joyousness of conversion. The audience listens attentively, in complete silence. At the end of the sermon, which lasts about forty-five minutes, the foreman resumes the podium and leads another hymn. A committee of women from the community then brings out coffee and pastries, and the audience spends the next half hour eating and conversing with their neighbors at the table. The speaker may follow with a shorter sermon, summarizing his earlier points and adding some inspiring message. Finally, the foreman stands to lead another hymn or two, and the assembled flock departs.

The calm tone of these meetings, in which the speaker preaches quite literally to the converted, differs radically from meetings during the awakening. Today, outsides almost never attend Mission meetings, which function more as community gatherings than as instruments for conversion. In the movement's early years, local leaders and missionaries would canvass their villages, inviting neighbors and relatives to attend the meetings. They avoided coffee and conversation, focusing the meetings on the sermons. These sermons affected their listeners profoundly; a good meeting would attract a hundred or more listeners and produce several converts, who might tearfully confess their sins afterward to the priest in attendance. Meetings during the awakening sent shocks through village communities, sometimes producing an active body of missionsfolk in the course of a few weeks. Missionsfolk held them as often as possible, and local Grundtvigians and nonbelievers often fought to keep them from occurring.

The written record of the Mission on Mors provides no detailed description of such a meeting. We can get a sense of their tone, however, from Hans Kirk's account of a Mission meeting in *The Fishermen*. Set in the Limfjord town of Gjøl, the novel describes the establishment of a Mission community by a group of fishermen from Harboøre. For their first revival meeting, the fishermen invite the priest from Harboøre to speak in the Gjøl church. Despite his reputation for powerful rhetoric, the priest begins the service quietly:

> When the hymns were over, it became quiet in the church. The light in the chandelier cast flickering shadows on the white limed walls, and the tall arches over the choir lay in darkness. The priest had knelt before the altar during the psalm, now he stood up in the pulpit, brimming with power and dangerous in the black robe. One could almost hear people gasp in the great room. For a moment he stared without moving down into the church. His eyes passed from one to another. It strained the atmosphere in a strange way. People bowed their heads under his keen gaze. The stillness lasted and lasted, no one dared move, it felt as though a thunderclap must now come that would tear down everything.

But when he finally began to speak, it was with a rather gentle, almost mild voice. It hit the strained minds in an even more violent manner. His words reached in to the farthest corners, and people felt painfully insecure. He spoke of peace in Jesus. [The fishermen] sat with open, ecstatic eyes and followed along. Yes, this was truth, such was mercy, an eternal peace, a brotherhood between God and men ...

Soon, however, the tone of the sermon changes:

He spoke now about humanity's betrayal and evil. It was a message that hit home. The women sat with downcast eyes and felt a terror when he spoke of immorality. The priest knew all about every secret mischief, every hidden and improper longing in the depths of the soul. He placed reputable people in front of a mirror, where they saw themselves in hideously distorted form, and the devil stood behind them and laughed. In a thundering voice, the priest raged against drink, dance, card playing, ungodliness, lechery, and – he raised his clenched fist as if to break the pulpit to splinters, but in stead of a bang, he whispered: Hell. The word gave a sense of deep dread. A woman gave a choked whine. And now he set to with a voice that rang and echoed in the beams. He whipped people with rods of brimstone and fire. His raging eloquence struck them like an axe in the head. He bored with unerring accuracy just where it would hurt. He drove them together with a common feeling, like sheep in a storm. Women mumbled quietly or wept. Men sat with frozen expressions or rocked uneasily back and forth. He had them in his power. He raged like a magician over them, until they no longer had will or sense, and had completely forgotten who they were. The [missionsfolk] were beside themselves with excitement ... Each of them felt the terror and lifting as a movement in their souls. Never had the priest spoken as tonight. Never had the spirit of the faithful thundered with such power from his lips. With a sweeping gesture, which stirred the air, the priest finally stopped. One could hear the sobbing of the women and the men's dry breathing. Deep sighs rose from hard-pressed hearts. The white room with the flickering candles swam in a fog. Shake and dispirited, yet with a certain earnest joy in their minds, the people waited for what would come.

Finally, the priest brings forth the promise of redemption:

... now the priest turned peaceful and gentle in tone, and spoke of mercy and peace in Jesus. Reform yourselves and come to Jesus! He spoke with plain, almost artless words and called on every one of the listeners as an equal and brother. After the common terror came a feeling of common happiness and peace.

When the closing hymn rang through the church, there was a buoyancy in the sound. The familiar words had become new, and taken on a special meaning. (Kirk 1978 [1928]: 61-63)

The Inner Mission in the Lives of Its Members

A century has passed since Jens Bertelsen died, and the last ripples of the Mission awakening have long since faded away. Mission houses today serve coffee, not brimstone, and few strangers ever come to drink it. For its remaining members, the Mission is a remnant of a community, not an awakening; it preserves a circle of friends and fellow believers from decades ago, when God's children thrived in the countryside. Missionsfolk still believe in the doctrines of conversion and salvation, which they proclaim in the religious images and mottoes that hang on the walls of their homes. They teach their children pietist morals, and bring them to church and Sunday school. The Mission no longer defines their social world, though, or limits their daily activities. It is not a community, but a circle of believers, one which offers a gateway to future salvation and a reminder of a world gone by. As an example, let us look at its place in the life of a member.

Peder Svenningsen, 65, was born in Sejerslev, in a small thatched farmhouse just north of the village center. His parents had grown up during the first Mission awakening in the parish, and they participated actively in the life of the Mission community. Peder attended KFUM and Sunday school classes as a boy, like his brother and all of his friends; on a given Sunday, up to 170 children might pack the meeting hall of the mission house. Peder's father died of pneumonia when Peder was 10, and series of assistants moved in to do the heavy work of the farm. After graduating from the Folkeskole at age 14, Peder worked as a farmhand at a number of farms around the island, supplementing this practical education with a winter at an agricultural institute on Fyn. A few years later he moved back home and took over the operation of the farm. He also began working as a counselor at the Sejerslev KFUM/K, leading classes and outings. While on a summer trip to the Mission camp at Bjørneborg, he met a Mission girl from Øster Assels named Hanne Vestergaard; the pair fell in love, and when Peder was 24, they decided to become betrothed. Before they could announce the betrothal, though, Peder's mother died, so they married immediately and moved into the farmhouse. They had two children, both of whom are now grown and married; one lives in Ålborg, the other on a farm on Mors. They also expanded the farm, which now has several dozen pigs, twenty cows, horses, chickens, and about 38 tdr. of grain. Peder has run the Sunday school since his mid-20s, and has been the foreman for the Sejerslev Mission Society for the past ten years. He lives in the house where he was born, and can still see the low roof of the mission house from his bedroom window.

The Mission still means a lot to Peder; most of his old friends belong to it, and the biweekly meetings at the mission house recreate part of the community in which he grew up. He believes firmly in the forgiveness of his sins through Jesus Christ, who will one day welcome him into the eternal kingdom of the holy. Peder sees that forgiveness as a priceless gift, a source of happiness and comfort in his daily life, and he hopes that all men will find their way to accepting it. He does not, though, try to impose it on his neighbors through proselytizing. One cannot force a man to believe something, he says, and one must respect the rights of one's neighbors to their own views. Nor does Peder follow the ascetic lifestyle of early Mission communities; while he would not think of drinking or dancing, and his tastes are not extravagant, his clothing and furnishings look just like those of his non-Mission neighbors. His children have blended even more with the non-Mission world; they believe in most Mission doctrines, but they keep very little contact with their own local mission houses. Peder still enjoys teaching Sunday school, even if his classes seldom exceed five children, and he looks forward to meetings and Bible studies at the mission house. But they are an activity, not a world; while Mission work may keep him in touch with the members of his old KFUM classes, it cannot recreate the community in which they all once lived.

Future Prospects for the Inner Mission

Missionsfolk on Mors are frank about the future of the Mission; as they watch their local circles grow smaller every year, they express little hope that it will survive the next quarter century. The demographics of the movement support their pessimism. The Mission on Mors has few young members, and the young people who participate tend to have looser ties to the movement than their elders. The past decades have seen mission houses close and Mission communities disappear, with only a few of the largest local Societies remaining viable. Moreover, the conditions that undercut the movement show no signs of changing. The smaller villages continue to lose businesses and population, while improving agricultural machinery makes farming less and less labor intensive. The small rural communities that provided the best soil for the Mission will probably never return.

The organizational structure of the Inner Mission makes a recovery particularly difficult. As local circles grow smaller, the costs of keeping up a mission house become increasingly burdensome; after a certain point, the mission houses must be sold, and the local chapters lose their centers. One solution would be to develop regional circles, rather than local ones, as the Grundtvigians did. While the local Grundtvigian population in most northern Mors parishes could never support even a small free church, together they can easily maintain the Ansgarskirke. The island's missionsfolk, likewise, have enough members to support a strong Mission chapter on a regional basis. Their structural association with the Folkekirke, however, makes such collaboration very difficult. Any regional association would cross parish and pastorate lines, potentially undermining the authority of local Folkekirke priests – an authority that the Mission hierarchy has worked diligently to safeguard. Allegiance to the Folkekirke makes a regional solution to the Mission's problems difficult to carry through.

We should be careful, however, not to write premature obituaries for the Inner Mission. Its decline in recent years has stemmed not so much from its theology as from its organization; the ideas that lie behind it build on a tradition of Danish pietism that has endured since the late 17th century, and that still has powerful supporters today. The doctrines of sin and redemption, of mercy and salvation, can still terrify and exhilarate the souls of men. Through reorganization and youth work, the Inner Mission could well solve the problems that have plagued it since the 1950s. It might even create another awakening. As missionsfolk like to say on Mors, an awakening is like the wind, sent by God according to His own schedule, capable of bursting across the fields of the island at any moment.

7. The Apostolic Church

ᘓ   ᘓ   ᘓ

Et liv i stadig sejr,
i stadig tak og pris,
det er din ret på jorden,
på vej til Paradis;
for sejren er jo vundet
på korsets smalle sti
ej synd i dig skal råde
i Jesus er du fri!

Om du den kunst vil lære
at modstå fjendens list,
da luk vidt op dit hjerte
for helten – Jesus Krist!
Når ånden, brudt og bøjet
bli'r grebet af hans magt,
du altid sejr vil vinde,
for værket er fuldbragt!

A life in constant triumph,
in constant thanks and praise,
this is your right on earth,
on the way to Paradise;
for the victory has been won
on the cross's narrow roads,
sin shall not rule in you
for in Jesus you are free!

If you wish to learn the art
of resisting the Enemy's charge,
then open wide your heart
for the hero – Jesus Christ!
When the spirit, bowed and broken
is seized with His might,
you will always win the battle,
for the work has been completed!

— Evangelie Sangbog

Gunnar followed nervously through the dark hallway of the parsonage, the girl's form barely visible in front of him. A floorboard creaked beneath his feet, and he cringed as he thought of the priest drinking coffee downstairs; he had never been here at night before, and he wondered whether the entire household could trace his progress past the servants' rooms. He hadn't imagined such a scene yesterday, when the priest had

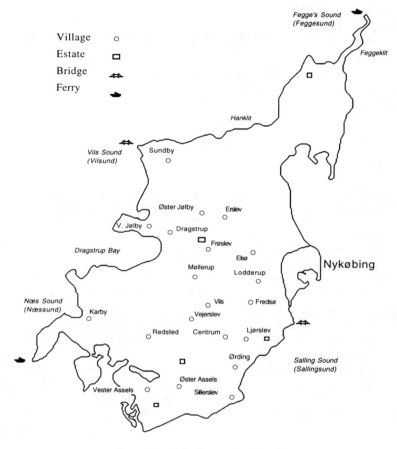

Map 8: Mors Island Apostolic Church
Important Sites

invited him to the party. The priest had called it a youth gathering, a way for the young workers dispersed around the parish's farms to meet one another. A promising young farmhand like Gunnar, he had said with a smile, surely would want to meet some nice girls. Though he usually avoided secular gatherings, Gunnar had accepted. What could happen, after all, in the pastor's own house? But the priest had been conspicuously absent for much of the evening, leaving the youths to flirtatious and increasingly suggestive party games. Some took place in the dark, with boys sitting on girls' laps or dancing with a string of partners. And now, just after midnight, Gunnar found himself tiptoeing through the darkness, his face flushed, his heart pounding, his eyes and mind fixed on the dim figure of a serving maid he had met only a few hours ago. He saw her stop at a door, turn a handle and step inside; as he reached the threshold, he saw her standing by her narrow bed, holding her hand out toward him. He nearly went in.

Then suddenly a booming voice froze him in place. It was not the priest, or the deacon, or the girl's angry father standing in the hallway. It came from within, and Gunnar knew without thinking that it was the voice of God. "Don't go inside, Gunnar!" it commanded, driving all other thoughts from his mind. And for an instant Gunnar saw before him not a cramped bedroom but the fiery chasm of hell, not a seductive young woman but grinning Satan himself, hungrily awaiting the surrender of another Christian soul. Gunnar knew then, as certainly as he had ever known anything, that to step through that doorway was to step into hell; once across the threshold, his soul would be lost. Without a word, he pulled himself back and turned around. He marched grimly back down the hallway, oblivious to the creaking floor, clattered down the steps, and strode out the door without saying good-bye. He leaped on his bicycle and rode home, through the blinding fog of the southern Mors winter. When he arrived at the farm, he threw down the bicycle and fell to his knees, his eyes closed, whispering fervent thanks to God for his salvation.[1]

God's intervention in Gunnar's life was dramatic, but hardly surprising. A few months earlier, in the summer of 1939, he had joined a Pentecostal movement on Mors called the Apostolic Church. This church

---

1. This story was told to me by a member of the Apostolic Church in Nykøbing, in essentially the form presented here. He recounted it as one of the most important moments of his life. It bears a striking resemblance to a passage in Kirk's *The Fishermen*, in which a Mission adherent tells about his conversion (1978). *The Fishermen* is an extremely well-known book in Denmark, and I assume that my informant had read it; his anecdote may well have been influenced by it.

preached an energetic and extroverted Christianity, in which each member had a personal connection to God through the Holy Spirit. Only a few Morsingboer had joined the church since its founding in 1935, but their dramatic rituals and tireless proselytizing had given them a fame out of proportion to their numbers. The church's size and importance on Mors would never approach that of the Folkekirke, the Inner Mission, or the Free Congregation; still, faithful members like Gunnar would make it one of the most active and cohesive religious communities in the history of the island.

The Apostolic Church on Mors derived from a nationwide Pentecostal expansion in the early 20th century. The movement began in Copenhagen, where a Pentecostal evangelist from Norway attracted a small circle of followers in 1907. His converts included a well-known actress, Anna Larsen, who subsequently left the stage to proselytize for her new faith. Using her celebrity as a draw for their meetings, Larsen and her husband, Sigurd Bjørner, soon built the circle into a congregation of several hundred. It built its own church in Copenhagen in 1922. The group originally called itself "The Evangelic Congregation" *(Evangeliemenigheden),* and had no formal ties to any larger organization. In 1923, however, while attending a conference in Wales, Bjørner converted to a particularly structured Pentecostalism called the Apostolic Church. The Church had emerged from a Welsh Pentecostal awakening in the previous decade, and it stressed the organization of the earthly congregation according to the example of the apostles. Bjørner's conversion created a schism in the Evangelic Congregation, but the majority joined him in the new faith. The church changed its name to "The Apostolic Church in Denmark" *(Apostolsk Kirke i Danmark),* and it began a vigorous campaign to evangelize the nation.

By 1930, the Church had established outpost congregations in the major cities of Sjælland, Fyn, and Jutland. Most of its converts came from the ranks of the Inner Mission; the Church attracted them with dramatic tent meetings, featuring fiery sermons and speaking in tongues. The city congregations divided the countryside into districts, with each city responsible for evangelizing its own region. The island of Mors lay within the territory of the Århus congregation. At the end of July 1935, therefore, three traveling evangelists from Århus conducted a series of meetings on Mors, first in the Temperance Hotel in Nykøbing, and then in the fields of an Inner Mission farm owner in Sundby.

Neither written sources nor living memory retains any detailed record of those meetings. Indeed, the Apostolic Church on Mors has extremely few historical records of any kind. Members say that their task is to make history, not write history, and they have discarded almost all the materials that could have helped reconstruct the development of the congregation. All we know for certain is that the meetings produced eight converts, who underwent baptism in the Limfjord near Sundby, and that unsympathetic neighbors heckled and ridiculed the participants. We also know that within a year the movement had made twenty-one converts on the island, who together founded an Apostolic Church congregation in Nykøbing. The members came from around the island, with a large contingent from Sundby; its elders, or local leaders, were two farm owners from Sundby and Sillerslev. For the first few years, itinerant preachers from Århus took turns leading Sunday services in a rented hall in Nykøbing. In addition, the elders held prayer meetings at the homes of the various members. In 1942, however, the national Apostolic Church assigned a full-time minister to Nykøbing, who took over leadership of the congregation.

The new church threw itself immediately into aggressive evangelism. At "outposts" around the island, members held tent meetings regularly to attract converts. They conducted dramatic and controversial full-immersion baptisms in the Limfjord, always surrounded by throngs of curious onlookers. They testified in homes and meetings to miraculous healings and ecstatic glossolalia. They even traveled off the island, setting up satellite congregations in Thisted and Skive. The war slowed them down only slightly, since the Germans took little notice of their activities; when the Germans withdrew, the Church experienced the greatest wave of success in its history. Between 1949 and 1952, twenty-eight young Morsingboer underwent baptism into the Apostolic Church. Their enthusiasm gave the Church a sense of progress, as well as an important financial boost; by 1952, it was able to buy its own building in Nykøbing to hold services.

This success aroused fierce opposition from the nonmembers, as the Pentecostal movement had all over Denmark. Just as anti-Grundtvigians had stabbed Grundtvigians with hatpins in the 1840s, and Grundtvigians had sabotaged Mission meetings in the 1890s, both missionsfolk and Grundtvigians fought the incursion of the Apostolic Church in the 1940s and 1950s. Priests and missionaries inveighed against it in churches and mission houses. Villagers heckled speakers at the Apostolic tent meetings and ridiculed participants in the baptisms. In some cases, they went so far as to vandalize the property of the evangelists. One Apostolic missionary recalls being called in the middle of the night by the voice of God, who ordered him to go out and check his tent. He arrived there just in time to prevent its collapse; local mischief-makers had pulled up all but a few of the tent stakes. Evangelists' reminiscences describe a constant battle in its first decades against the abuse and ill-will of the Church's neighbors.

This battle eventually came to a sort of draw, as both sides moderated their tones in the late 1960s. Proselytizers never gave up their faith or renounced their quest to evangelize the island. On the other hand, the meetings never gained large numbers of converts, and by the 1960s the Church had begun to scale down its outpost work. The congregation and its proselytizing centered increasingly around the headquarters in Nykøbing; the congregation never grew much beyond sixty members, nor fell much below thirty-five. Leaders cultivated better relations with the other religious groups on the island, even holding meetings together and cooperating in charitable activities. The stream of converts slowed to a trickle, with less aggressive proselytizing producing just enough converts to keep the membership steady.

In recent years, the active leadership of Søren Viftrup has rekindled some of the energy of the Church's early years. Members have launched several new projects, which they hope will spark a new awakening on the island. In 1980, the church established a bookstore and café on the ground floor of its Nykøbing headquarters. The café offers free coffee to visitors, who also receive gentle proselytizing from the staff. The café gained an added attraction in 1988, when a farm owner in Vester Jølby donated religious statuary for a "Bible garden" in the back yard. The homemade figurines depict a series of charming scenes from the Old and New Testaments, amidst a garden of carefully tended flowers and shrubs. The church advertises the café and garden heavily, and they bring in a good number of visitors during the tourist season. Except for Church affiliates, however, few native Morsingboer ever venture inside.

More recently, the Church has built a boutique and craft workshop in Karby, where it plans to attract prospective members through craft classes and Bible meetings. The Church has also purchased a property in northern Thy for use as a summer camp and meeting center. Both projects have started successfully, and working on them has given the members a sense of common purpose and achievement. Their ultimate effectiveness in spreading the faith, however, remains to be proven.

On the whole, the Church today appears to be thriving. It has forty-six members, a dozen more than it had a decade ago; another thirty or so nonmembers occasionally attend its services. The members are active and enthusiastic, attending services faithfully and providing ample financial support. The Church has an established, capable leader, and it maintains friendly relations with most of the other religious groups on the island. It also keeps close contact with the national Apostolic Church and other Scandinavian Pentecostal groups. It remains peripheral to most of Mors society, a far cry from the electrifying religious force that its founders envisioned. Yet within its limited domain, the Apostolic Church constitutes a vital, powerful, and enduring religious community.

Apostolic Church Theology

Basic Tenets

The Apostolic Church's theology flows from the same vein of pietism that inspired Grundtvig and Vilhelm Beck, and most of its doctrines mirror those of the Inner Mission. Members believe in the Trinity, the necessity of personal conversion, the salvation of the faithful, the damnation of the unbelieving, and the importance of living according to biblical moral principles. But they also hold two beliefs that clash violently with both Mission and Grundtvigian doctrine: the necessity of baptism after conversion, and the special powers of believers.

Baptism, according to Apostolic teachings, marks the transition from ignorance and evil to faith in Christ. It formalizes membership among the holy, and serves notice to the forces of Satan that the initiate is beyond their reach. Since this transition is based on faith, only those who have consciously converted may undergo it. The child baptism of the Danish Lutherans, therefore, has no validity; it tries to confer redemption on infants who cannot possibly have undergone conversion. Moreover, the light sprinkling of water in Folkekirke baptisms bears little resemblance to the full-body immersions that John the Baptist conducted in the New Testament. The Apostolic Church recognizes only baptisms of converted adults, and it requires complete submersion of the initiate in the water. This teaching provides the Church with one of its most colorful rituals, but it has also inspired the bitter resentment of many Folkekirke members.

Even more controversial are the gifts that the Church says accompany conversion. Those who join Christ's flock gain special powers, which help them evangelize the unbelieving and give comfort to their congregations. They can speak in tongues, for example, when the Holy Spirit fills them; some of them can prophesy the future, perform miracles, exorcise demons, or heal the sick.[2] The Church puts great emphasis on these powers, especially prophecy and speaking in tongues, which occur in virtually every Sunday service. Like adult baptism, however, they provide a very visible focus for opposition to and ridicule of the faith.[3]

Members tend to be extremely well versed in this theology, able to explain its bases and provide scriptural documentation for it on the spur of the moment. They also adhere to it quite rigidly; whereas Grundtvigians have significant disagreements over theological matters, and even missionsfolk tend to interpret their doctrines in varying ways, members of the Apostolic Church present a remarkably uniform vision of their faith. Their detailed and regimented knowledge makes them impressive proselytizers, able to explain and justify their positions to anyone who challenges them. At the same time, their rigidity often irritates members of more mainstream denominations.

Conceptions of This World and the Next

Like the Inner Mission, the Apostolic Church sees this world as a battleground, on which the forces of God and Satan contend for the souls of mankind. The world is inconsequential in itself, its ephemeral sorrows and pleasures meaningless in comparison with the everlasting world to follow. Yet it offers people their only chance to receive Jesus's blessings and gain entry into the kingdom of God. Accordingly, the Church places scant weight on the trappings and traditions of earthly society; the only social distinction that really matters is that between believer and nonbeliever, between the future resident of heaven and the future inmate of hell. The community of the holy must have certain structures to maintain itself, of course, and members must live according to a certain moral code. But such arrangements are merely means, not ends, and matter only insofar as they promote the increase and steadfast belief of the congregation of the faithful.

2. This doctrine is based partly on Paul's discussion of such powers in his letters to the Corinthians; see 1 Corinthians 12:8-11, 14:26, also Mortensen et al. (1974: 134).
3. I use the phrase "adult baptism" here, since it corresponds to *voksendåb*, the term that most Danes use to describe the practice. It should be noted, though, that many Apostolic Church members object to this term, preferring "baptism of the faith" *(troens dåb)*; the issue, they say, is not one of adulthood, but of ability to understand the concepts of sin and redemption. A particularly bright seven-year-old might well be allowed to undergo the ritual.

Apostolic conceptions of the afterlife also resemble those of the Inner Mission. The Church posits a divine judgment of the individual after death, and the subsequent passage of the converted into heaven and the unconverted into hell. Its members tend to describe those realms in more detail than missionsfolk; whereas Mission adherents seldom say anything concrete about the conditions of the afterlife, Apostolic churchgoers often cite biblical clues about the nature of existence there. Certain passages indicate that punishment in hell varies in severity, for example, while others indicate that heaven will involve a corporeal existence and city-like architecture. In addition, the Church makes less of a connection between the earthly and heavenly communities. Both Grundtvigians and missionsfolk tend to see the kingdom of God as an extension of the community of the godly on earth, a transposition of the congregation into the eternal. The Apostolic Church, in contrast, emphasizes the individuality of salvation and judgment. Though the earthly congregation can support one's faith in this life, one always enters God's judgment hall alone; no one can predict whether another person will be saved, or who will end up in the kingdom of God. Indeed, some other faiths may also lead to salvation. The Church concerns itself not with its perpetuation as a group, but with the individual fate of each of its members.

Indeed, the Apostolic Church places relatively little emphasis on the corporate community of believers in this world. It has no doctrine resembling the Separation of the Inner Mission, or even the folk community of the Grundtvigians. Members on Mors live scattered around the island, working and socializing freely with members of other faiths. They often attend services and functions with other pietistic groups in the area, such as the Pentecostal Church and the Salvation Army. Though members spend a tremendous amount of time on church activities, the religious community does not circumscribe their world as the Mission did in its heyday.

The Apostolic Church also envisions a greater interpenetration of the earthly and heavenly worlds than its rivals. Even more than the Mission, the Church gives Satan an active role in this world. The devil routinely brings misfortune, illness, and even spirit possession to the unconverted; indeed, nearly all worldly ills can be traced to his intervention. Likewise, the good and happy things in life stem directly from the agency of God. Members of the Church enjoy a certain protection from misfortune, and they can marshall the power of the Holy Spirit to battle the evils that Satan creates. They can drive out demons, illness, and even bad luck from those whom Satan has afflicted. This tactic differs radically from that of the Inner Mission God; whereas missionsfolk achieve a consciousness that makes worldly pain irrelevant, the Apostolics receive the power to combat that pain directly.

This difference reflects a basic contrast in the Mission and Apostolic views of this world. Both religions follow the pietistic tradition of denigrating earthly existence, whose pleasures and pains pale in importance before the prospect of eternal life. Yet the Apostolic Church still values the enjoyment of this life. Its literature proclaims the importance of a joyous existence, and stresses the effectiveness of its faith in combating the evils that prevent a comfortable life. The Holy Spirit brings its followers not only future salvation, but also present health, wealth, and wisdom. In their proselytizing, members frequently cite their faith's ability to bring happiness in this world as proof of its validity. While this world is ephemeral and illusory, it is important both to man and to God.

Conceptions of God and Other Deities

The Apostolic cosmology uses the same major deities as the Inner Mission, a beneficent tripartite God and a malevolent Satan. The deities' personalities also follow the Mission pattern. God the Father sits in judgment in heaven; Jesus tends His flock on earth; the Holy Spirit communicates with the faithful; and Satan uses misfortune and guile to lead people astray. The Church differs sharply from the Mission, though, in its view of God's relationship to the holy. Whereas the Mission God appeals almost entirely to the spirit, leaving earthly pains and pleasures to Satan, the Apostolic God takes an active interest in His followers' worldly well-being. Through the agency of the Holy Spirit, He intervenes directly and dramatically in the temporal lives of His people. Every convert, moreover, becomes a vessel for the Holy Spirit, imbued with a power that can defy physical laws and vanquish the forces of darkness. The Apostolic deities, both good and evil, maintain a visible, tangible presence in the lives of human beings.

This presence shows itself most commonly through speaking in tongues *(tungetale)*. At rituals and during prayer, church members regularly undergo glossolalia, usually during specific parts of the services. They find themselves uttering words they cannot understand, words that flow out effortlessly, as though generated by an independent force. That force, they say, is the Holy Spirit, speaking through them in a language intelligible only to God. Such speech sometimes serves simply to praise God, while other times it may suggest prophecies or truths to

those who hear it. In all cases, it exhilarates those who experience it.
Speaking in tongues places the speaker in direct contact with God; the
Holy Spirit seizes direct control of the believer's body, using it to proclaim the faith for Its own purposes. The Lutheran denominations never
imagine such a physical union with the Almighty, one that implies an
intimate connection between the deities and the physical world.

The deities also intervene in the everyday activities of life, guiding the
faithful to happiness and success. God may warn an Apostolic member
against committing a sin, as He did for Gunnar; He may advise a member to begin a project that will bring him happiness, or give up an enterprise that will not. He may even grant worldly wishes. One member on
Mors recalled winning the soccer lottery after entreating God to help
him pick the right teams. Often this divine assistance operates to help a
religious project; in the latter case, the lottery winner donated some of
the proceeds to the Church's missionary work.[4] God's concern for the
well-being of His congregation, however, clearly extends beyond the
desire to build a stronger Church. He wants His people to be comfortable and happy, and He will deploy His divine powers toward that end.

Faith healing furnishes the most vivid symbol of this concern. Neither members nor leaders of the Apostolic Church claim to have personal medical powers. But just as the Holy Spirit sometimes inspires
them to speak in tongues, It can give them the power to relieve bodily illnesses by the laying on of hands. Such healings do not happen often on
Mors; to the best of my knowledge, none occurred during my time on
the island. Members of the Church firmly believe in their veracity,
though, citing them as proof of the power of the Holy Spirit. Healings
provide a tangible symbol of Apostolic belief, an indisputable demon-
stration that the Holy Spirit is not simply a figment of the members'
imaginations. At the same time, they clearly depict God's benevolence.
While Satan's work on the earth brings suffering and misery, the intervention of the Apostolic God brings only relief and joy.

Conceptions of the Individual and Society

Like most of its theology, the Apostolic Church's view of the individually
generally agrees with that of the Inner Mission. It gives human beings a
divided nature, partly sinful and worldly, partly longing for the divine.

---

4. Members of the church see no contradiction between their edicts against card gambling and their avid participation in the soccer pools.

Ordinary society appeals mostly to the sinful side; it draws people into traps set by Satan, appealing to their natural avarice, ambition, and lust to separate them from God's Word. The Church congregation provides an alternate social world, which can support rather than degrade its members' faith. This view of the secular and holy communities runs through most pietistic denominations, and the denunciations of worldly evils at an Apostolic service could pass equally well at a Mission tent meeting.

Compared with the Mission, however, the Church puts a tremendous amount of power in the hands of the individual. Conversion makes each member an agent of the Holy Spirit, a proxy warrior for Jesus in the crusade against Satan. Whereas missionsfolk can merely spurn the devil, scorning his attacks and temptations, Apostolic converts can actively fight him with such powers as exorcism and faith healing. Moreover, each member communicates directly with God, without the intervention of any priest or social organization. The individual does not depend on the community for salvation or spiritual strength; he can stand on his own, armed with the weapons of the Holy Spirit, able to face down any demon that threatens his soul.

Such a strong conception of the individual implies a relatively weak role for the community. The Apostolic Church does grant the holy society a greater role than do some Pentecostal groups; the priest has an important role, and the members need guidance from the Church to interpret what God says to them. And in practice, the congregation tends to constitute a huge part of the individual's social circle. But society has none of the vital conceptual importance that it has in the Grundtvigian and Inner Mission worldviews. It is not so much a community as a corporation, a group of individuals united in the pursuit of a common purpose. They need not live together, work together, or have a common heritage to achieve their goals; their interaction need only involve common worship and cooperative evangelization. The Church's society is a collection of discrete individuals, all united in a spiritual mission, but each the captain of his own soul.

Apostolic Church Organization

Authority Structure

The Apostolic Church differs from most Pentecostal groups in the importance of its central authorities. It contends that Christ ordained a specific form of leadership for the earthly congregation; in Ephesians 14, the apostle Paul describes a church structure composed of apostles, prophets, evangelists, shepherds, teachers, and elders (cf. Mortensen 1974: 139-144). Accordingly, the Church vests most of its authority in a central council. The National Council consists of twenty-one theologically trained members, led by a foreman, who convene twice a year to decide positions and policies for the Church. One member also operates the National Secretariat, which administers the Church on a daily basis. These agencies have sole control over the Church's theology, and they assign ministers to the local congregations. Through committees, they also oversee the Church's finances and administration, mission work, as well as the seminary and boarding school that the Church operates.

Local laymen share authority only in the organizational work of the congregation. Each chapter has a minister *(forstander)*, assigned by the National Council; the minister preaches during Sunday services, administers sacraments, supervises church administration, and officiates at all congregation activities. Most ministers have received some training at the Apostolic seminary, but particularly able laymen may also rise to the position.[5] Congregations can neither hire nor dismiss ministers, though in extreme cases individual members can request such action from the National Committee. A council of three to five older members of the congregation helps the minister organize the Church's local activities. Since congregations tend to be small, this Council of Elders *(ældsteråd)* operates rather informally, without a standard division of tasks and functions. Its members, moreover, carry little real authority; they make decisions about church affairs, but they tend to follow the lead of the minister. Local authority, like national authority, rests primarily with theologically trained appointees.

Financing

Funding for the Apostolic Church comes mainly from its members, most of whom contribute about a tenth of their yearly incomes to the

5. The current minister for the Nykøbing congregation, Søren Viftrup, has no formal theological training. He assured me, however, that he has a great deal of practical experience in the ministry, and his talent for the job is indisputable. "Minister," incidentally, is probably a poor translation for *forstander*; "foreman" or "leader" conveys the term more directly. Neither of these, however, connotes the theological authority and education implicit in the position. Members of the Nykøbing congregation often refer to Søren Viftrup as "the priest," and his role is clearly analogous to that of a Folkekirke priest.

Church. Individuals determine their contributions themselves, but Church doctrine and peer pressure strongly suggest tithing.[6] Some members also make special contributions for the Church's mission work in other countries. In addition, the Nykøbing congregation draws some funds from its subsidiary activities; the bookstore and café turn a small profit, and the Church generates some income with its offset printing equipment. The Church uses the majority of this money to pay for local expenses, such as the upkeep of the church building and transportation of elderly members to services. It also sends a generous contribution – up to 40 percent – to the Common Fund of the national Church.

The Nykøbing congregation currently stands on a stable financial footing. In 1990, its income totaled just over 180,000 kroner (US$ 30,000), 147,000 of which came from members' tithes. This income compares favorably with that of other religious organizations in the area; it represents a sixth of the income of the Free Congregation, for example, despite a membership only one thirtieth the size. The congregation contributed 70,000 kroner, almost 40 percent of the total, to the Common Fund.

Associated Organizations

The Apostolic Church has no equivalent to the Danish Society, the Grundtvigian free schools, or the KFUM/K. The church's activities focus almost entirely on services and evangelization, without any cluster of associated secular organizations. Its subsidiary projects, such as the bookstore and the Karby craft workshop, operate directly under its control; the Church views them as alternative evangelization strategies, not as independent organizations. This approach distinguishes the Apostolic Church sharply from the Mission and the Free Congregation. Those groups were each part of an integrated community, centered on a religious view but encompassing a broad range of social activities. The Church focuses directly and almost exclusively on the salvation of souls.

6. I was not permitted to examine the Nykøbing congregation's financial records in detail, so I cannot say with any certainty that the tithing doctrine is adhered to. All members with whom I spoke said that they and the other members tithed. This assertion seems dubious, however. If all 46 members tithing together only generated 147,000 kroner (the 1990 total), the average individual income of the congregation would be less than 32,000 kroner, or about US$ 5,325; this figure is far below even the standard pension wage. Even if only two-thirds of the members were of an age to contribute, that figure would rise only to 49,000 kroner, still below the pension level. Clearly, members are not actually contributing a tenth of their income. I do not have any reliable way of determining how much they actually do contribute.

The Church does maintain close contacts with some of the other free churches in the area. Many of its members occasionally attend services at the Nykøbing Pentecostal Church *(Pinsekirken),* which lies on the other side of town. The Pentecostal congregation has fewer members than the Apostolic one, and its theology differs slightly. Members have trouble explaining the differences between the churches, however, and they regard the separation between them as an administrative fiction. The two churches hold revival meetings together, socialize together, and turn out in force for each others' baptisms. Both churches also lend support to the town's small Salvation Army chapter. They have less theology in common with the Salvation Army, a pietist group that denies the efficacy of sacraments. They regard it as a fellow soldier in the battle for salvation, though, and they boost attendance at its meetings and festivals.

Membership

The sparse records of the Apostolic Church make its early membership difficult to reconstruct. We cannot reliably estimate its demographic constitution, its occupational groups, or even its exact size for most of its history. Members' recollections, however, give us a general sense of its development. The movement first took hold in Sundby, led by a local farm owner; a number of members also clustered around a farm owner in Sillerslev. They came primarily from farm families, recruited along kinship and neighborhood lines. The outpost work in the 1930s and 1940s brought converts from a number of villages in southern Mors; most were young men, also from farm families. Their conversions took place individually, often in connection with crises of illness or employment in their personal lives. Never did a wave of conversions sweep an area, nor did Church members ever form even a large minority in any single village. The total membership on the island ranged around sixty in the middle of the century. A network of members developed in the countryside, though, and converts sought each other out for counsel and common prayer. The membership met as a whole at Sunday services in Nykøbing.

The end of the outpost work in the 1960s slowed the stream of new converts, and during the 1970s the congregation aged and shrank. By 1980, membership had fallen to about thirty, most of whom were middle aged or older. The congregation centered increasingly around Nykøbing, as village evangelization ended and older members moved into the town. During the past decade, the congregation has experienced a moderate revival. It has received more than a dozen new members, most of them immigrants to the island from other Apostolic congregations in Denmark. These members have worked energetically for the Church, participating regularly in its services and leading some of its new projects. The Church remains focused in Nykøbing, where all but a few of it members live.

No clear pattern dominates the demographic structure of the congregation today. Its members come from a broad range of occupations, including farm owners, nursing assistants, workmen, maids, a teacher, and several artisans. Professionals are almost absent from the congregation, and farm workers few; factory workers form perhaps the largest single occupational group, but they do not approach a majority. The congregation has no unusually wealthy members, and only a very few with university educations. Women outnumber men about three to two in the congregation, and they attend services more regularly than the men. Three or four families in the congregation have young children; most of the members are past middle age. The lack of available membership lists makes a precise demographic profile impossible. It seems clear, however, that such a profile would reveal a fairly heterogeneous group, without the predominance of regional or occupational groups that characterize the Free Congregation and the Inner Mission.

Leaders

The Apostolic minister occupies a stronger and more central position than his counterparts in the Free Congregation and the Inner Mission. In Sunday services, for example, all of the activity focuses on him; where the Free Congregation priest leaves much of the ritual to assistants, the minister conducts almost all of it himself. He delivers energetic, bombastic sermons with a theatrical flair. He sings loudest and best during the hymns. He reads the scriptural passages himself, interjecting his comments on the important sections. Even when members rise to give testimonials and prophecies, he assesses their merit and adds his own comments. In other meetings, he always presides and directs the discussions and festivities. Throughout his work, the Apostolic minister must exercise a degree of authority and self-confidence that would outrage the independent Grundtvigians or the self-effacing missionsfolk.

Perhaps as a result, the congregation's leaders have generally come from outside the community. The first ones traveled all the way from Århus to deliver Sunday sermons. When the first resident minister arrived in 1942, he and his wife moved to Nykøbing from Sjælland. Few leaders since then have had any prior connection to the island or its inhabitants. Ministers receive their appointments and their salaries from the National Council, and only the National Council can dismiss them. Moreover, their long-term membership in the community is limited; after five to ten years, the Church normally transfers them. They do become close to the members during their tenure, and their positions make them important players in the social life of the congregation. Members always speak warmly of past ministers, for whom they seem to have genuine affection. Ultimately, though, the minister has a certain independence, an outsider status that allows him to exercise a power that community members could not.

Some leaders, of course, have come from local ranks; the ministers in 1949-52 and 1971-78 were already members of the congregation. These ministers received their positions on the recommendations of their predecessors, owing to to their zealous belief and their gifts as speakers. Such leaders can be effective, but the position places them under a tremendous emotional strain, requiring them to behave in ways sharply at odds with the island's norms. The last local minister eventually suffered a nervous breakdown and resigned the position. Local members can occupy less formal leadership roles; the latter minister now sits on the Church's Council of Elders, and he supervises work on the Bible Garden. Likewise, a local lay woman runs the craft workshop and meeting center in Karby. Such roles are limited, though, and distinctly informal, with none of the demonstrative authority required of the minister. Their holders need not copy the minister's flagrant violation of the strictures of the Jante Law.

Ritual in the Apostolic Church

The Apostolic Church, like the Folkekirke and the Free Congregation, performs a broad range of seasonal and life-cycle rituals. It conducts Sunday services, communions, baptisms, weddings, funerals, and holiday services; it also holds a number of less formal events, such as prayer meetings, Bible studies, and singing evenings. The church does not practice confirmation, and it substitutes a naming ceremony for the infant baptism that inaugurates life in the Folkekirke. Otherwise, its ritual system corresponds closely to that of most churches on the island.

While the names and timing of the rituals mirror those of the Folkekirke, the format and character differ radically. Apostolic rites involve much more direct oral and physical participation by the members. In addition, they focus much more directly on the person of the minister. To convey a sense of the differences, I will briefly describe two of the Apostolic Church's most important rituals: the Sunday service, its most frequent; and baptism, its most prized.

Sunday Services

The Apostolic Sunday service takes place in Nykøbing, in a modest brick shop that the congregation bought and converted to a church in 1952. By ten o'clock in the morning, a crowd of fifteen to twenty people has made its way up the winding staircase to the second floor, to a roughly rectangular room holding a dozen rows of wooden chairs. A raised platform extends across the front wall; at one end a modern wooden podium faces the room, at the other an electronic keyboard stands against the wall. The minister sits in a chair behind the podium, waving and talking to the arriving members, while the organist reviews his music at the keyboard. Members sit in groups of families or friends, talking as they wait, each holding a pair of evangelical hymnals.

When everyone has arrived, the minister stands and announces the first hymn. The congregation sings sitting down, though the minister stands to lead; he sings loudly and well, into the podium's microphone, carrying the congregation through the more complicated melodies. The hymn may be a standard Folkekirke song, with a stately melody and poetic lyrics. More commonly, though, it comes from the Church's own songbook of simple, lively, and very modern hymns. These hymns normally contain only one or two verses and a chorus, all of which are repeated as many times as the minister sees fit. The congregation sings them enthusiastically, sometimes clapping along to the syncopated rhythms. One popular hymn goes as follows:

Vi vil give Dig ære	We will give You honor
Tak være til dig o far	Thanks be to You, o Father
Og vi vil frembære	And we will carry forth
Alt som vi har	All that we have
Jeg gi'r ære	I give honor
Ære til min fader	Honor to my father
Ære til min frelser	Honor to my savior
Ære, ære til min fader	Honor, honor to my father
Jeg gi'r ære til min far	I give honor to my father

The verses repeat again and again, perhaps five or six times, as long as the minister senses an energy in the congregation. When enthusiasm for the song begins to wane, he signals an upcoming stop, and the hymn ends at the finish of the next chorus.

After a pair of these hymns, the minister delivers the sermon. The sermon usually lasts for about half an hour, during which he explicates a passage of scripture and relates its meaning to the lives of the Church's members. His speaking style contrasts sharply with the almost regal manner of a Folkekirke priest. His body sways, his arms wave, his voice rises and falls; he does not merely read the sermon, he performs it, emphasizing the major points with vivid tones and gestures. He wears a beatific smile throughout, personifying the joy that the word of the Lord should bring to its hearers. He also provokes smiles among the congregation with frequent dry jokes.[7] The congregation listens attentively throughout the sermon, laughing at the humor and softly voicing their approval. Whenever the minister makes an important point, a wave of soft mutterings – "Thank you, Jesus," "Alleluia," "Praised be His name" – sweeps through the congregation.

After the sermon, depending on the time available, the minister may call upon members to give testimonials. The members called upon take the minister's place at the podium, while he sits back down behind them. Many are slightly reluctant to be called upon, but they all speak with considerable confidence once they begin. They tell of moments in their lives when Jesus has helped them, or when Satan's temptation has reared its ugly head. They may read a passage of scripture that has special meaning for them, or tell an anecdote that illustrates a scriptural truth. They may even relate a prophecy that they feel God has told them. Testimonials are short, perhaps two or three minutes each, and their tone varies with the speaker. The minister nods his head and listens closely, interjecting an "Alleluia" or "Thank you, Jesus" occasionally. When each testimonial concludes, he resumes the podium and adds his own comments. He may call the words wise, helpful, or even a message from God. His comments are always positive, and he encourages speakers to give more testimonials in the future.

Another pair of hymns follows the testimonials. At the end of the second hymn, the singing does not die; the singing voices gradually

---

7. Such a technique is common on Mors; I never heard a minister give a sermon that did not include at least a few jokes. Indeed, virtually all speeches and conversations on the island are suffused with them, and a person who does not make jokes and laugh at them stands out.

blend with a sort of group prayer, which can last up to fifteen minutes. The song slowly dies away, replaced by a whispered chorus of amens, which are repeated over and over at irregular intervals. The minister keeps up a quiet singing, repeating "Thank you, Jesus," "Amen," and "Alleluia" with his head tilted slightly back, his eyes closed, his body swaying slowly back and forth, his arms raised, palms upward, and a serene but concentrated expression on his face. Sometimes speaking in tongues replaces his Danish phrases, as an unintelligible stream of speech flows from his lips. He stands in one place, not shifting his feet. In the congregation, people stand with their eyes closed, rooted to their spots like the minister, swaying slowly. Some have their arms outstretched, but none as far as the minister's. Some hold out both arms with the elbows close to the body, palms upward; some hold out one arm the same way; some hold one arm across the body, hand near the heart, the other arm held up with the hand facing forward, as if taking an oath; some keep their hands down, either clasped next to their bodies or resting on the chair in front of them. The latter tend to have their faces cast downward, while the rest gaze slightly up. Most are praying aloud, softly breathing thanks to Jesus or glossolalia at intervals of three to five seconds. Many of the voices are not whispers, but low moans, as though the speakers had just run long distances. Some whisper longer prayers in barely audible voices. The voices are not coordinated, and together they sound like flowing water, a steady low whispering sound with random soft moans rising above it.

After a minute or so, one member's voice rises in a real prayer, aloud for the rest of the congregation to hear. Anyone who is seized with the spirit may give such a prayer, though the more active members of the congregation tend to do it most. The prayer is coherent, and thanks Jesus for his blessings and his forgiveness of their sins, and also asks his blessing in the coming times. Once the praying aloud begins, the sounds start to get a kind of rhythm. The speaker says two or three words, then pauses for about two seconds before saying the next two or three. In the interval, the rest of the congregation interposes their own thank you Jesuses, alleluias, and amens. Beneath it all, some of the congregants continue their whispered prayers, making a steady stream of prayer beneath the rhythm. The prayer goes on for as long as the speaker wants, and is ended by the speaker simply stopping. The waves of prayer continue for half a minute or so, then another speaker takes over. The process can continue for as long as the congregation wishes, usually for fifteen minutes or so.

Eventually, the priest takes over, saying a prayer like all the others, but in a louder, more composed voice, not moaning but speaking. His prayer is longer, more coherent, and better rehearsed, though he does not change his position. He finally ends with a fervent "Amen," which the congregation echoes; the group then begins a standard hymn from memory, praising God and His works. When it ends, the minister intones a few praises to God, opens his eyes, and tells the congregation to sit back down. Once seated, they sing a final hymn, and the service ends.

Baptism

Baptism takes place during a regular Sunday service, but the logistics of the ritual require several departures from the regular format. Since the Apostolic Church recognizes only full-immersion baptism, the ceremony must take place by a body of water; the Church uses the beach if weather permits, but usually it borrows the baptismal pool at the Nykøbing Pentecostal Church. In addition, the entire service centers around the event. The testimonials relate to the joys of baptism, the sermon addresses the initiates directly, and the group prayer is shortened or left out.

The baptism itself follows directly after the sermon. When the minister has finished talking, he leads the initiate into a room behind the baptismal pool. The pool is a concrete basin about eight feet by ten feet by four feet deep, with stairs leading into it from the back; it stands at the front of the Pentecostal Church's main hall, covered by a platform when not in use. The congregation sings a hymn as the two principals prepare themselves. As the hymn ends, the minister emerges at the top of the pool's stairs, clad in white from head to foot. He descends slowly into the water, then gestures to the initiate to follow him. The initiate, also clad entirely in white, descends hesitantly under the eager and delighted gaze of the congregation. He stands by the minister in the water, facing the congregation, as the minister explains the purpose and meaning of the ceremony. The minister then turns to the initiate and intones the three questions of the Nicean Creed, to which the initiate responds affirmatively. Finally, the minister stands to the left of the initiate, placing one hand behind the head, the other on the initiate's clasped hands, and tips him backward into the water. As he does so, he proclaims, "I baptize you in the name of the Father, the Son, and the Holy Ghost." The initiate's body remains rigid as it dips briefly under the water, then rises again in the firm clasp of the minister. The congregation then breaks into a standard baptismal hymn, and the two white figures remount the steps, dripping wet, to change their clothes in the back room.

I did not personally witness an Apostolic baptism, since none occurred during my time on the island. Members spoke of them in glowing tones, though, vividly describing the circumstances, procedures, and people in attendance. They clearly regarded the ceremony as the most important and most joyous of their rituals. Baptisms represented the triumph of their mission, the victory of the forces of Jesus over the forces of Satan, moments never to be forgotten by either the participants or the spectators.

The Apostolic Church in the Lives of its Members

The Apostolic Church has no Apostolic butchers or bakers, no Apostolic villages or Apostolic lineages. Its members belong as individuals, not as part of an integrated community that structures and limits their lives. Nonetheless, their commitment to and activity in the Church equal anything in the history of the Inner Mission and Grundtvigian movements. Members attend services regularly and participate enthusiastically; they serve frequently in the café and bookstore; they attend Church social events and socialize mostly with other members. Many attend Apostolic seminaries or workshops, and all try to evangelize their neighbors and family. The Church community occupies most of the time that work and home do not, demanding an avid and durable interest from those who belong to it. In return it offers another home, an intense and secure social group that accepts and loves all who enter. We can get a sense of its role by considering the life of one of its members.

Anders Madsen grew up in Sillerslev, the youngest child of a poor smallholder and his wife. The family owned a small plot of land, a few pigs, and two cows; to supplement these meager means, Anders's father spent summers digging ditches for swamp drainage projects. Anders attended the parish school from ages 7 to 14, like all children in the area. In the summer after his graduation, his father caught a serious illness in the swamps. None of the family had been particularly religious before that, but the father underwent a pietistic conversion in the hospital. As the mortal nature of his illness became clear, the father talked increasingly to his children about religion; in his last conversation with Anders, he made Anders promise that they would meet again in heaven. The boy took no action on the promise at the time, even when a voice came to him in the fields one day, saying "Anders, convert!"

At age 20, after several years as a farmhand, Anders was conscripted into the army. The life of a soldier at the base in Holstebro marked a radical change in his world; he had only visited Nykøbing a few times in his life, and the bustling life of the city caught him wholly unprepared. He fell into the habits of the soldiers, drinking heavily, gambling excessively, and dancing at the base's raucous balls. After a few months, he fell seriously ill, and the army doctors gave him little hope of surviving. His mother visited him from Mors, convinced he would die; after she left, she sent him a letter that said simply, "Anders, pray!" The letter moved him deeply. The same night he received it, as he lay shivering and feverish in the hospital, a young woman from the local Pentecostal Church came to visit him. He realized then that his life had to change, that he must put his faith in Jesus and reform his ways. An hour later his fever broke, and he soon left the hospital in good health.

He returned to Mors a convinced pietist, and resumed his work as an itinerant farmhand. The local Inner Mission, Pentecostal, and Apostolic circles all sought him as a member, and he liked all three, but the voice of God told him to affiliate with the Apostolic Church. He underwent baptism in the Limfjord, a rite that some spectators mocked, but that most of his friends respected. He stopped attending dances, balls, and other secular affairs. He sometimes found himself sorely tempted to join them; in one instance, he went so far as to ask God for permission. Anxious to attend a party at a large estate, he told God that he would go if the sky was clear after seven o'clock. The rain began falling as the clock chimed seven, and Anders knew that something terrible would happen if he went to the affair. He spent the next two winters at the Apostolic seminary in Kolding, then spent a year doing door-to-door evangelizing around the country.

After his year of evangelization, Anders married a girl he had met at the seminary and returned to Nykøbing. His wife, Pia, worked as an assistant at a clothing shop in town, and Anders took a job at the slaughterhouse. In time Pia took over management of the shop, which she developed into one of the town's larger boutiques. After fourteen years at the slaughterhouse, Anders spent another year as an itinerant evangelist; when he returned, he helped Pia with the shop until their retirement. During the early 1970s, he served as minister for the church. His tenure went well, but the strain of managing it proved too much for him; he finally suffered a nervous breakdown, and gratefully accepted the Church's offer of a replacement. The couple has raised four sons, all of whom married and had children of their own. Today they live in a large house in Nykøbing, subsisting on state pensions and their proceeds from the sale of the boutique.

The Apostolic Church is an intimate part of Anders's life. It shapes his understanding of the God who directs his actions, and it brings him close to fellow believers. Anders attends services every week, together with his wife; he also attends Bible studies, Council of Elders meetings, and assorted Church functions. He works in the café two afternoons a week, helps tend the Bible garden, and frequently visits services at the Pentecostal Church and Salvation Army. Most of his friends belong to the Church as well. But most importantly, the Church is with him in the form of the Holy Spirit. The Apostolic Church is God's congregation on earth, the worldly incarnation of the body of Christ. It is thus intimately associated with the Spirit that is ever-present in Anders's life. Anders consults God in moments of doubt, prays to Him in times of sorrow, praises Him in times of happiness. Each of these myriad cries to God, whether during a Sunday service or in the quiet of his home, invokes the doctrines and community of the Apostolic Church. Despite its small size and loose organization, the Church infiltrates the lives of its members to an extraordinary degree.

Future Prospects

The Apostolic Church relies on a different sort of community than the Free Congregation or the Inner Mission. Its bonds do not derive from a common folk tradition, a shared village society, or old family affiliations. Its members are connected only by a shared faith, by the fact that at some point in their lives, each has renounced the beliefs and traditions of his neighbors in favor of an ecstatic union with Christ. This foundation insulates the Church from many of the social changes that have undermined such groups as the Inner Mission. The restructuring of Mors society does not weaken its community, as long as individuals continue to have the sorts of experiences that lead to Apostolic conversion. Indeed, social upheaval may well benefit the Church. Many of its members join at times of personal crisis, when changes in their families or social worlds place them outside of their accustomed roles. Social crises breed such personal crises, and the Church's greatest revivals have occurred in times of societal disruption.

The Church's prospects for survival, therefore, look very bright. It has grown moderately over the past decade, and its members are energetic and committed. Though aging may soon thin its ranks, its younger members promise active and enduring support. It stands on a solid financial base, and it has an experienced and effective leader. Even if such bulwarks should fail, moreover, the Church can rely on the support of the National Council. As long as even a few converts remain active on the island, the Council will ensure that the Apostolic Church on Mors continues to spread the faith.

How far they can spread it remains a question. Even during its greatest expansion, following World War II, the Church has never gained a large following on Mors; its converts have come singly and sporadically, never in the sort of wave that characterized the Grundtvigian and Mission movements. The Church requires an unusually strong conversion, one which rejects the Folkekirke entirely and often incurs ridicule from friends and family. It cannot offer an alternative social world to buttress that conversion, as the Mission did, nor can it invoke the folk tradition that united the Grundtvigians. Membership demands a renunciation of one's old community, but does not provide any truly integrated community in return. For most Morsingboer, such a price is too high; despite its problems, the island's society does provide a rewarding identity and social environment for most of its inhabitants. Unless that society changes radically, the Apostolic Church will probably remain what it now is, a small enclave of ecstatic belief on the island's religious fringe.

Part III

MORS AND THE MEANING OF RELIGION

The people who walked in darkness have seen a great light; those who lived in a land of deep darkness – on them light has shined. You have multiplied the nation, you have increased its joy; they rejoice before you as with joy at the harvest, as people exult when dividing plunder. For the yoke of their burden, and the bar across their shoulders, the rod of their oppressor, you have broken as on the day of Midian.

— Isaiah 9:2-4

8. Religion, Science, and Secularization on Mors

ॐ ॐ ॐ

What ails religion in Denmark? Everyone knows the answer, from the detached sociologists who populate the Danish news programs to the doleful patriarchs of the old Inner Mission. Religion in Denmark has gone the way of the thatched roof and the horsedrawn carriage, swept into irrelevancy by the tide of modernity that has flooded the country over the past century. People have lost faith in religion's simple beliefs and quaint explanations of the world; they have turned to the less comforting, but more realistic, teachings of science. Some mourn the death of religion, which once gave Danes a sense of morality and belonging in the community. Others rejoice at Denmark's liberation from the confining morality and prejudices that the Church once imposed. All agree, though, that it is modernity and science that have discredited and dethroned the mighty power of the old church. The modern and the scientific are irresistible juggernauts, destined to roll over and crush the religions of the world.

A quick glance at the religious movements on Mors seems to confirm this view. The Inner Mission, so large and energetic a half century ago, has seen its numbers and activities gradually dwindle away. Free Congregation members speak seldom of God nowadays, and many almost never go to church. Even the Apostolic Church has moderated its message and failed to increase its flock. To an outsider, and to many insiders, Mors's religious history presents a textbook case of the secularization of modern society. The eclipse of religious movements, especially the Inner Mission, provides convincing evidence of the process.

On closer inspection, however, the situation becomes less clear. The Free Congregation, for example, has actually grown over the past decade, while the Apostolic Church has held its membership steady. The Inner Mission has indeed declined, but it maintained strong communities on the island as late as the 1960s; its fall seems to reflect organizational problems more than discredited philosophy. Moreover, insofar as the religious movements have declined, their losses do not relate clearly to the rise of science or modernity. Grundtvigian and Mission farmers have embraced the past century's agricultural innovations. New technologies and education have rarely conflicted with their faith. Today, in fact, the Free Congregation's growth derives primarily from the medical personnel and professionals who personify scientific progress in Denmark. Something has obviously changed about religion on Mors, but the religious movements have not died, and the scientific juggernaut does not seem poised to kill them.

This situation recalls some of the questions raised in the first part of this book. The notion of secularization has dominated studies of modern religion since the dawn of social science, and secularization theory remains the most influential approach to understanding religion in contemporary Europe. This theory is especially important in Scandinavia, which is associated both by scholars and by laymen with extreme modernity and a dearth of religion. On Mors, however, in the heart of Scandinavia, the oppositions between science and religion predicted by the theory may not exist. If they do not, the ability of secularization theory to explain religion in Scandinavia, and by extension throughout the modern world, must fall into doubt. In this chapter, I will consider this issue in depth. Does the history of religious movements on Mors reveal the sorts of patterns and oppositions predicted by secularization theory? If not, how are we to understand the ebb and flow of religious movements in modern society?

I will begin with theory, discussing some of the theoretical issues involved in secularization's definition of religion. I will also consider another approach to understanding modern religion, one drawn from symbolic anthropology, and focusing on religion's role in creating identity and community for its members. I will then discuss how each of them might interpret the religious history of Mors Island, and the implications of this interpretation for their empirical validity.

Secularization Theory and the Nature of Religion

In Part I, I discussed some of the premises and predictions of secularization theory. First developed in the 19th century, secularization theory argues that modernization must ultimately destroy religious institutions. Through such processes as rationalization, societalization, and social differentiation, modern society pushes religion out of the public sphere, relegating it at best to the peripheral world of private belief. This paradigm dominated the sociology of religion until quite recently, and it continues to shape understandings of religion throughout the social sciences. In recent years, however, a number of scholars have offered penetrating critiques of the theory. Most have attacked it on empirical grounds, pointing out that religion has failed to die according to the theory's schedule. Some have also attacked the theoretical foundations of the theory, decrying the conceptual inconsistencies and unexamined assumptions that riddle the theory. With the rise of highly visible religiosity in the United States, Eastern Europe, and the Muslim world, the credibility of secularization theory has suffered profound setbacks over the last decade.

In a real sense, however, the essence of the theory remains largely intact. Despite stinging attacks on its methods and predictions, most critics have accepted the basic premises that underlie secularization theory. They agree, for example, that there is a basic opposition between religious and nonreligious ways of understanding the world. They agree that the non-religious worldview is essentially equivalent to that of Western science, which provides both an index of and a reason for secularization's progress. They agree as well that a tension between religious and scientific worldviews is the defining feature of the modern age in religion. For most of its critics, the weakness of secularization theory lies primarily in its overreaching, its grandiose predictions of the end of religion. That end, they say, is neither as inevitable nor as final as the theory would have it. But the basic conflicts that lie behind these predictions are sound; by recasting it as a more complex, limited, and reversible process, much of secularization theory can be salvaged. For all the critiques leveled at it in recent years, secularization theory continues to set the terms in which modern religion is understood.

Yet these terms themselves pose some of the paradigm's most serious problems. In particular, they require a definition of religion as a system of belief in the supernatural. This definition, as noted in Part I, produces a drastically impoverished understanding of religion; it portrays a complex set of social and cultural classifications as a small group of ideas

217

about nonexistent beings. In the notion of the supernatural, moreover, it has a deeply flawed concept at its core. Indeed, the importance of the supernatural to secularization theory raises serious questions about its cross-cultural applicability.

The Supernatural and Secularization Theory

Secularization theory generally builds on a more or less Tylorean definition of religion. In his 1871 study *Primitive Culture*, Edward Burnett Tylor portrayed religion as a primitive explanatory system, a way of explaining puzzling facts in a prescientific world. Its defining characteristic was its belief in supernatural beings; originally invoked by early humans to explain dreams, these beings eventually came to explain virtually all confusing aspects of the natural world. Tylor therefore defined religion in its broadest sense as belief in supernatural beings. Secularization theories have elaborated this definition considerably, but they have largely retained its central premise (e.g., Wilson 1985: 11-12, Stark and Bainbridge 1985: 3, Martin 1978: 12, Wallace 1966: 264). Human beliefs are religious insofar as they invoke supernatural agencies; religions are social institutions devoted to the maintenance or spread of such beliefs.[1]

This definition of religion reserves a special place for science, since it depends on a specific definition of the supernatural. Secularization theory usually defines the supernatural as anything whose existence conflicts with the doctrines of Western science (e.g., Martin 1978: 12, Wallace 1966: 264). Science, therefore, stands in a fundamental opposition to religion; in a sense, it defines what religion is not. A view of the world based on science is thus categorically different from all religious understandings of the universe. It is this view, drawn from the principles of reason and the discoveries of empirical science, that constitutes the secular way of thinking.

By seeing the scientific world view as an objective reality, theorists can apply their models of secularization cross-culturally. Whatever the reli-

---

1. Theorists today seldom put this definition as simply as Tylor, but the essential notion of the supernatural remains a basic ingredient of almost all secularization theory. Spiro (1964) and Stark and Bainbridge (1985) both provide sophisticated defenses of this approach, arguing forcefully that institutions without supernatural beliefs should not be called religions. They refute Durkheim's famous example of Theraveda Buddhism as naturalistic religion, each pointing out that this philosophy never achieved significant popular followings.

gion a society may once have practiced, its transition to secularism has something in common with all religious declines. Secularization is not just the transformation of one religion into another, but a transition from religion in general to nonreligion. Scholars can therefore develop theories of secularization independent of any particular cultural context, drawing on general theories of human belief rather than endless analyses of individual cultures.

This approach, however, presents serious theoretical difficulties. The notion of the supernatural, to begin with, is far from universal; not all cultures distinguish between a realm of the ordinary and a realm of the otherworldly (Douglas 1982). Even where they do draw such a distinction, cultures vary widely in their specific delineations. The Azande studied by Evans-Pritchard, for example, considered witchcraft as ordinary and explicable a phenomenon as could be imagined; it derived from physical traits, it operated in predictable ways, and it could be controlled by mechanical operations (1937). The Azande notion of the natural covered powers that would be clearly supernatural in a Western context. Conversely, many Native American groups attached spiritual value to homosexuality. One became a *berdache* after a spiritual visitation, and the homosexual relationships involved in the role were justified by the nature of the guardian spirit (Whitehead 1981). Such cultures assigned a supernatural cause to an activity defined in the modern West as a matter of preference or biological drive. No single division of the natural and the supernatural can encompass these various viewpoints without doing violence to some of them.

A number of authors have tried to evade this dilemma by introducing variations on the term. Melford Spiro, for example, uses "superhuman" instead (1966); Orru and Wang, among others, vary this with "supra-human" (1992). By focusing on the belief in beings with powers greater than human ones, these definitions seem to skirt the problems associated with the supernatural. The improvement, however, is illusory. After all, many beings have superhuman powers – an elephant, a bird, and a man with an airplane can each do things impossible for humans in their natural condition. No theorist would regard the belief in such beings as evidence of religion. It is only when the powers of such beings exceed those recognized by science that they are cited as religious figures. The superhuman, in other words, is of interest only insofar as it is also supernatural.

Such objections may arise with any substantive definition when used cross-culturally, as secularization theorists are quick to point out; the fact that a definition fails to fit indigenous categories does not necessarily make it useless. Even if the Nuer do not recognize the term pastoralist, the term can still be useful when anthropologists try to understand them (cf. Wallis & Bruce 1992: 9-10). "Natural" and "supernatural," however, are much vaguer and more culturally specific than terms like "pastoralist." To use them cross-culturally, one must first make a compelling case that they have some universal validity. So far, secularization theory has failed to make such a case. Even if it did, this approach to defining religion would remain highly problematic. It defines institutions as religious or nonreligious based not on their internal properties, but on the degree to which they correspond to a foreign system of thought, namely science. It is not a church's form, its functions, its organization, or its culture that define it as a religious institution – it is the fact that certain aspects of its belief system disagree with scientific doctrines, doctrines that may be partially or wholly unknown to the church's members. In any area but religion, such an approach would appear hopelessly ethnocentric. No anthropologist would define deviancy, for example, as behavior that departs from middle-class American notions of correct behavior; why then define religion as belief that departs from one particular notion of reality? Doing so smacks more of moral judgment than of cultural classification.

Moreover, this approach depends perilously on the immutability of scientific doctrines. A substantial change in the beliefs of science might require a complete reclassification of religious institutions, without any changes in the institutions themselves. The controversy over acupuncture illustrates the problem. Until fairly recently, Western medical researchers dismissed acupuncture as a hoax, and attributed belief in it to superstition, suggestion, and the invocation of supernatural forces. Belief in acupuncture thus fell into the realm of religious activity. In recent years, scientists have reconsidered, and while they do not fully understand acupuncture, they consider its effects part of natural reality. Belief in it is thus no longer superstition or religion. The people in Asia who use acupuncture have not changed their opinion of it during this time; yet that opinion has changed from religion to science, according to this definition of religion. We can only imagine our predicament if a researcher should prove the existence of God. The variability and ethnocentrism inherent in the term "supernatural" make it a poor candidate for defining religion.

This objection is more than a quibble over definitions. The distinction between science and religion lies at the heart of secularization theory; if the scientific worldview is not regarded as separate from religion, as an essentially acultural constant, then secularization theories cannot be applied cross-culturally. Transition from traditional religion to secularism becomes simply another religious change, related to the specific features of the culture involved, not an example of a worldwide decline or resurgence of religion. Unless one draws a clear line between the religious and the secular, the most interesting and ambitious claims of secularization theory become moot.

It is not clear that such a line can or should be drawn. Some religions coexist fairly easily with science and secularism, and incorporate scientific doctrines into their beliefs (Hunter 1985: 152).[2] More importantly, attitudes toward science in secular societies bear a strong resemblance to religious attitudes (Yinger 1970). Many Americans, for example, believe that science can explain virtually anything about the world; they look to science to explain physical events, social problems, even their own emotions. They do so not because they understand scientific methods, of which most Americans are largely ignorant. They do so out of faith, out of a conviction in the rightness of the scientific establishment that strongly resembles faith in a priesthood. If secularized culture adopts an attitude toward science that mirrors earlier attitudes toward religion, why not describe that attitude as religious? Doing so allows us to apply illuminating models of religious activity to our own society. Failure to do so renders our culture opaque to the analyses we have used so productively in others.[3]

Religion as a Symbolic System

While secularization theory has dominated the study of religion in the modern west, anthropologists looking at other societies have developed

2. In the 19th century, for example scientific theories of race and intelligence dovetailed neatly with religious justifications of racial inequality in the United States. Moreover, one could argue that the secularized Western worldview conflicts with areas of science more than do non-western ones. In the West, for example, the individual is conceived as a relatively autonomous actor, with an identity and motivation distinct from all others. Many other cultures see the individual instead as a member of an extended family, whose identity and interests are inseparable from his own. The latter view accords fully with recent work by behavioral biologists, who have used the concept of inclusive fitness to produce more convincing models of evolution.

3. Or is that in fact the point? Much of the sociological work on secularization resembles a frantic attempt to distinguish the sociologists' own worldview from all others. By establishing a bright line between religion and science, social scientists identify

very different understandings of religion. In these models, particularly the ones proposed by symbolic anthropologists, ideas about the supernatural play little or no part. Instead, religion appears as a system of classification, a way of defining what the world is and how people and nature fit into it. Religion's concerns overlap with those of science, in that they define the nature of physical forces and the types of beings in existence. Religion defines much more, however, including things that science inherently cannot. It describes the nature of the individual, the connection between the individual and the community, the nature of moral action, and the relationship between the temporal and the eternal. Such issues have no objective answers, and the definitions that any religion uses are essentially arbitrary. From the viewpoint of an adherent to any one religion, therefore, all others appear irrational and unreal. His or her own, however, feels uniquely real (Geertz 1973). It is not a theory of the supernatural, but a sensible and demonstrable description of a plainly intelligible world.

For these models, religion is perhaps best seen not as an institution or a set of beliefs, but as a field of human activity (Goodenough 1974, Yinger 1970). In this view, human society and psychology are seen to require answers to certain basic questions, such as the connection of mankind to the universe and the types of beings in existence.[4] The process of answering such questions is the process of religion, and human action is religious to the extent that it relates to these questions. The answers that people devise resonate throughout their cultures; work for a New England Congregationalist or an Indian untouchable, for example, has a direct connection to ideas about the nature of the divine and the moral order. Every action thus has a religious dimension, just as it has an economic dimension and a political one (cf. Leach 1954). Religion appears as an essential aspect of human activity, not a particular set of beliefs or institutions.

---

their own way of seeing the world as uniquely true. Whatever its theoretical validity, such an approach is certainly reassuring to social scientists.

4. As Goodenough points out, the difficult part of this definition of religion comes when one must define the particular questions at issue. Those questions revolve around the essential natures of human beings, and around the connection between those aspects of the world that are defined as human and those that are defined as nonhuman. Their specifics, however, require considerable elaboration, which I believe must ultimately rest on a psychological foundation. Even reaching this level of discussion, however, represents a fundamental change — and, I think, a fundamental improvement — from the conventional understanding of religion as a particular set of beliefs.

Since they define the natural and moral order, religions have enormous significance for ordering the social system (Evans-Pritchard 1965, Douglas 1970, Turner 1969, Ortner 1989, Geertz 1973). They imply definitions of the social group, the proper attitude of the individual to the society, the proper relations between members of family groups, the proper organization of work and exchange, and other aspects of social action. In defining them, religious systems also legitimate and buttress social arrangements. In some cases, they impose divine sanctions against disorderly conduct; marital infidelity, for example, may be viewed not simply as a breach of family law, but as a sin punishable by illness or damnation. Even without such sanctions, religion's role in defining reality subtly supports the social system. It roots social categories in the nature of the universe, not in the arbitrary decisions of human beings. People accept social roles and requirements as part of essential reality, as unalterable aspects of an objectively defined world (Geertz 1973). [5]

Beyond its importance to the social order, religion has powerful psychological value for the individual. Religion defines the universe in which the individual exists, and in doing so it defines the individual himself (Berger 1967, Geertz 1973). It tells him how he fits into the world around him, how he is like and different from other people, how to understand his own sensations and emotions. The individual builds his own personal identity on a foundation that religion provides him. This religion may come to him from an established church, or from less localized sources in his social network. Either way, they are an integral part of his identity, which is in turn one of the essential elements of his psychological make-up (Freud 1922, Fromm 1947, Wallace 1970, Lindholm 1990).

In a relatively stable society, religion dovetails neatly with social systems and individual identities. Incremental changes in the social world prompt corresponding changes in religious views; religions change their doctrines over time to accommodate new social or environmental arrangements. Such gradual changes represent little threat either to the society or to the individual. If society changes drastically, however, reli-

---

5. This view of religion does not require the assumption of a homogeneous society; different groups within a society tend to have different religions. Even where elements of religions may be common to opposing groups, each group may have a different understanding of those elements. The 19th-century Grundtvigians and missionsfolk, for example, believed in the same cosmology of God, Jesus, the Holy Spirit, and Satan, but the personality and attributes of each character were defined very differently.

gious views may lose credibility. Their definitions of groups, of motivations, even of physical reality may come into conflict with a newly refigured world. A system of divine kingship, for example, faces a crisis if the king is overthrown and the monarchy abolished. A religion linked to a caste system faces trouble if economic changes obliterate traditional occupational groups. A religion that classifies people according to their land holdings and location loses its basis if land reforms relocate people and redistribute property.

A discredited religion threatens the social order, since it can no longer effectively support social and cultural classifications. Its divine sanctions lose their force, and its definitions of reality lose their power. Partly as a result, substantial economic and political changes tend to generate problems throughout the social system. Family structures, local exchange networks, local power arrangements, gender relations, and age classifications all come under attack when the religious system can no longer buttress them. Such changes disorient individuals, who lose confidence in the social framework that has previously defined their world. More importantly, they lose confidence in their own identities. If the nature of their universe falls into doubt, so too do their own natures; a fundamental shift in the order of ones world means that ones own identity, the concept of self that forms the basis of individual perception and action, is essentially flawed. The social changes that undermine a religion, therefore, also undermine the psychological security of the religion's adherents. They produce a crisis of identity, which leads to deep-seated individual anxiety (cf. Zablocki 1980, Lindholm 1990, Wallace 1970).

Individuals can resolve this crisis by affiliating with new religious movements.[6] An alternative religion can provide a different understanding of the world, with a different understanding of the person, that meshes better with the individual's changed social circumstances. By redefining the world and the individual, it relieves the anxiety associated with the old, discredited definitions. Such a reformulation of the self requires a wrenching conversion process; once converted, however, the adherent finds himself at ease with a previously unsettling and confusing world. Religious movements may actually recreate the social world itself,

6. Religious movements are not, of course, the only means of settling identity problems. Other options might include romantic love (Lindholm 1982, Buckser 1986) or attachment to a charismatic leader (Lindholm 1990, Zablocki 1980). Religious movements, however, with their emphasis on the group and community, provide a more secure and potentially enduring solution than the fragile bonds of individual affection.

gathering its members into new communities with a common religious outlook. Such communities often suffer organizational problems, and many founder; where successful, however, they may provide viable alternatives to the social system and worldview of the larger society (Wallace 1970, Zablocki 1980, Kanter 1972, Fitzgerald 1986).

This approach sees the secular worldview as a religion in itself, a set of definitions and assumptions about the nature of the world and the place of human beings in it. Its appeal, like that of any religious system, lies not so much in its fit with any objective scientific reality, as in its fit with the social world that modern society has created. Its rejection of a divine being or plan makes sense in a society without a clear center of authority or social hierarchy; its refusal to attribute personality to nonhuman entities accords with a society that treats the nonhuman as a commodity. Certain common aspects of modern Western social organization, such as industrial production and bureaucracy, lend common features to Western secular worldviews. Even so, the cultural differences among Western nations give each of them its own version of secular thinking.[7]

The question of secularization is not, then, a question about the death of religion, but a question about a particular religious change. This approach does not ask why religion has lost its validity in modern society, but why many modern societies have adopted the sorts of religious views implicit in secular thought. It answers that question with the same models it applies to other instances of religious change. Secularization theory often implies that there is something inherently unique about modern thinking, something unprecedented in the history of humanity that has enabled modern culture to break the age-old chains of religious thought. A symbolic approach begins from the opposite assumption, that the way humans think in the modern West is continuous with the way they think everywhere else.

Applying Theory to Mors

The two approaches outlined above lead to radically different ways of characterizing religious phenomena. Each has a long tradition of research and theory, and each has ardent defenders and detractors. The proof of the pudding, however, lies in the data. I will therefore turn to the religious movements on Mors, and consider how each of these approaches would characterize their development. To what extent does each model

7. A rather crude example would be the different relationships between the individual and society among "secularized" residents of Denmark and the United States.

describe, illuminate, or distort religious history in the area? Through which theory do we get a richer and more persuasive view of the meaning of Grundtvigianism, the Inner Mission, and the Apostolic Church? The answer will help us judge the utility of these explanations for Danish religion, and for modern religion in general.

Mors and Secularization Theory

Both popular and scholarly stereotypes portray Scandinavia as the epitome of the progressive modern society. With their superbly functioning welfare states, their unusually well-educated population, their high-technology industry, their commitment to racial and sexual equality, and their embrace of rationalism in government, Denmark and its neighbors embody both the aspirations and the fears of modern Western social reformers. Their religious systems are no exception. As far back as the beginning of the century, English accounts described Denmark as a land almost devoid of religion. Its people no longer believed in the archaic superstitions of the church; they, like their government, had cast off religion in favor of a rational secular approach to the problems of the world. Writers today, in the English-speaking world and in Denmark itself, frequently echo the same thoughts. Despite extremely high membership in the state church, only about 3 percent of the Danish population attend church on any given Sunday, and a relatively low percentage profess a belief in the central doctrines of the Lutheran church. For most writers, Denmark offers a shining example of the relationship between the rise of modern society and the decline of religion.

Mors, then, offers an appropriate test for secularization theory. If the secularization paradigm works anywhere, it should work here, in a well-off and well-educated corner of one of the most modern societies in the world. And at first glance, Mors seems to confirm every expectation of secularization theory. The spacious church in Nykøbing attracts only a few dozen of its eight thousand parishioners every week; in the countryside, most priests count themselves lucky if twenty souls attend a Sunday service. Few people speak openly of God or Jesus, and few homes display religious imagery on their walls. When asked about the origin of the world, most Morsingboer refer to the cataclysmic cosmogenesis of scientific theory, not to the creation myth of the Old Testament. When asked about their morality, they speak not of sin and the Ten Commandments, but of the rights and responsibilities of citizens. Most observers think of Mors as many Morsingboer think of themselves: as an entity that has cast aside its religion for the clarity and reason of secular scientific thought.

This image oversimplifies the situation considerably. While few Morsingboer attend Sunday services, for example, almost all of them belong to either the Folkekirke or the Free Congregation. They flock to their churches at Christmas and Easter, and they send their children to church for confirmation instruction. Most still hold their weddings in churches, and nearly all participate in such church rituals as baptisms and funerals. If such rituals hold real significance for the society, as anthropologists generally say they do, then the church clearly retains an important place in the community. Moreover, the worldview of the supposedly secular society has a considerable continuity with traditional religious ideas. As Jakob Rod has argued, even Danes who disavow any attachment to the church tend to have a sort of unspoken folk religion (Rod 1961, 1972). The church has certainly lost much of its authority on Mors, but popular views tend to exaggerate religion's demise.

What then of the religious movements we have discussed? How do they fit in with this image of Mors as a secular society? How does secularization theory explain their existence? The answer depends on ones view of the irreversibility of secularization. If one considers secularization an inevitable and irreversible process, one would argue that these movements are holdouts; for a number of reasons, their members have managed to retain religious worldviews for longer than the members of the larger society. Those reasons might have something to do with the relative backwardness of rural society. Out in the countryside, where these movements have been strongest, people have held on to traditional ways of working and thinking. They have resisted the influences of the outside world, in a way which towns and cities cannot. Traditional religion, traditional dialects, traditional kinship networks, and traditional occupations all hold out the longest in the countryside. As a result, movements aimed at buttressing traditional religious views have thrived there. In time, though, the modern world will reach even the furthest corners of the society.[8] Indeed, the disruption of village social systems beginning in the 1950s has already crippled the Inner Mission and stopped the spread of the Apostolic Church. As the years go by, even the Free Congregation will lose its members, as the secular worldview overthrows the most stalwart religious opposition.

8. Berger (1969: 11) made such an argument regarding conservative Protestantism in the United States in the 1960s, which he said was restricted to the fringes of modern society. Hunter (1985: 152) points out some flaws in this position, which Berger himself later reconsidered.

This answer has an intuitive appeal to it, and it is indeed an answer that many Danes would give. It involves a simplistic view of the movements, however, which has little connection to reality. The rural Morsingboer who stoked the island's awakening in the 1840s were not backward peasants ignorant of the outside world; they were among the most educated and innovative members of the agricultural community, and they had extensive contact with thinkers from off the island. Their network of itinerant preachers and speakers, as well as their active political involvement, kept them in closer touch with the world outside than most of their neighbors. Indeed, one of the central institutions of the Grundtvigian movement was its system of progressive schools. The Inner Mission had less contact with the outside world, and it did reject many of the fashions of 20th-century urban Denmark. But its members had no lack of exposure to secular and scientific ideas; rationalist priests and visiting Grundtvigian lecturers abounded on Mors throughout the 19th century. The Mission was not an enclave that the modern world never penetrated, but a community that deliberately turned away from a secular worldview it knew quite well. It even boasted considerable strength for some time among Nykøbing factory workers, one of the groups most directly acquainted with the new industrial society.

Indeed, the Mors religious movements were never particularly conservative. The Grundtvigian awakening was predicated on a violation of traditional local social structures; it united members across village, parish, and kinship lines, often to the annoyance of established authorities. The schools and societies associated with it also challenged traditional village-based institutions. The building of the Ansgarskirke created a wholly new force on Mors that divided the island's priests and eventually drove out its provst. If anything, its political and social agitation accelerated the demise of the traditional social system. Likewise, the Inner Mission did not seek a return to any holy society of the past. It aimed to remake the social world on a newly revealed pattern, one that was fundamentally different from the sinful traditions of village society. The Apostolic Church took a similar position, aspiring to "make history, not write history" (Mortensen 1974: 5). Religious movements on Mors have not been isolated refuges from the changes of the modern world, but active agents for particular types of directed social change.

The image of the countryside as isolated from modernity owes a great deal to the romantic imagination of the Grundtvigian movement, which saw rural culture as the repository of Danish folk tradition. The Mission

228

also idealized the isolated rural society, whose small scale could nourish the sort of community essential to the holy life. These images had something to them; a lack of industry and a relatively poor communication system do insulate the countryside from many aspects of modern urban society. But rural Mors has always had some contact with the larger trends of Danish society, and over the last two centuries it has had a lot. If the countryside has failed to join the secular trend, it has not done so out of ignorance or mindless conservatism.

Theorists like Stark and Bainbridge, who regard secularization as a reversible process, might therefore take a different tack. They might argue that the religious movements represent a rejection of the secular world; disenchanted with its impersonal and ultimately cynical scientific worldview, some Morsingboer have affiliated with groups that promise moral guidance in this world and eternal life in the next. These groups reassert the existence of supernatural agencies, and thus give greater comfort and security to their members. In doing so, they oppose the doctrines of modern scientific thought. The Inner Mission and the Apostolic Church, for example, explicitly reject some of the most disturbing findings of science, such as the falsity of the Christian Genesis story and of supernatural forces. And contrary to scientific doctrines, all of the movements assert a divine purpose to the social arrangements they espouse. They impose a supernaturally sanctioned order upon the world, producing a more reassuring vision of existence than the cold, inhuman world of scientific reality.

The difficulty of this position lies in its presumed opposition between the religious movements and modern science. Secularization theory must contain such an opposition; without it, the opposition between the religious and the secular itself breaks down. Yet no such opposition has really characterized the religious movements on Mors. All of them have at various times rejected various specifics of scientific theory, but they have never disputed the validity of scientific work in general. Grundtvigian farmers in the19th and 20th centuries embraced scientific advances in agriculture as an essential element of rural empowerment. Mission farmers likewise participated in cooperative dairies and agricultural development societies, both of which were heavily associated with scientific research in farming. Mission leaders have frequently decried such technological developments as television and the cinema; however, their opposition has focused not on technical development as such, but on the access to the sinful world that it gives the communities of the holy. The Apostolic Church generally regards science as having confirmed most of its own doctrines.[9] The Free Congregation has always regarded science as an ally, and it has devoted a substantial part of its time to spreading scientific knowledge among its members. Indeed, its recent growth in membership consists largely of professionals and medical workers, the very people who personify the advance of science and modernity on Mors. Secularization theory's opposition between science and religion does not accurately describe the religious system on Mors.

Moreover, a focus on the supernatural does not convey the complexity and richness of these movements. Secularization theory presents religions as flawed explanatory systems, as more or less successful ways of resisting the painful verities of science. Yet the movements did far more than explain the physical world through the supernatural; indeed, such explanation was perhaps their least important function. Grundtvigianism provided a reconceptualization of the folk tradition, an exhilarating vision of the free individual, and a comforting picture of the nurturing community. It was these ideas, as much as any ideas about God and salvation, which drew people to the Free Congregation in 1870, and which continue to attract them today. Likewise, the Inner Mission presented little in terms of explanation that did not already exist in Folkekirke tradition. Its newness lay in its reevaluation of the world, its division of society into the holy and the sinful, and its creation of a particular kind of community. These were not peripheral elements of the movements, but lay at their very heart. It was not a decline of belief, but the crumbling of the village community, that eroded the Inner Mission in the 1960s; it is not a uniform faith in God, but a coherent vision of the community, that sustains the Free Congregation today. The richness of these movements lies in areas that have little to do with anything that conflicts with scientific explanation. By characterizing religion as a supernaturally based system of explaining the world, secularization theory ignores some of its most important dimensions.

A secularization approach, then, at once distorts and impoverishes the history of the island's religious movements. It supposes an opposition between religion and either science or modernity that has not actually characterized the movements. In addition, by seeing religion and science as competing explanatory systems, it misses much of the richness and complexity that make Mors's religion such an interesting subject.

---

9. Scientists would certainly disagree; but Apostolic Church members on Mors frequently cite scientific research to back up their views on morality and social organization.

Religion, Identity, and Social Change on Mors

The second approach that I have discussed puts less emphasis on issues of scientific knowledge, focusing instead on the significance of religious symbolism for community and individual identity. It asks a rather different set of questions about the movements than secularization theory. What kinds of social change, for example, accompanied the emergence and development of these religious groups? How did these changes affect established conceptions of the individual and society? What transformations of self and community did the various religious movements proposed? What sorts of people turned to which movements? And what factors affected the survival or demise of each group?

The answers begin in the early 1800s, with the social changes that followed from land reforms in the late 18th century (see pp. 31-32). The land reforms had initiated the breakup of the old estate system, which for centuries had bound most Morsingboer to large landed estates. They had released peasants from mandatory work at the estates, and they had allowed estate owners to sell land to independent farmers. As the 19th century opened, the massive estates began a slow transformation into a patchwork of independent farms, owned for the first time in memory by autonomous free farmers. These farmers gained influence and political power as their numbers grew, and they became a formidable political bloc by the middle of the century. At the same time, those peasants who could not buy land found themselves pushed increasingly to the margins of rural society. They became poor smallholders or laborers, and were often forced to leave the countryside altogether for Nykøbing or America. A new social order came to the Mors countryside, an order centered around farm owners, smallholders, and artisans. The old village society, built on common peasant status and allegiance to a common landowner, evaporated in the course of two generations.

These changes implied profound shifts in the natures of the individual and the community. The individual's ties to the village and the estate loosened or disappeared. Formerly defined by his peasant status and village residence, he suddenly found himself enmeshed in a whole complex of new categories, based on land ownership and social mobility. His horizons expanded beyond the self-contained, inwardly directed village community to a wider economic and cultural world. This world offered exciting possibilities for wealth and upward mobility, as well as the freedom to travel and live where he pleased; it also offered grim poverty and dispossession, and possible eviction from the only home he knew. But whether he prospered or failed in this new social system, he had no choice but to enter it. The village community that had defined his existence had disappeared irretrievably by the middle of the 19th century. The community that would replace it, the social order that would emerge from the chaos of land transfers and peasant displacement, had yet to be created.

This social dislocation undermined the core of the established Lutheran Church. Churches on Mors, like those in the rest of Denmark, were intimately connected to the traditional hierarchical structure of village society. The priest acted as a local representative of royal authority; at the end of each Sunday service, for example, he stood outside the church and read a list of government proclamations. His approval gave official sanction to births, marriages, and funerals. Church rituals meshed tightly with the social classifications of village organization. Confirmation, for example, implied not only a passage into full church membership, but also into formal adulthood, completed education, eligibility for agricultural employment, and eligibility for legal rights. Likewise, the seating in Sunday services reflected the divisions of village society. Men and women sat on separate sides of a central aisle, while the estate owners sat in an enclosed and often elevated private booth. Memorial plaques and portraits of former estate owners often adorned the walls; indeed, the church itself usually belonged to the local landowner. In its organization and outlook, the church had its roots in a social order that was rapidly disappearing.

By the middle of the 19th century, therefore, the social classifications that formed the foundation of Morsingbo identity lay in disarray. Old ideas about the place of individuals in society, about the nature of the community, about the rights and obligations of rural individuals, no longer described the world within which Morsingboer found themselves. Their reality had changed, and they needed a new system of categories and ideals to understand it. The old church, with its feet cemented in the old village order, could offer no such innovation. As time went by it seemed increasingly out of step with the lives of its parishioners, and many Morsingboer came to disdain it as a lifeless relic of days gone by. Their cries for church renewal echoed their need for a new religious vision, a recreation of the cosmos in the image of their recreated world.

Peter Larsen Skræppenborg offered just such a vision when he arrived on Mors in 1837. His Grundtvigian pietism proposed not only a new picture of God, but a new understanding of society centered around the rural population (see p. 93). His godly meetings, for example, shifted religious leadership from the village priest to the villagers, and thereby from the representative of the king to the representatives of the folk. The meetings violated traditional parish boundaries, linking people of different villages and kin groups on the basis of a common faith. Their common status as free farmers and artisans, members of a divinely blessed folk culture, overrode the village and estate attachments that had previously defined them. The community was redefined as a community of faith, not of location or common fealty. Its members, moreover, shared equally in the community. God's love for humanity involved an appreciation of their folk heritage, a heritage to which every farmhand and serving maid had a full claim; landlords, merchants, and priests had no greater access to the blessings of God than ordinary farmers. The discredited social distinctions of the old order had no place in Skræppenborg's congregation.

Along with this new vision of the community came a new idea of the individual. Grundtvigians imagined a new free farmer at the heart of their new society. This farmer knew and valued his folk heritage, and actively studied and celebrated it. He understood his close attachment to his community, which he strengthened through participation in its activities and piety in his home. His connection to home and heritage, however, did not mean shutting out the world outside; to the contrary, he learned as much as he could about the world, and sought to increase his community's influence in it. He attended lectures at the Danish Society, classes at the folk high schools, and meetings of the Left Party. So did his wife, whose femininity in no way diminished her capacity for enlightenment.[10] This individual was liberated from the confining roles of the old estate society. He provided a new model of the self for the farmers of Mors, one that fit in neatly with the new community that they were about to build.

10. Not much has been written about the status of women in the Grundtvigian movement, particularly in the movement's early stages, and it is difficult to make general statements about how women participated and were viewed. My reading of the documentary evidence for Mors, though, suggests that they played an active and important part in the movement. Many of Christen Kold's first converts, for example, were wives in the farms of Solbjerg and Øster Jølby. Most leaders of the Grundtvigian movement on Mors have been men, as they are to this day. Yet anecdotes about the movement make frequent reference to assertive and articulate women, some of whom clearly affected the decisions of the leadership. Women were enthusiastic participants in such activities as the Danish Society, the folk high schools, and the gymnastics associations.

This reconception of the world resonated well with the experience of the farm owners, smallholders, and artisans of Mors. It gave them a framework within which to understand the cultural, social, and political power that they suddenly found in their hands. It gave them a new picture of themselves; the ideal of the Grundtvigian farmer, aware of his cultural heritage and in command of his spiritual destiny, replaced the outdated image of the obedient peasant as the archetype of rural society. Perhaps most importantly, it gave them a new basis on which to build a community. The Grundtvigian community was based on a shared faith and social vision, not on the antiquated geographical divisions of traditional society. Those who followed Skræppenborg found a new and vital community in which their own roles were clearly and pleasantly defined. They found an exhilarating solution to the confusion of identity that recent social changes had given them.

By the 1860s, this vision of society had found a following all over the northern half of the island, and in large parts of the southern. Its members, though spread out among a number of villages and attending a number of different churches, considered themselves a community of believers, all part of a single movement. They expressed this belief in their agitation for a single Grundtvigian communion for the island (see p. 109). This communion would not provide simply a central place of worship, but a distinct symbol of the new community they had created. Around it would spring up a new society of Grundtvigian farmers, artisans, schools, banks, clubs, and festivals. In 1870, with the building of the Ansgarskirke, they set this vision in stone. With each brick that they laid in the vacant fields of Øster Jølby, they cemented their community as a visible, viable alternative to the traditional world of the peasantry.

In doing so, however, they unwittingly reimposed some of the structures that the movement had originally opposed. By fixing the congregation in a distinct location, the Grundtvigians reawakened some of the regional rivalries and antagonisms that had characterized the old system. Members from the southern *herred*, for example, felt uncomfortable affiliating with a church in a northern village. Even within northern Mors, residents of villages such as Solbjerg and Sundby had longstanding rivalries with Øster Jølby, which they could not easily put aside. Beyond such outright antagonism, simply traveling to Øster Jølby imposed a hardship on members from the south and east of the island. By building a church, the Choice Congregation introduced geographically based cleavages into a previously unfocused movement.

To those who could not join the new congregation, the building of the Ansgarskirke came as a betrayal. A movement to which they had committed themselves had cast them aside, leaving them out of a new community that they had helped to build. Without it, moreover, they found themselves cast again into the old quandary of identity; the old estate community had dissolved, yet they were unwelcome in the new Grundtvigian order. Where now would they find a model of self, through what framework would they understand themselves and their world? Their resentment was reflected in the bitterness of the splits that followed both the building of the Ansgarskirke in 1970 and the establishment of the Free Congregation in 1883. Disaffected members castigated the new congregations as arrogant hypocrites, deluded by their own vanity and a misunderstanding of their faith. The leading opponents of the congregations soon left the island altogether, and others were left with smoldering resentments that would last a lifetime.

Many of these people found an alternative in the 1890s, when the Inner Mission began building its own congregations on Mors. Like the Grundtvigians, the Inner Mission proposed a radical refiguring of society and the world – but along profoundly different lines. The Mission cast the world in terms of sin and salvation, with most aspects of the traditional world attributed to the machinations of Satan. The world felt alien, unkind, and hostile because it was; no true happiness or salvation could be found in it. The Mission's solution, like that of the Grundtvigians, was to recreate the community, this time as an intense local society of the holy. Its ideal man was not a disciple of folk tradition, but a devotee of pietistic morals, wholly and exclusively committed to the teachings of Jesus. Like that of the Grundtvigians, this world was to be self-contained, with its own societies, institutions, and moral codes. Like the Free Congregation, it provided a clear model for identity and action, along with strict supervision over thought and conduct. Yet unlike the Free Congregation, it rooted this new community in the geographic structures of the old one, with a local focus and attachment to the old church that could not be taken away. For those who felt rejected by the Grundtvigians, or who could not identify with its idealization of folk culture, the Inner Mission provided an energetic alternative solution to pressing problems of identity.

These two movements thus provided different solutions to a common problem. The old world of the estate society had disappeared, leaving rural Morsingboer without a clear framework for understanding themselves and their surroundings. The Grundtvigians and the Inner Mission proposed new understandings of the world, each built around powerful new visions of the community and the individual. The Grundtvigians based their community on a shared folk tradition, the free individual, and the breaking of old geographical divisions; the Inner Mission built its societies on a shared rejection of the world, a stringent moral code, and an intense attachment to the local group. Both offered viable solutions to problems of identity. In addition, both constituted effective ways of organizing society. The Grundtvigians' regional appeal united farmers and artisans from a large area over Mors, and their systems of education and political action dramatically improved the welfare of their members. The Inner Mission communities remained strictly local, but their youth and trade associations made them powerful and well-integrated social groups. In the first half of the 20th century, therefore, both movements became solid institutions with adherents all over the island.

The rise of the Apostolic Church in the 1930s does not appear to have drawn on the same sort of widespread social disorientation that fueled the two larger movements. Its early members tended to come from established Inner Mission communities, which at the time functioned effectively for most of their residents. The scanty data for the period make it hard to assess the motives of these first converts, but many appear to have joined following crises in their personal lives. This pattern may reflect the individualist emphasis of the group. The Apostolic Church, like other religious movements, offered a redefinition of the world and the individual, one that placed enormous power and moral authority in the hands of the individual. Where the Grundtvigians and the missionsfolk emphasized the importance of the community, the Apostolic Church gave the individual a personal pipeline to the divine. Each member had direct, unmediated contact with the Holy Spirit, which the community could only support and interpret. Such contact implied a very particular idea of the individual. It cast the believer in an epic conflict between good and evil, between the omnipresent demons of Satan and the omnipotent powers of God. Issues like residence, occupation, family background, and cultural heritage mattered little in such a context; the individual was defined, and validated, by his personal alliance with God.

For its converts, the Apostolic Church promised a new world in which they could be powerful, secure, and loved by God Himself. Such a redefinition of self had considerable appeal to Morsingboer who had lost touch with their communities due to a personal crisis. Converts often joined while traveling, for example, or working on a farm far from home. Some joined after life-threatening illnesses, or after the death of a loved one. After World War II, the Church found many converts among young men unsure of their place in postwar society. In general, experiences that separated individuals from their social groups made them more likely to join the Church.[11] Such experiences occur in any society, and they provided the Church with a small but steady stream of converts after its arrival. At the same time, the Church's weak vision of the community kept it from challenging the island's mainstream groups. As a haven for the disaffected, the Church became established in, but restricted to, the margins of Mors society.

Times changed for the larger movements after World War II. The mechanization of agriculture, coupled with the expansion of industry in Nykøbing and elsewhere, undercut the foundations of the village social system (see pp. 31-32). Village populations declined and aged, and their shops and social activities disappeared. At the same time, automobiles and mass communications brought the national culture directly to the villagers who remained. The rural social system that had emerged out of the collapse of the estates came itself under strain.

For the Free Congregation, this change created a relatively minor problem. The Congregation had never based itself on the village social system; indeed, in many ways it constituted a rejection of that system. Nor had it ever resisted the ideas and influences of the outside world. The mechanization of farming hurt the Congregation demographically, by reducing the rural population available to it. It particularly affected youths, who provided much of the manpower and energy for the Congregation's social activities. But for those who stayed in the Mors countryside, the Grundtvigian worldview remained as viable as ever. The ideal of the free farmer, the celebration of folk culture, and the commitment to the community of believers still made an effective foundation for understanding the self and the world. Thus the postwar social changes created hardships for the Free Congregation, but they posed no real threat to its existence.

For the Inner Mission, in contrast, these changes were a catastrophe. The Mission had built its ideology around the village community, an intensive and insular holy society separate from the world outside it. This community was an essential part of the movement, providing the entire social and moral environment for its adherents. Its existence

---

11. This tendency has been observed among religious and communal movements in the United States. See Zablocki (1980).

required a nearly total renunciation of the customs and company of nonbelievers. As the villages foundered, therefore, so did the Mission. Farm mechanization forced many members to seek work in the shops and factories of the sinful; many had to leave the villages entirely, to enter the society of Nykøbing or the cities beyond it. Even for those who remained in their established occupations, the insular community became increasingly difficult to sustain. As shops closed and roads opened, the markets of Nykøbing became an important part of villagers' experience. Cars made the world outside more accessible, while radio and television brought it into the home. The walls that the Mission had built around its communities crumbled and fell in the course of two decades. Without these communities, the definitions of self and society that the Mission had provided lost their credibility. Members dropped out of active Mission participation, and they increasingly understood the world and themselves through the rationalist models of the national culture.[12]

It is tempting to view these events as a triumph of reason over ignorance, as an example of modernity's inevitable invasion and destruction of backward, insular worldviews. But the decline of the Mission did not stem from any intellectual dissatisfaction with its theology. Members who entered mainstream culture usually kept many of their ideas about God, Jesus, and the Bible; after all, Mission theology was entirely consistent with standard Folkekirke doctrines. What had been distinct about the Mission was not so much its image of God, as its image of the earthly community. The Mission declined because social and economic changes made this community untenable, not because rationalist argument discredited its worldview.

Indeed, recent changes in Danish society have sometimes benefited religious groups. Among the fastest-growing occupational groups in contemporary Denmark, for example, are professionals and medical workers. Members of these groups exist in a poorly defined area of society, pursuing occupations that have often been made up or dramatically

12. This thesis is a study of the religious movements on Mors, not of the religious presumptions of the Danish national culture. We will not, therefore, explore here the worldview that the missionsfolk adopted when they left the Mission. Such an exploration would require a far larger volume than this one. Readers interested in this issue should consult some of the intriguing studies of contemporary Danish folk religion, pioneered by Jakob Rod (1961, 1972). Salmonsen (1975), Iversen (1986), and Gronblom (1984) also provide sophisticated studies of current Danish religious belief, though they focus primarily on organized church worship.

redefined in the very recent past. In many ways, they find themselves in much the same position as the free farmers of the early 1800s: outside of the old economic order, upwardly mobile, possessed of political power, articulate, and in need of a coherent vision of themselves and their society. Many of them have therefore turned to the same Grundtvigianism that had appealed to the earlier farm owners. Over the past decade, the Free Congregation on Mors has drawn an increasing following among the island's professionals and medical workers. This trend has kept the Congregation growing during a time of declining farm population, when it might have been expected to shrink. These new members seldom invoke theology to explain their affiliation; they say that they have joined the Congregation because they agree with its views of the individual, of society, of education, and of folk culture. Such ideas have the same power in the changing modern society of the 1990s as they had in the brave new world of Mors in 1837.

In summary, a focus on identity and community reveals a complex evolution of the Mors religious movements since 1800. At the opening of the 19th century, the breakup of the estate system produced social dislocation and confusion of identity for former peasants on the island. The Grundtvigian movement provided an appealing and coherent worldview that resolved this quandary of identity, and during the middle of the century it generated a large and diffuse community of believers. In 1870, the building of the Ansgarskirke focused that community around a single location; in doing so, however, it created geographical cleavages within the movement. These splits drove many members out of the movement, and back into the identity problems which Grundtvigianism had relieved. In the 1890s, the Inner Mission provided an alternative solution, based on insular holy communities deeply rooted in the village social system. These two movements developed into powerful institutions on the island in the early 1900s. After World War II, however, farm mechanization produced another drastic social change that transformed village society. For the Free Congregation, whose community had little attachment to the village social system, these changes had relatively minor effects. For the Mission, though, the decline of the villages destroyed the heart of its communities. By the 1990s the Mission had nearly collapsed, while the Free Congregation actually benefited from the increase in professionals and medical workers. Each movement has arisen and declined in concert with particular social changes that have made its vision of the individual and the community appealing for different people at different times.

Comparison of Approaches

Of the two approaches discussed in this chapter, the symbolic approach to religion gives a clearly more satisfying explanation for the religious movements on Mors. Secularization theory provides a simple and intuitively appealing picture of religious change, one which seems at first to apply to the island's history, and one which the people of Mors themselves would largely accept. On closer examination, however, it tends to distort and oversimplify the actual character of the movements. Since it opposes science to religion, it must portray the movements either as holdouts from or reactions against the scientific worldview. In reality, their relationship to science and modernity was much more complex; they were never the conservative or isolated entities supposed by the theory. The second model, which focuses on religion's role in providing community and identity for members, produces an account more true to the development of the movements. It effectively links the rise and decline of the various groups to specific social and economic changes. It also explains how the specific ideologies and theologies of the different movements relate to their differential success. By using a broader understanding of religion, the symbolic approach provides a richer picture of the culture it describes.

Religion and Identity Beyond Mors

The sorts of social change and identity dislocation that seem to have driven religious developments on Mors are by no means unique to the island. The mechanization of agriculture, the decline of rural society, changes in government, family, and education – these patterns have swept through most of the Western world over the past century. In many cases, they have been accompanied by changes more severe and more disorienting than those experienced by Morsingboer. In the United States, for example, the past thirty years have seen a radical reorientation of gender roles; a massive shift in the structure of the industrial economy; a collapse of faith in the national political system; a reallocation of power among ethnic and racial groups; profound changes in the nature of childcare and domestic life; and a host of other social and cultural changes. Using the model outlined here, we might expect these upheavals to produce tremendous strains on individual identities. Finding a reliable and coherent sense of self, one rooted in a relationship to

240

a community and a culture, ought to become increasingly difficult. Some evidence suggests that this is the case; Christopher Lasch, for example, has argued that identity disorders have become endemic in American society (1979; see also Zablocki 1980, Lifton 1970, Bellah 1985, Lindholm 1990). The same forces that generated awakenings and restructuring of the religious world on Mors have arisen in equal or greater strength elsewhere in the West.

If this is the case, then the model that we found most effective for understanding Mors may serve us equally well elsewhere. Resurgences of religion in the United States, the Middle East, and Eastern Europe have puzzled secularization theorists in recent decades. Religious movements have surfaced not only among the poor and dispossessed, but also among educated middle classes well versed in the teachings of science. Religious revival does not clearly correspond to any decline in the legitimacy or explanatory efficacy of science. It does, however, tend to coincide with periods of profound social change, change which calls for a redefinition of the individual and the world. Russians after the fall of communism, Iranians during the rise of Khomeini, even "yuppies" in Reagan's America shared a common sense of separation from the old social order. In their longing for a divine recreation of the world, they echoed the feelings of the free farmers of Mors during the 1830s. A focus on identity may provide a common model for all of these movements, and thus a true cross-cultural theory of religion.

It is beyond my scope here to address these areas in detail. I can suggest the general approach, however, by briefly discussing two intriguing religious movements in the United States: conservative Christian fundamentalism and the New Age.

Identity and American Fundamentalism

Christian fundamentalism is a longstanding force in American religion (Finke and Stark 1992). Since the early 1970s, however, it has taken a leap forward in visibility and power, largely on the basis of its involvement in social and political issues. Since the late 1970s, American fundamentalists have made social policy an integral part of their religious message. Leaders such as Jerry Falwell, Pat Robertson, and Ralph Reed have connected fundamentalism to a variety of worldly issues; they argue that there is a Christian position on such matters as abortion, childrearing, taxation, health care, and even defense policy. In doing so, they have welded a vast number of independent churches into a single movement known as the Christian Right. This strategy has drawn criticism from many observers, who view Falwell and his allies as Bible-thumping demagogues. Critics have scolded the Christian Right for mixing religion and politics, and they have often suggested that the movement's religious principles are simply a cloak for a conservative political agenda. Members of the group disagree violently, contending that their political views are a legitimate extension of strongly held religious beliefs.

The situation of the Christian Right exhibits striking parallels with that of the Grundtvigian movement in the late 19th century in Denmark. In each case, religious views were inseparable from social ones, and they had important political repercussions. In each case, a common religious and political position united a large number of independent congregations. And in each case, opponents interpreted the movements' social activism as a perversion of the proper role of religion. When explaining the power of the fundamentalist movement, critics have often located its strength in the power of its belief – because of the intensity of their faith, it is argued, fundamentalists can be led to join a variety of conservative political and social causes. My analysis of the Grundtvigians, however, suggests that we might do well to focus also on community. The political and social aspects of New Right fundamentalism may not be secondary spinoffs of strong belief; it may be that by linking the cosmological world with the social one, they help create religious communities within which identities may be safely established.

Indeed, creating community is one of the greatest strengths of contemporary American fundamentalism. Fundamentalist churches tend to have active outreach programs, which ensure that new or prospective members are quickly integrated into the social world of the group. Prayer meetings, youth groups, social service networks, and an active clergy keep members in ongoing contact with each other. Theologically, an emphasis on the wages of sin and a personal relationship with Christ keep the church relevant to even the most private moments of life. Membership in the church, moreover, is more than a matter of affiliation; it requires a change of heart, a rebirth, an explicitly new identity as a member of the congregation. To become such a Christian is to become a new person, one enlivened with the power and joy conferred by a personal experience of Christ. The community created by the church can therefore become extremely intense. It draws tightly together a group of people whose individual identities and experiences are bound up tightly in their status as members.

The social and political dimensions of the fundamentalist movement, then, may function in much the same way as those of the Grundtvigians – to create a total world for adherents, in which all aspects of everyday experience can be brought into accordance with the identity implied in membership. There is a "Christian" way, just as there was a "free" way or a "Mission" way, to pattern virtually every piece of daily activity. Christian childcare books tell mothers how to raise children in a holy manner. Christian business manuals tell businessmen how to incorporate Christ into their workplaces. There are Christian guides to breastfeeding, entertaining, home decorating, vacation planning, tax preparation, storytelling, and marital relations. Beyond them, an array of self-help books, support groups, radio shows, and telephone banks exists to help translate individual emotions and experiences into Christian allegory. For members of the movement, the world is not the disorienting chaos of a society in constant transition. It is a place where every activity and every experience can be understood as an expression of a comprehensible universal order.

This worldview, whatever its limitations as a theological system, offers a solution to the predicament of contemporary America. In a society that has lost its moorings, where established roles and expectations have little relation to the present or the future, the new Christian fundamentalism offers a solid, integrated, comprehensive understanding of the world. It offers a large community within which that worldview makes sense. It ties daily experience tightly to that worldview, and provides extensive support to ensure that no event or emotion need be understood in any other terms. In its rhetoric, moreover, it appeals to precisely the sort of anxieties generated by contemporary social change. It appeals to "biblical truth," to "traditional family structures," to "old-fashioned American values." It promises a community that will not change over time, one whose timeless values will provide a firm foundation on which members may build their identities. It offers a rock of unchanging truth amid the shifting sands of contemporary America.

The rise of fundamentalism in the past two decades may derive less from its specific ideas about the supernatural than from the sort of identity it offers. If so, the standard criticisms of the Christian Right may be unfair, or at least unrealistic. Opponents often attack the movement for exceeding the proper bounds of religious expression, for suggesting that God cares about such mundane matters as clothing styles or the strategic arms limitation treaty. Yet the strength of the new fundamentalism may lie precisely in its ability to encompass the mundane as well as the divine. By insisting on a common logic for cosmology, politics, social life, and expressive culture, the movement gives its members a coherent picture of the world, and a clear understanding of how they fit into it. It makes their world a place within which they themselves can make sense.

Identity and the New Age

The increasing visibility of Christian fundamentalism in the United States has been paralleled by the apparent expansion of a radically different religious movement: the New Age, a loose assortment of fringe groups and cults far removed from the Christian Right. The New Age spans a broad range of phenomena, including trance channeling, alternative healing, psychic divination, shamanism, crystal therapy, and interaction with extraterrestrial beings. Most of its beliefs and practices have a long history in the United States, deriving in some cases from 19th century spiritualist movements. In the 1980s, however, the New Age achieved an unprecedented amount of interest and publicity. Thanks in large part to the activities of actress Shirley Maclaine, the New Age became one of the most visible elements of the American religious world, attracting the devotion of thousands and the curiosity of millions. It has exercised an influence far out of proportion to its tiny membership; indeed, in the eyes of much of the Christian Right, it represents the most potent threat in existence to the success of Christianity in the United States (Friedrich 1993, Finke and Stark 1992, Burrows 1987).

The rise of the New Age seems to defy both the predictions and the basic assumptions of secularization theory. It enjoys some of its greatest strength in areas where the theory suggests religion should be weakest: in intellectual and artistic communities, often in university centers, where science is familiar and widely accepted. Much of the New Age does not, in fact, see itself as opposed to science. While they resent the establishment that supposedly controls scientific research, for example, many New Age healers feel confident that science will ultimately vindicate them. New Age groups draw heavily on the social sciences, particularly anthropology, and some pattern their organizations on scientific institutes.[13] Secularization theory's opposition between religion and science is therefore difficult to apply to New Age groups. The theory's focus on belief, likewise, sorts poorly with the nature of New Age affiliation. Some peo-

---

13. In Berkeley, California, for example, one of the most visible New Age groups calls itself the Berkeley Psychic Institute, and explicitly describes itself as a research and education foundation.

ple do join New Age sects, avowing a true belief in their theological and philosophical doctrines. Many more, however, simply dabble in New Age literature and ritual, sympathizing with its viewpoints but reserving judgment on their ultimate truth. While sales of crystals, books, workshops, and other New Age products have skyrocketed in recent years, the number of Americans who regard New Age groups as their primary religious affiliation remain quite small (Finke and Stark 1992: 245). The rise of the New Age seems to represent neither a decline in scientific awareness nor a surge of supernatural belief.

It may be more fruitful to see the success of the New Age in terms of its statements about individual identity, rather than its views about supernatural forces. A recurrent theme in the New Age is the search for an authentic self, a true identity rooted in nature, the cosmos, or the past. Trance channelers connect themselves to a series of past lives, some of which feel truer and more dramatic, more of an expression of their true natures, than the current one. Shamanists pick and choose chants and spells from a variety of tribal cultures, each supposedly closer to the true rhythm of the earth than is the West. Members of Wicca celebrate the community of witches, and understand their own identities as part of a larger diabolical tradition. Users of crystals impute a sort of wavelength to themselves and to the universe, and understand their feelings as results of harmony and dissonance with an authentically correct tone. Through all of them runs the message that the self as constituted by mainstream society is inadequate, unsatisfying, and incomplete. The movements do not, by and large, offer a particularly satisfying replacement; very few people actually join them. They remain of interest, however, because their depiction of mainstream society rings true for many Americans. In a world of dizzying change, where the foundations of personal identity are constantly eroding, the notion of a true self rooted in the authentic past or the unchanging rhythms of the universe has strong appeal. The number of Americans who dabble in the New Age, then, may say less about the spiritual power of the New Age movements than about the tenuous basis for identity in the larger society.

The approach to religion outlined here allows a richer understanding of contemporary religious development than the theoretical approaches that have so far dominated the subject. It views religion as an aspect of social life, and regards its social classifications as seriously as its supernatural ones. It can also help us move beyond the ethnocentrism that has all too often characterized the study of Western religion. It can place the inhabitants of the modern West in the same analytical framework as the people of the rest of the world, and the rest of history. We need not assume that our own scientific worldview stands above all other understandings of the universe; science can stand, rather, as one of many worldviews, responding like the others to a common need for identity and community. While acknowledging its unique features, we can incorporate modern thought into a general theory of human belief.

If the scientific worldview is like others, moreover, then it will not last forever; another transformation of society will one day bring in something new, or perhaps bring back something old. On the island of Mors, social change may one day even bring the renewal of faith for which the missionsfolk so devoutly pray. Members of the religious movements on Mors often compare awakenings to the wind, which comes and goes for reasons beyond human understanding. An awakening could come anytime, they say, arising next week or next year or next decade as unpredictably as a summer storm. They may be right. Perhaps even now, out somewhere in the icy North Sea, the winds of awakening gather over the waters, building their strength and biding their time, waiting for their signal to sweep once more down into the Limfjord, and rekindle the fire of God in the hearts and souls of Morsingboer.

APPENDIX
Membership Statistics

෨ ෨ ෨

*C*hapters 5, 6, and 7 of Part III present statistics on membership for the three religious movements discussed in this work. Statistics tend to be presented, here as elsewhere, in terms of very exact numbers, which lend an air of precision to an often incomplete or unsatisfactory body of data. Compiling statistics, moreover, involves decisions about interpreting data that are inevitably largely arbitrary. I believe that the membership statistics presented in the body of this study accurately reflect the compositions of the different groups. For the benefit of interested readers, however, I would like to describe the data used for each group, and some of the decisions that went into compiling the statistics.

The Free Congregation

The Free Congregation has an unusual amount of archival material available for investigators, much of it stored in a large wooden box in the basement of the parsonage. Records include *kirkebøger*, the large bound volumes that record births, deaths, confirmations, and weddings in the congregation; *protokoler*, bound volumes that record the people present and issues discussed at congregation meetings; *bidragslister*, lists of contributors to the Congregation, often listing the amounts given; assorted correspondence, including the copy books of Rasmus Lund; various historical documents, such as newspaper articles about the congregation and announcements for congregation functions; and an original hand-written history of the congregation by editor Henrik Fog of the *Morsø Folkeblad*. This wealth of information allows a very rich historical recon-struction of the movement from about 1870 onward. In addition, a number of historians have written about the congregation. In terms of membership information, the best sources are treatments by ethnologist Margareta Balle-Petersen and former priest Per Fisker.

The data presented here about the movement's early membership come largely from the work of Fisker and Balle-Petersen, both of whom present statistics on the occupational makeup of the congregation's early members. It should be noted that the two authors do not always agree; in cases of dis-agreement, I have sided with Balle-Petersen, who has made a particularly rigorous study. I have checked the figures of these authors with my own reading of the congregation's early membership, and have found them con-vincing. I have not, however, made an independent analysis of the issue.

The data on current membership are my own work, based on a list of Free Congregation members given to me by the current priest, Erik Overgaard. Members include all those who pay dues to the Congrega-tion, as well as their children who have undergone confirmation. The Congregation does not maintain any systematic records of the occupa-tions of its members. I therefore found the occupations myself, based on those listed in the island's address register; because of the frequent repe-tition of names in Denmark, public records identify individuals by occu-pation as well as name. After entering every member and his or her address into a dBASE III+ database, I cross-referenced the list with the 1991 Mors *Addressebog*, and entered the occupations listed there.

This procedure presented two problems. First of all, not all members had listed occupations in the book. For such people, how could one fix an occupation? In some cases, doing so was clearly impossible, and I did not include those people in the summary statistics. In others, the per-son's address made identification possible. A person living at the address of a retirement home, for example, without any listed occupation, could be safely assumed to be a retiree. Likewise, a woman living on a farm, married to a man whose occupation was listed as farm owner, could be safely assumed to be pursuing the role of a farmer's wife. These assump-tions involve a certain degree of risk, but I believe that they have not compromised the statistics.

It is impossible at this point to say anything for certain about those for whom I was unable to find occupations. Many of them are certainly children, who have not yet entered the workforce. Most of the rest are probably retirees. Since agricultural employment has declined in recent years, I suspect that the retirees include a greater percentage of agricultural workers than the younger members; if we were to ascertain occupations for all members, therefore, I believe that the percentage of agricultural workers in the congregation would be slightly higher than that listed in the text. The recent rise in wage work among women, likewise, means that the figures in the text may understate the number of housewives in the congregation.

The other problem related to classifying occupations into categories. Most occupations were fairly easy to categorize; a carpenter is clearly an artisan, for example, and a smallholder is clearly an agricultural worker. Others involved more arbitrary judgments. A *sygehjælp*, for example, is an assistant in a hospital setting roughly equivalent to an orderly. Should such a worker be classified in the same group as the nurses, or in a group with janitors and laborers? A plausible case could be made for either grouping. The ultimate decision on classification must rely on an intuitive sense of the place of the work in the local culture.

The Inner Mission

The Inner Mission presents many more statistical difficulties than the Free Congregation, primarily because its membership is less clearly defined. Officially, the organization has no members; since it is allied with the Folkekirke, any Dane who wants to may participate. Almost everyone involved in the Mission contributes to his or her local mission house, and contributor lists are sometimes used as a guide to effective membership; some contributors, though, seem to contribute out of habit or family tradition, so that contributor lists may tend to exaggerate the amount of active participation. Without the clear membership criteria of the Free Congregation, the Mission presents a challenge for statistical analysis.

In this chapter, I have dealt with this problem by allowing a local expert to define membership for me. I asked the head of the Mission circle in Sejerslev, Jørgen Bruun Bendtsen, to draw up a list of all active missionsfolk in the village. The sixty-five names which he gave me represent his assessment of the local Mission community, and they have formed the basis of the statistics presented here. I determined occupations in the same way as for the Free Congregation.

The Apostolic Church

As mentioned in the text, the Apostolic Church has few records of any kind with which its early membership could be reconstructed. Indeed, even current membership is difficult to ascertain, because church officials are reluctant to give out the information. My own efforts at obtaining a list of members met with little success. This lack of membership information is puzzling, since converts are encouraged to proclaim their belief to the world; it may stem from a discrepancy between the church's ideology of constant expansion and its actual small size. For a group devoted to evangelization and proclaiming the Word, a small congregation is an indictment of its success. The figures on membership cited in the text are drawn from anecdotes and estimates given to me by members.

To get a sense of the occupational and gender breakdown of the congregation, I relied on my own observations and on the few written sources available. Each year, the congregation publishes a brief annual report, which often includes the names of people who worked on particular projects; such reports provide a limited list of the Church's most active members. In addition, a *jubilæumskrift* published in connection with the Church's fiftieth anniversary celebration in 1986 contained scattered information about its membership and history. None of these sources, including my own observations, provides a satisfactory list of the Church's members; accordingly, I have used general statements, rather than statistics, to describe occupations in the church.

BIBLIOGRAPHY

❧ ❧ ❧

Abildtrup, Jens, *Iver Viftrup: En lægprædikant fra de gudelige forsamlingers tid.*
Copenhagen, 1930.

Anderson, Barbara Gallatin, *First Fieldwork: The Misadventures of an Anthropologist.* Prospect Heights, IL, 1990.

Anderson, Robert, *Denmark: Success of a Developing Nation.* Cambridge MA, 1975.

Anderson, Robert and Barbara Gallatin Anderson, "Sexual Behavior and Urbanization in a Danish Village," *Southwestern Journal of Anthropology* 16:1(1960).

_____, *The Vanishing Village: A Danish Maritime Community.* Seattle, 1964.

Aron, Raymond, *Main Currents in Sociological Thought: Durkheim, Pareto, Weber.* New York, 1967.

Asad, Talal, *Genealogies of Religion: Discipline and Reasons of Power In Christianity and Islam.* Baltimore, 1993.

Ausmus, Harry J., *The Polite Escape: On the Myth of Secularization.* Athens, Ohio, 1982.

Bainbridge, William Sims, "Utopian Communities: Theoretical Issues," in Hammond, Philip E.,ed., *The Sacred in a Secular Age.* Berkeley, 1985: 21-35.

_____, *A Theory of Religion.* New York, 1987.

Balle-Petersen, Margareta, "Guds Folk i Danmark," *Folk og Kultur,* 1977.

_____, "Grundtvigske Kulturmiljøer," in Jørgen Jensen and Erik Nielsen, eds., *Efterklange: Et Grundtvig-Seminar.* Århus, 1983.

_____, "Vækkelserne som Religiøse Minoriteter," in Ragnhild Kristensen and Ole Riis, eds., *Religiøse Minoriteter.* Århus, 1987.

251

Barnes, J.A., "Class and Commitment in a Norwegian Island Parish," *Human Relations* 7:1(1954): 39-58.

Barth, Frederik, *Ethnic Groups and Boundaries: The Social Organization of Culture Difference.* Boston, 1969.

Begtrup, Holger, *Dansk Menighedsliv i Gruntvigske Kredse: En Historisk Fremstilling.* Vol. 5: *Nord-, Midt-, og Vestjylland.* Copenhagen, 1934.

_____, *N.F.S. Grundtvigs Danske Kristendom.* 2 vols. Copenhagen, 1936.

Berger, Peter L., *The Sacred Canopy: Elements of a Sociological Theory of Religion.* Garden City, 1967.

Bellah, Robert N., *Beyond Belief: Essays on Religion in a Post-Traditional World.* New York, 1970.

_____, *Habits of the Heart.* New York, 1985.

Blauenfeldt, Louis, *Den Indre Missions Historie.* Copenhagen, 1912.

Borg, Anton, Erik Hesselager, Holger Jørgensen, Arnold Kæseler, and Per Vegger, *Kirker på Mors.* Nykøbing, 1989.

Borish, Steven, *Land of the Living: The Danish Folk High Schools and Denmark's Non-Violent Path to Modernization.* Nevada City, 1991.

Breiner, Magne, *Vækkelsen og Indre Mission på Fur.* Nederby, 1986.

Bruce, Steve, ed., *Religion and Modernization.* Oxford, 1992.

Brusgaard, Sven Aage, Ingrid Marie Madsen, and Kirsten Ulrich, eds., *Mors og Morsingboerne: Tanker og Billeder ved et Jubilæum.* Copenhagen, 1977.

Buckser, Andrew S., "Sacred Airtime: Church Structures and the Rise of Televangelism," *Human Organization* 48:4: (1989): 370-76.

_____, "Religion and the Supernatural on a Danish Island: Rewards, Compensators, and the Meaning of Religion," *Journal for the Scientific Study of Religion* 34:1(1995): 1-16.

_____, "Tradition, Power, and Allegory: Constructions of the Past in Two Danish Religious Movements," *Ethnology* 34:4(1995): 257-72.

Burrows, R., "A Christian Critiques the New Age," *Christianity Today* 16 (1987).

Chaves, Mark, "Secularization as Declining Religious Authority," *Social Forces* 72:3(1994): 749-774.

_____, "Intraorganizational Power and Internal Secularization in Protestant Denominations," *American Journal of Sociology* 99(1993): 1-48.

Christiansen, Palle Ove, "Forms of Peasant Dependency in a Danish Estate 1775-1975," *Peasant Studies* 7:1(1978).

_____, *Fire Landsbyer: En Etnologisk Rapport om nutidige livsformer.* Copenhagen, 1980

Christensen, Christen, *Nykjøbing paa Mors 1299-1899.* Copenhagen, 1902.

Clifford, James, *The Predicament of Culture: Twentieth-Century Ethnography, Literature, and Art.* Cambridge MA, 1988.

Crippen, Timothy, "Further Notes on Religious Transformation," *Social Forces* 71:1(1992):219-223.

Dal, Frode, *Digte og Sange.* Nykøbing Mors, 1943.

Danish Ministry of Education, *Folkeskole: Primary and Lower Secondary Education in Denmark.* Skive, 1988.

Dawson, Christopher Henry, *America and the Secularization of Modern Culture.* Houston, 1960.

Det Danske Selskab, *The Limfjord: Its Towns and People.* Ålborg, 1964.

Dobbelaere, Karel, "Secularization: A Multi-Dimensional Concept," *Current Sociology* 29(1981):1-216.

_____, "Secularization Theories and Sociological Paradigms: A Reformulation of the Private-Public Dichotomy and the Problem of Societal Integration," *Sociological Analysis* 46(1985): 377-78.

_____, "The Secularization of Society? Some Methodological Suggestions," in Jeffrey K. Hadden and Anson Shupe, eds., *Secularization and Fundamentalism Reconsidered.* New York, 1989: 27-43.

"Some Trends In European Sociology of Religion: The Secularization Debate," *Sociological Analysis* 48(1987): 107-37.

Douglas, Mary, *Purity and Danger: An Analysis of the Concepts of Pollution and Taboo.* New York, 1966.

_____, *Natural Symbols: Explorations in Cosmology.* New York, 1970.

_____, *Implicit Meanings: Essays in Anthropology.* London, 1975.

_____, "The Effects of Modernization on Religious Change," *Daedalus* 3:1(1982): 1-19.

Durkheim, Emile, *The Elementary Forms of the Religious Life.* New York, 1965.

Eilstrup, Per and Nils Eric Boesgaard, *Fjernt fra Danmark: Billeder fra vore Tropekolonier, Slavehandel og Kinafart.* Copenhagen, 1974.

Eister, Allan W., *Changing Perspectives in the Scientific Study of Religion.* New York, 1974.

Ejerslev, M.P., *Bette Wolle fra Mors: Et Gruntvigske Tidsbillede.* Kolding, 1947.

_____, "En Religiøs Bevægelse i Jørsby," *Historisk Aarbog for Thy og Mors* 1970.

Eliade, Mircea, *The Sacred and the Profane: The Nature of Religion.* San Diego, 1959.

Evans-Pritchard, E. E., *The Nuer: A Description of the Modes of Livelihood and Political Institutions of a Nilotic People.* Oxford, 1940.

_____, *Theories of Primitive Religion.* Oxford, 1965.

_____, *Witchcraft, Oracles, and Magic among the Azande.* Oxford, 1958.

Fabricius, L.P., *Danmarks Kirkehistorie I: Middelalderen.* Copenhagen, 1934.

_____, *Vor Kirkes Reformation.* Copenhagen, 1936.

Fenn, Richard K., *Toward a Theory of Secularization.* Society for the Scientific Study of Religion Monograph Series No. 1, 1978.

Finke, Roger, "An Unsecular America," in Steve Bruce, ed., *Religion and Modernization*. Oxford, 1992.

Finke, Roger, and Rodney Stark, *The Churching of America 1776-1990*. New Brunswick, 1992.

Fisker, Per, *Morsø Frimenighed, 1871-1971*. Nykøbing Mors, 1971.

Fitzgerald, Frances, *Cities on a Hill*. New York, 1986.

Freud, Sigmund, *Group Psychology and the Analysis of the Ego*. New York, 1922.

_____, *Totem and Taboo: Resemblances between the Psychic Lives of Savages and Neurotics*. New York, 1918.

Friedrich, Otto, "New Age Harmonies," in A. Lehmann and J. Myers, ed., *Magic, Witchcraft, and Religion*. Mountain View, CA, 1993.

Fromm, Erich, *Man for Himself: An Inquiry into the Psychology of Ethics*. New York, 1947.

Frykman, Jonas and Orvar Lofgren, *Culture Builders: A Historical Anthropology of Middle-Class Life*. New Brunswick, 1987.

Fuchs, Estelle, "The Danish Friskoler and Community Control," in E. Leacock, ed., *The Culture of Poverty*. New York, 1971.

Geertz, Clifford, *The Interpretation of Cultures*. New York, 1973.

_____, *Writing Culture: The Poetics and Politics of Ethnography*. Berkeley, 1986.

Glock, C.Y. and P.E. Hammond, eds., *Beyond the Classics?* New York, 1973.

Glyn-Jones, W., *Denmark: A Modern History*. Dover, 1986.

Goodenough, Ward E., "Toward an Anthropologically Useful Definition of Religion," in Eister, ed., *Changing Perspectives in the Scientific Study of Religion*. New York, 1974: 165-84.

Greenhouse, Carol., *Praying for Justice: Faith, Order, and Community in an American Town*. Ithaca, 1986.

Gronblom, Gunnar, *Dimensions of Religiosity: The Operationalization and Measurement of Religiosity With Special Regard To the Problem of Dimensionality*. Åbo, 1984.

Guthrie, Stewart, *Faces in the Clouds: A New Theory of Religion*. Oxford, 1993.

Hadden, Jeffrey K., "Toward Desacralizing Secularization Theory," *Social Forces* 65 (1987): 587-611.

Hadden, Jeffrey K. and Anson Shupe, eds., *Secularization and Fundamentalism Reconsidered*. New York, 1989.

Hamberg, Eva, "The Religious Market: Denominational Competition and Religious Participation In Contemporary Sweden," *Journal for the Scientific Study of Religion* 33:3(1994): 205-16.

_____, "Stability and Change in Religious Beliefs, Practices and Attitudes: A Swedish Panel Study," *Journal for the Scientific Study of Religion* 30:1(1991): 63.

Hammond, Philip E., ed., *The Sacred in a Secular Age*. Berkeley, 1985.

Hansen, Dorthe, *Turisme på Mors: Valg af Målgruppe*. Nykøbing Mors, 1990.

Hansen, Judith Friedman, *Danish Social Interaction: Cultural Assumptions and Patterns of Behavior*. Doctoral dissertation, University of California, Berkeley, 1970.

Hartling, Poul, *The Danish Church*. Copenhagen, 1964.

Hegnsvad, Herluf, "De Stærke Jyder," in Anders Pontoppidan Thyssen, ed., *Vækkelsernes Frembrud i Danmark i første Halvdel af det 19. Århundrede*, Vol. IV, *De Ældre Jyske Vækkelser*. Aarhus, 1967: 179-269.

Hendin, Herbert, *Suicide and Scandinavia*. New York, 1964.

Holch Andersen, Karl Georg, *Rofærge og Dampdrift: Færgefart på Sallingsund*. Nykøbing Mors, 1974.

_____, *Nykøbing-borgerne og Deres Kirke*. Nykøbing Mors, 1975.

_____, *1864 og Morsingboerne*. Nykøbing Mors, 1976.

_____, *Hestekraft og Motorvogn*. Nykøbing Mors, 1978.

_____, *Typer og Tryk i en Lille By: Morsø Avis og Morsø Bogtrykkeri i 125 År*. Nykøbing Mors, 1980.

_____, *Gamle Postkort fra Mors*. Nykøbing Mors, 1981.

_____, *Kammerherrens Højris*. Nykøbing Mors, 1983.

_____, *Det Hvide Lys Tændes*. Nykøbing Mors, 1985.

_____, *Vilsund-overfarten*. Nykøbing Mors, 1989.

_____, *Nykøbing Mors i Tekst og Billeder 1800-1940*. Nykøbing Mors, 1990.

Holt, Paul, *Kirkelig Forening for den Indre Mission i Danmark Gennem 100 År, 1861-1961*. Copenhagen, 1961.

Hovmøller, Hans Kristjan, ed., [1871] *Barnesyn og Ønske af Anders Svendsen Hovmøller*. Vester Jølby, 1982.

Hunter, James Davidson, *American Evangelicalism: Conservative Religion and the Quandary of Modernity*. New Brunswick, 1983.

_____, "Conservative Protestantism," in Hammond, ed., *The Sacred in a Secular Age*. Berkeley, 1985.

Hunter, Leslie Stannard, ed., *Scandinavian Churches: A Picture of the Development and Life of the Churches of Denmark, Finland, Iceland, Norway, and Sweden*. London, 1965.

Hvidt, Kristian, *Flugten til Amerika: Drivekrafter i masseudvandringen fra Danmark 1868-1914*. Copenhagen, 1971.

Højmark, Asger and Uffe Hansen, *De Grundtvigske Fri- og Valgmenigheder: En Historisk Oversigt med en Kort Fremstilling af Hvert Enkelt Menigheds Tilblivelse og Virksomhed*. Odense, 1944.

Iversen, Hans and Anders Pontoppidan Thyssen, eds., *Kirke og Folk i Danmark: Kirkesociologisk Dokumentation*. Copenhagen, 1986.

Iversen, Hans and Ole Riis, "Nyreligiositetens Baggrund i Danmark," *Nyt Synspunkt* 11(1980): 24-40.

Jakobsen, Frode, *Da Leret Tog Form.* Copenhagen, 1976.

_____, *Alt Hvad der Jæger Min Sjæl.* Copenhagen, 1977.

Jensen, F. Elle, "En Kysse-Sekt paa Mors," *Historisk Aarbog for Thisted Amt.* Copenhagen, 1944: 118-27.

_____, "Pietismen i Thy," *Historisk Aarbog for Thisted Amt.* Copenhagen, 1946: 363-375.

Jørgensen, Alfred T., *Nordens Kirker og Nordiske Aandsstrømninger Efter Verdenskrigen.* Copenhagen, 1921.

Jørgensen, Erik Lau, ed., *Morslandet.* Nykøbing Mors, 1975.

Kanter, Rosabeth Moss, *Commitment and Community.* Cambridge MA, 1972.

Kirk, Hans, "Religion og hartkorn," *Clarte,* 1926.

_____, *Fiskerne.* Copenhagen, 1978 [1928].

Koch, Hal, *Danmarks Kirke gennem Tiderne.* Copenhagen, 1960.

Kornerup, Bjørn, Hal Koch, N.K. Andersen, and P.G. Lindhardt, *Den Danske Kirkes Historie I-VIII.* Copenhagen, 1950.

Krogh, J.C., *Gamle Danse fra Mors og Thy.* Copenhagen, 1973.

Larsen, Kurt E., *Indre Mission i Ny Tid.* Fredericia, 1986.

Lasch, Christopher, *The Culture of Narcissism.* New York, 1979.

Lauring, Palle, *A History of the Kingdom of Denmark.* Copenhagen, 1963.

Lausten, Martin Schwarz, *Danmarks Kirkehistorie.* Copenhagen, 1987.

Lavsen, Jens Mathias, *Mindebog.* Nykøbing Mors, 1942.

Leach, Edmund, *Political Systems of Highland Burma: A Study of Kachin Social Structure.* Cambridge (UK), 1954.

Lechner, Frank J., "The Case Against Secularization: A Rebuttal," *Social Forces* 69:4(1991): 1103-19.

Lemberg, Kai, *Dominant Ways of Life in Denmark, Alternative Ways of Life in Denmark.* Tokyo, 1980.

Lifton, R. J., *History and Human Survival.* New York, 1970.

Lillelund, Charlotte, *Erindringer.* Unpublished manuscript, Morsø Frimenighed Archive.

Lindberg, P. "Biskop Lind og Bevægelsen paa Mors." *Morgenbladet* 51(1883):1.

Lindhardt, P.G., *Vækkelse og Kirkelige Retninger.* Copenhagen, 1959.

Lindholm, Charles T., *Generosity and Jealousy: The Swat Pukhtun of Northern Pakistan.* New York, 1982.

_____, *Charisma.* London, 1990.

Luckmann, Thomas and Peter Berger, *The Social Construction of Reality: A Treatise in the Sociology of Knowledge.* New York, 1966.

Martin, David, *The Religious and the Secular: Studies in Secularization.* London, 1969.

_____, *A General Theory of Secularization.* New York, 1978.

Michelsen, Peter and Holger Rasmussen, *Danish Peasant Culture.* Copenhagen, 1955.

Mills, C. Wright, *The Sociological Imagination.* New York, 1959.

Morsø Kommune Tekniske Forvaltning, *Statistisk Information 1979.* Nykøbing Mors, 1979.

_____, *Befolkningsprognose 1988-2003.* Nykøbing Mors, 1988.

Mortensen, Kurt, *Apostolsk Kirke i Danmark, 1924-1974.* Roskilde, 1974.

Mulder, D. C., ed., *Secularization in Global Perspective.* Amsterdam, 1981.

Munck, Knud, *Grundtvig og Grundtvigianerne: Indføring og Kilder.* Copenhagen, 1984.

Nielsen, Ernest D., *N. F. S. Grundtvig: An American Study.* Rock Island, IL, 1955.

Nørgaard, Anders, *Grundtvig og Danmark.* Copenhagen, 1941.

Nygaard, Jens Jørgen, *Kristne Samfund i Danmark.* Copenhagen, 1982.

Oakley, Stewart, *A Short History of Denmark.* New York, 1972.

Orru, Marco, and Amy Wang, "Durkheim, Religion, and Buddhism," *Journal for the Scientific Study of Religion* 31(1992): 47-61.

Ortner, Sherry, *High Religion: A Cultural and Political History of Sherpa Buddhism.* Princeton, 1989.

Overgaard, Suzanne, "C.B. Godskesen: Købmand, Værtshusholder og Sparrekassedirektør," *Jul på Mors* 26(1988): 26-31.

Pedersen, Gerhard, *Om Kirken: Indføring i Kirkekundskab.* Copenhagen, 1970.

Pedersen, Valdemar, *Indre Mission paa Mors gennem et Halvt Aarhundrede.* Struer, 1937.

Piø, Iørn, "Harald Blåtand på Mors i 974," in E. Lau Jørgensen, ed., *Morslandet.* Nykøbing Mors, 1975.

Pontoppidan, Erik, *Danske Atlas.* Copenhagen, 1769.

Pontoppidan Thyssen, Anders, *Den Nygrundtvigske Bevægelse med Særligt Henblik paa den Borupske Kreds.* Vol. 1: 1870-1887. Aarhus, 1957.

_____, "Brødremenigheden i Christiansfeld og herrnhutismen i Jylland til o. 1815," In Anders Pontoppidan Thyssen, ed., *Vækkelsernes Frembrud i Danmark i første Halvdel af det 19. Århundrede,* Vol. IV, *De Ældre Jyske Vækkelser.* Copenhagen, 1967: 11-175.

_____, "Sækulariseringsprocessen i Danmark," *Nyt Synspunkt* 11(1980):7-23 .

Pontoppidan Thyssen, Anders and Frands Ole Overgaard, *De Senere Jyske Vækkelser: Herrnhutismen, forsamlingsbevægelsen og grundtvigianismen i*

Nørrejylland ca. 1815-1850. Volume V of *Vækkelsernes Frembrud i Danmark i første Halvdel af dte 19. Århundrede.* Copenhagen, 1970.

Rod, Jakob, *Folkereligion og Kirke.* Copenhagen, 1961.
_____, *Dansk Folkereligion i Nyere Tid.* Copenhagen, 1972.
Roof, Wade Clark, "The Study of Social Change in Religion," in P.E. Hammond, ed., *The Sacred in a Secular Age.* Berkeley, 1985: 75-89.

Salmonsen, Per, *Religion i Dag.* Copenhagen, 1975.
Sandemose, Aksel, *A Refugee Crosses His Tracks.* New York, 1936.
Sappington, A.A., "The Religion/Science Conflict," *Journal for the Scientific Study of Religion* 30:1(1991):114-20.
Schade, Caspar, *Beskrivelse over Øen Mors.* Aalborg, 1811.
Schmidt, August, *Fra Mors.* Brabrand, 1957.
Schrøder, Ludvig, *Peter Larsen Skræppenborg.* Fredericia, 1991.
Silverman, William, "Images of the Sacred: An Empirical Study," *Sociological Analysis* 49:4(1989): 440-94.
Skyum, A.C., *Vers på Morsingmål.* Aarhus, 1953.
Spiro, Melford, "Religion: Problems of Definition and Explanation," in Michael Banton, ed., *Anthropological Approaches to the Study of Religion.* New York, 1966: 85-126.
Stark, Rodney and Lawrence Iannaccone, "A Supply-Side Reinterpretation of the Secularization of Europe," *Journal for the Scientific Study of Religion* 33:3(1994): 230-52.
Stark, Rodney and William Bainbridge, *The Future of Religion: Secularization, Revival, and Cult Formation.* Berkeley, 1985.
_____, *A Theory of Religion.* New York, 1987.
Stromberg, Peter G., *Symbols of Community: The Cultural System of a Swedish Church.* Tucson, 1986.

Tambiah, Stanley J., *Magic, Science, Religion and the Scope of Rationality.* Cambridge (UK), 1990.
Taussig, Michael, *The Devil and Commodity Fetishism in South America.* Chapel Hill, 1980.
Thodberg, Christian and Anders Pontoppidan Thyssen, *N.F.S. Grundtvig: Tradition and Renewal.* Copenhagen, 1983.
Turner, Victor, *The Drums of Affliction: A Study of Religious Processes among the Ndembu of Zambia.* Oxford, 1968.
_____, *The Ritual Process: Structure and Antistructure.* Ithaca, 1969.
Tylor, Edward Burnett, *Primitive Cultures: Researches into the Development of Mythology, Philosophy, Religion, Language, Art and Custom.* Boston, 1874.

Wallace, Anthony, *Religion: An Anthropological View*. New York, 1966.
_____, *Culture and Personality*. New York, 1970.
Wallis, Roy and Steve Bruce, "Secularization: The Orthodox Model," in Steve Bruce, ed., *Religion and Modernization*. Oxford, 1992: 8-31.
Weber, Max, *The Protestant Ethic and the Spirit of Capitalism*. New York, 1976.
Whitehead, H., ed., *Sexual Meanings*. New York, 1981.
Wilson, Bryan, *Religious Sects: A Sociological Study*. New York, 1970.
_____, "Secularization: The Inherited Model," in P.E. Hammond, ed., *The Sacred in a Secular Age*. Berkeley, 1985: 9-20.

Yinger, Martin, *The Scientific Study of Religion*. New York, 1970.

Zablocki, Benjamin, *Alienation and Charisma: A Study of Contemporary American Communes*. New York, 1980.

INDEX

